Understanding Wall Street

Fourth Edition

Jeffrey B. Little
and
Lucien Rhodes

McGraw-Hill

New York   Chicago   San Francisco   Lisbon
London   Madrid   Mexico City   Milan   New Delhi
San Juan   Seoul   Singapore   Sydney   Toronto

To
Helen T. Walbran
Years Ahead of Her Time

Understanding Wall Street – 4th Edition

Table of Contents

Preface

Over the years, the public has been encouraged to "Own a Share of America." Yet, how many individuals have been prepared to invest wisely?

The stock market is rarely taught in high school, and even on the college level, investment courses are typically selected only by students with specialized business interests. Moreover, investors have found it difficult to educate themselves, even with the flood of literature available to date. Free pamphlets and superficial guides have not provided substance, encyclopedic texts have been too intimidating, and the "get-rich-quick" books have deluded investors with false hopes of easy gains.

Understanding Wall Street provides a good, practical education by combining investment fundamentals and many useful analytical techniques. It was written for two readers: first, the individual who knows little or nothing about the stock market but has always wanted to understand it; and second, the "experienced" investor who recognizes that there is much more to learn. This book offers more than just a colorful history of Wall Street or how to read the stock tables. It also describes, for example, the reinvestment rate, and the computation of current equity in a short seller's margin account. In addition, new investments such as ETFs are included.

With the substantial presence of mutual funds, banks and other large institutional investors, it is widely believed today that the so-called "small investor" is at a disadvantage in the marketplace. To the contrary, many smaller investors have found it possible to prosper handsomely in this challenging environment, whether the market is going up or down. Armed with an equal degree of common sense, vast quantities of information from companies as well as the internet, and great portfolio flexibility, the average investor actually has the upper hand. After all, the basics and the psychology of investing, which are explained in this work, never change.

New Video

The author is pleased to offer a new, inexpensive color video (available in VHS, CD, or DVD formats) based on the major elements of this text.

The *Understanding Wall Street Video* was developed with the help of the New York and American Stock Exchanges and features extensive, lively graphics throughout. Details can be found on the last page of this book.

What is
a share
of stock?

Introduction Every business day millions of shares of stock are bought and sold. How did these shares originate and how are the prices determined? For shares to be traded from one person to another, a company must be created. How does it begin? Where does the money come from?

In this chapter, the New-Design Chair Company is born and its officers confront the problems all successful corporations must solve. Directors are elected, shares are issued, profits are reinvested into the business, and dividends are declared. In the process, the reader will see capitalism at work and will gain an appreciation for a system that has produced the most advanced economy in the world.

The New-Design Chair Company

Charlie, a young inventor, has just built a new light weight, folding chair having a superior design. Encouraged by family and friends, he decides to turn his hobby of building chairs into a full-time business rather than sell his patents to a large furniture company.

Although Charlie has savings that could be put into the venture, the amount is far short of the total capital necessary. He estimates the total cost of the factory, machinery, and initial money needed for product inventory to be approximately $2 million.

These "assets" (the factory, machinery, inventory, and remaining capital) would be used to produce the chairs and maintain the new business. The more chairs Charlie can produce using these assets, the more profitable the business would be.

Charlie has calculated that if he could make and sell at least 100,000 chairs annually, it would cost about $20 to manufacture each chair. In addition, he estimates the sales and marketing expenses for each chair to be roughly $10. Since each new chair would be sold to his customers at the competitive price of $35, his profit (before paying federal, state, and local taxes) would be $5 per chair.

– One Chair –

	Selling Price	**$35.00**
Less	Cost of Manufacturing, Materials, Salaries, Labor, Other Direct Costs	**$20.00**
	"Gross Profit"	**$15.00**
Less	Advertising Expenses, Sales Commissions, Other Expenses	**$10.00**
	Profit Before Taxes	**$ 5.00**

Charlie believes his new enterprise would be beneficial in several ways. Thousands would enjoy using the new chairs, many people in his community would be earning a living by making and selling the chairs and the business would also contribute to the welfare of his community, state, and country through the payment of taxes. If Charlie could, indeed, manufacture and sell 100,000 chairs, this activity would no longer be a hobby; it would be a sizable business.

Now Charlie faces a major problem. Where will he get almost $2 million for the factory, machinery, and working capital? He is unable to borrow such a large amount without collateral.

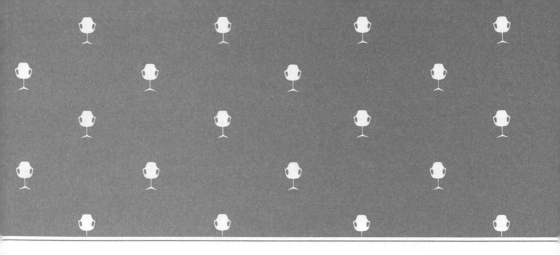

– 100,000 Chairs –	
Total Sales	**$3,500,000**
Less Cost of Manufacturing, Materials, Salaries, Labor, Other Direct Costs	**$2,000,000**
"Gross Profit"	**$1,500,000**
Less Advertising Expenses, Sales Commissions, Other Expenses	**$1,000,000**
Profit Before Taxes	**$ 500,000**
Less Federal, State, Local Taxes	**$ 240,000**
Net Profit or "Earnings"	**$ 260,000**

He decides to find others, frequently called "venture capitalists," who might also see the potential for his idea and be willing to risk some capital to get the venture started. To interest others, Charlie must divide his new business into smaller pieces to give them some ownership. Charlie realizes, too, that by relinquishing some ownership, he would no longer be entitled to all the profits.

However, he is willing to do this to secure the help of others.

After exploring the advantages and disadvantages of the various legal forms of businesses, he decides to establish a "corporation." The principal reason for choosing a corporation rather than a partnership or any other form was *financial liability*. Charlie learned that no matter which legal structure is used, creditors always have first claim on the assets if the business fails. However, a corporation, as a legal entity, limits the financial risk of the owners to the amount of capital invested. In other words, stockholders of a corporation are not liable for more than they invest.

Charlie forms the corporation under the laws of the state, names it the "New-Design Chair Company," and selects a few individuals to act as the board of directors until the first annual meeting of stockholders. At that time, a board of directors will be formally elected by the stockholders. The directors decide to "issue" 250,000 shares of stock of the 400,000 total possible shares authorized by the company's founding charter (when the company was organized this was the number determined to be the most convenient for the company's needs). The 250,000 shares are divided between Charlie and the venture capitalists in proportion to their agreed ownership,

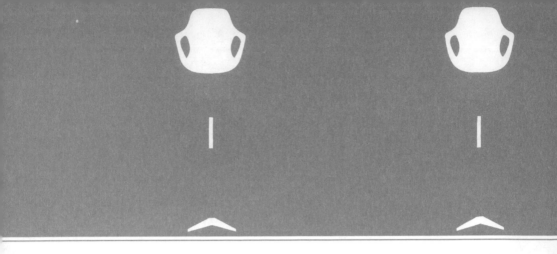

determined by the contribution of each. Charlie still owns a meaningful amount because of his importance to the company, his chair patents, and his initial capital. Now it can be said they are, indeed, "stockholders in common."

Each stockholder is a part owner in the company although the extent of ownership depends upon the number of shares held (an individual who holds 50 shares of the total 250,000 shares issued owns 1/5000th of the entire company, whereas a person who has 10,000 shares owns 1/25th of the company). The remaining 150,000 shares might be issued by the directors at a later date if the company finds it necessary. However, at the present time, the company's ownership is divided into 250,000 pieces. In other words, there are currently 250,000 shares *outstanding* of 400,000 shares *authorized*.

The members of the board of directors, including Charlie, are elected by these stockholders to oversee the affairs of the company. Each share outstanding, according to the company's charter, is entitled to an equal vote in the annual election of the directors.

The New-Design Chair Company is now a "private" corporation owned solely by its small group of founders. However, later, they might allow the public to participate. If so, stock would be sold to these new investors through the company's "Initial Public Offering" (or "IPO"). But, first, a "track record" needs to be established before "going public."

Most of the initial $2 million has been contributed in the form of "equity capital" by the venture capitalists. To raise the remaining capital, the company decides to go into debt. If the company were to borrow this money expecting to repay it in a relatively short period of time, a bank could be approached for a loan. If a longer time period is needed, a few years or more, the company might consider selling bonds.

The New-Design Chair Company, being a young, unproven business, would probably be unable to issue bonds solely on its word or good name (if it could, bonds of this type would be called "debentures"). Lenders are usually reluctant to loan money to a new firm without security. Consequently, the New-Design Chair Company might be asked to put up some property as collateral (bonds of this type are often called "mortgage bonds").

Although the New-Design Chair Company would have to pay interest on the money it borrows, present holders would not have to give up ownership as Charlie did when the new stock was issued for equity

capital. On the other hand, the lenders (the bondholders) do have first claim on the company's property if the company fails to repay the debt (such a failure is called a "default").

The Importance of Profits Why would Charlie and his associates risk their personal savings to build a factory to manufacture the chairs? They could have deposited their money into a bank account rather than investing in the new enterprise. The money would have been safe and the bank would have paid them interest. Why would anybody be willing to risk money – let alone $2 million – to start the New-Design Chair Company? The answer is simple: PROFITS.

Charlie and his associates saw an opportunity to make a good profit on each chair manufactured if the company met its business objectives. The stockholders also saw the possibility of increasing their profits in later years if more chairs could be manufactured and sold. In short, Charlie and his associates figured they could achieve a much better return on their money by investing in the new venture rather than receiving interest from the bank.

Now time has passed, Charlie's projections were accurate, and the venture has been successful. According to the statement of income in its recent Annual Report to stockholders, the New-Design Chair Company sold 100,000 chairs last year resulting in a net profit, also called earnings, of $260,000 – just as Charlie had anticipated. The stockholders of the company are now entitled to divide this money among themselves. Since there are 250,000 shares outstanding, dividing the earnings of $260,000 equally means that, for every share held, a stockholder would be entitled to $1.04 per share ($260,000 divided by 250,000 shares). This calculation is called "earnings per share." If, next year, or the year after, the New-Design Chair Company increases its production and earns, for example, $500,000, the calculation would be $2.00 per share ($500,000 divided by 250,000 shares outstanding).

Each year, the directors of the company must decide what to do with the earnings. If the company were to distribute to its stockholders part or all of last year's $260,000 earnings, this cash payment would be called a "dividend." The size of the dividend declared by the directors each year would most likely be determined by the amount of profits available. However, regardless of the total amount declared, each share would receive an equal dividend. The stockholder owning a greater number of shares would, of course, receive a larger dividend check from the company.

The directors of the New-Design Chair Company might declare only a small dividend or maybe none at all. If most or all of the $260,000 net profit is used to increase the size of the factory, hire more people, or add to the company's research program to design better chairs, the stockholders might enjoy higher earnings and bigger dividends in later years without having to invest any additional capital. This growth process is called "internal financing."

At the board meeting, the directors declare a dividend of $0.26 per share or a total of $65,000 (one-fourth of the earnings). In effect, the $0.26 per share dividend represents a 25% payout of the $1.04 earnings per share. The remaining $195,000 not paid out will be reinvested back into the business. These "retained earnings" will also enhance the financial condition of the company, expressed by reports that are released to shareholders periodically.

Financial Reports

The New-Design Chair Company, like most companies, will regularly provide financial reports to its shareholders and other people who might be interested, including lenders and potential investors. Financial reports will be discussed in detail later. However, for the purposes of this discussion, in general terms, two important reports are always included in the company's year-end Annual Report to shareholders:

(1) The balance sheet shows what the company owns, what it owes, and the value of the remaining amount, called stockholders' equity (i.e., the net worth of the stockholders' ownership) at the end of the year.

(2) The statement of income indicates the New-Design Chair Company's sales, costs, and profits earned during the year.

Obviously the stockholders will be watching the company's earnings progress closely. As they examine the profitability of the business, they will be asking two basic questions:

(1) How much profit was produced by each sales dollar?

(2) How much profit was produced by each dollar of stockholders' equity?

The typical U.S. company today earns only 7%, or about 7 cents profit after taxes from each sales dollar. This profit also represents approximately 14-15% of each dollar of stockholders' equity.

Clearly, profits are important to everyone in our economic system. Without profits to spur individual initiative and encourage

"There are two requirements for success on Wall Street. One, you have to think correctly; and secondly, you have to think independently."

—Benjamin Graham

investment, factories would not be built, people would not be using better products, and many more workers would be looking for employment.

The Stock Price Once a company's stock has been issued and is outstanding, how is the market price determined? To answer this question, there is an old Wall Street saying: "A stock is only worth what someone is willing to pay." Although the saying is somewhat shortsighted, there is some truth to it. A stockholder wanting to sell New-Design Chair Company shares, for example, could sell for no more than the price someone else would be willing to pay. The stock is rarely sold back to the company since the company's financial resources are tied up in the business. If the firm is prospering and the outlook is bright, there could be many eager investors ready to buy the shares at the asking price or maybe higher. A large demand to buy could lead to higher bids for the stock. On the other hand, if the business outlook is unfavorable, an anxious buyer might be scarce. Perhaps the asking price would have to be reduced to attract buyers. It is simply the supply/demand situation at that moment.

There are many factors to consider when estimating a value for the stock. However, an investor is most interested in the company's earnings outlook, dividend prospects, and financial condition. The stock price revolves around these three fundamental factors as investors compare the stock to all other investment opportunities.

Two Wall Street terms used frequently to appraise stocks are "Price/Earnings Ratio" and "Dividend Yield." They are not as complicated as they sound.

Price/Earnings Ratio

The "P/E ratio," or "P/E multiple" as it is also called, simply describes the relationship between the stock price and the earnings per share. It is easily calculated by dividing the price of the stock by the earnings per share figure. For example, if the price of the stock happens to be $30 and the annual earnings per share is $1.50, the P/E ratio is 20 ($30 divided by $1.50 per share).

Dividend Yield

The dividend yield, often just called the "yield," represents the annual percent return that the dividend provides to the investor. Yield is calculated by dividing the annual cash dividend per share by the price of the stock. If a company pays an annual cash dividend of $0.60 per share and the stock price happens to be $30, the annual return, or dividend yield, is 2.0% ($0.60 per share divided by $30).

Although a low P/E ratio is considered desirable, it is a common mistake to automatically assume that a stock having a low P/E ratio is more attractively priced than another stock having a higher P/E.

A stock with a P/E ratio of 8 times, for example, is not necessarily a better value than one with a P/E multiple of, say, 20 times earnings if future profits of the first company grow much more slowly, or maybe not at all, compared with the second company. A higher P/E ratio implies, but does not necessarily mean, greater investment risk.

The same applies to the dividend yield. A stock paying a dividend that yields a return of, say, 7.0% is not necessarily more attractive than another stock with a lower dividend yield of 2.0%, for example. How secure or safe is the dividend? What is the chance that the dividend will be increased in the future? How much of the company's profit is being paid out as a cash dividend to shareholders rather than being reinvested back into the business for future growth? These and other related questions must be considered.

Of course the P/E ratio and the dividend yield never remain constant. The P/E ratio increases and the dividend yield declines when the stock price moves higher. Conversely, the P/E ratio declines and the dividend yield increases when the stock price declines. Moreover, the P/E ratio and dividend yield will also vary as the company's earnings and dividends increase or decrease.

Over a period of days, weeks, or months, the price of a stock can fluctuate widely depending upon the direction of the overall stock market or news items affecting the company or its industry. Sometimes a stock will rise or fall at random for no apparent reason. Any number of circumstances or events can influence the confidence of investors and the delicate supply/demand balance of buyers and sellers. However, to repeat, over an extended time period – a few years or longer – the stock price will most likely rise or fall in line with the company's earnings, dividends, and financial condition.

Why Do People Buy Stocks? Where should that extra money go? Into the bank? Bonds? Real estate? Or art? Or will the stock market provide the best possible return? While each individual has a different investment objective, stocks are bought for one primary reason: To make money!

An individual can participate in the stock market in three ways:

Stocks Soar

Investing

This is generally the most successful approach because time can be used to an advantage. An investor buys shares to be a part owner of the company and to obtain at least an adequate return on the investment (enough to justify the risk and enable the investor to keep ahead of the rising cost of living). The investment time horizon is usually a few years or longer.

Speculating

The speculator is willing to assume great risk for a potentially great reward. Being a part owner is not important to the speculator since the time horizon is to be no longer than necessary.

Trading

A trader attempts to take advantage of small price changes and is less interested in intrinsic value. Stock certificates are merely pieces of paper to be bought or sold for a profit within a short period of time – sometimes weeks, days, hours, or even minutes.

In Wall Street parlance, the term "trader" is often used synonymously with the term "speculator," which is okay. However, it is best not to confuse the terms "trader" and "investor." They are quite different.

Whether investing, speculating, or trading, a stockholder makes money by receiving *dividends* from the company, usually paid quarterly, and/or by obtaining *capital appreciation* if the stock is sold at a price higher than the original price paid. Each day the stockholder can calculate the theoretical profit or loss on a piece of paper (hence, the popular terms "paper profit" and "paper loss"), but a profit or loss is not, as they say, "realized" until the stock is actually sold.

The stock market can be different things to different people. An older person, for example, might invest in stocks with an objective of obtaining a high, but fairly secure, dividend yield. A middle-aged couple might prefer buying only higher quality stocks with an investment objective of growth and modest dividend returns. A young investor, on the other hand, could be less interested in a current dividend return. Instead, he or she might be willing to assume greater risk and buy shares of small, rapidly growing companies for maximum capital appreciation. In any case, it is important for an investor to use only as much stock market capital as one can safely afford, to identify a realistic investment objective, and to know what to expect from each dollar invested.

Many years ago a popular slogan was used by brokerage firms to attract the small investor. "Own a Share of America," they used to say. With as little as a few thousand dollars of extra cash, inexperienced investors would buy shares of companies without any knowledge of their businesses, management, or investment potential.

Perhaps this explains why the "small investor" is so underrated by Wall Street "professionals." Many market observers figure that stock prices are too high once the "Average Joe" is fully invested. Conversely, they believe prices have finally reached attractive levels once the public, frightened by the possibility of further losses, has finished its selling in disgust. The small investor, as the stereotype goes, will then swear off this form of "gambling" and vow never to return to the Wall Street arena again.

For many nonprofessional investors, this is, indeed, a vicious cycle that will most likely continue for generations to come. But there have also been wise, patient individuals who have regularly invested modest amounts of money successfully over the years. Because they have taken the time to learn the basics of investing, they now have meaningful investment portfolios.

Stocks will always fluctuate and there will always be uncertainties. But as long as innovative men and women strive to profit from new ideas, or build new products, or offer new services, company values will rise. The profit opportunity for a long term investor is no less promising today than it was five years ago, ten years ago, or fifty years ago!

Common Sense Investing

Today's financial news is replete with dramatic headlines of every kind – big swings in stock prices, program-trading, large corporate mergers, etc. To those who do not follow the busy day-to-day happenings of Wall Street, it appears confusing and intimidating and many would-be investors become discouraged. Actually, for most, investing in the stock market can be a simple process. It can be educational, challenging, and with a little patience, very rewarding.

Many investment ideas have been identified by applying common sense to personal knowledge and using each observation as a starting point. "This new restaurant chain has just opened. It has a better menu and faster service than any other of its kind. Can I buy shares in this business?" Or, "This product is poorly constructed and inferior to its competition – I'd never want to own shares in this outfit." Or, "Just a few weeks ago I saw Charlie demonstrate a new chair. It is, indeed, superior in every way. Maybe the New-Design Chair Company is a great investment idea!"

Wall Street — How it works

2

Introduction Nearly 400 years ago Wall Street was an insignificant dirt path. Since then, history has changed the dirt path into the financial center of the World. Yet, Wall Street, perhaps the most famous of all streets, might also be the least understood.

Many people are frightened away by the apparent complexities of investing. They never learn of Wall Street's colorful history or its role in the American economy; the way stocks are bought and sold remains a mystery.

Wise investing is indeed a challenge that requires serious study, but a stock market transaction is much less complicated than buying or selling a car or a boat.

This chapter will provide a glimpse into the past and a brief explanation of Wall Street today.

Wall Street Defined Wall Street is a street, an address in New York City pointing straight from Roosevelt Drive near the East River to the old Trinity Church. But this is not the Wall Street people refer to when they ask, "How does Wall Street work?" or "What does Wall Street say?" That Wall Street is a marketplace.

Specifically, it is a marketplace where the merchants, agents, and customers of finance meet to buy and sell stocks and bonds. It is composed of all the individual marketplaces and the total community of interests that maintains them and is regulated closely by the Securities and Exchange Commission (SEC), created by the Securities and Exchange Act of 1934.

Thus, the name Wall Street is a short, convenient reference to the exchanges where stocks are traded in a two-way auction process: the New York Stock Exchange (NYSE), the American Stock Exchange (AMEX), and the regional stock exchanges. Also included are: the nationwide network of broker/dealers known as the NASDAQ over-the-counter market (OTC), the brokerage firms and their employees, and a variety of investors both individual and institutional.

Wall Street can also be defined with added precision according to its two major functions: to provide a PRIMARY market and a SECONDARY market. Through the primary market, corporations sell their stocks and bonds directly to the public, thereby obtaining the money needed for expansion. The process of bringing a stock issue to the market for the first time is called "going public." The term "initial public offering" (IPO) is more commonly used today.

After a company has gone public, its shares are traded in the secondary market, which provides the investor with an adequate number of bids to buy and offers to sell, as well as an opportunity to sell shares at any time. In the secondary market stock prices rise or fall according to supply and demand.

Each person using the Wall Street marketplace has one objective: To make money! The buyer is seeking to obtain an adequate investment return from a higher stock price or through dividend payments, or both. The seller, on the other hand, may already have a capital gain or loss and would like to free the money for investment elsewhere. Their efforts, in total, form a fundamental economic process that creates new industries, new jobs, and a higher standard of living.

A Short History The dirt path took its name from a wall of brush and mud built alongside it shortly after New York was founded as a Dutch trading post in 1609. The wall, later improved with a wooden fence, was built to keep cows in and Indians out. Although little is known about the wall's success with cows, by 1626, Indians were certainly allowed to enter the early business community — at least long enough to sell Manhattan for $24 and some beads. The street, however, quickly became a center of commercial activity because it connected the docks serving the Hudson River trade on one end with the East River importing business at its other end.

Early merchants had many interests. They bought and sold commodities such as furs, molasses, and tobacco; they traded in currencies; they insured cargos and they speculated in land. They did not, however, formally invest in stocks and bonds; for even as late as George Washington's inauguration, Wall Street had no securities exchange. In fact, this country's first stock exchange was established in Philadelphia in 1790.

In 1789, the first Congress of the United States met in Federal Hall on Wall Street, the place where George Washington had been inaugurated earlier that year as President. The first order of business was to authorize the issue of $80 million in government bonds to absorb the cost of the war. Two years later, bank stocks were added to government bonds when Alexander Hamilton, then Secretary of the Treasury, established the nation's first bank, the Bank of the United States, and offered shares to the public.

Now there were securities to trade, but still no organized market existed on Wall Street. Investors, by word of mouth, indicated their interest in any available issue through Wall Street coffeehouses or by advertising in newspapers. As the list of securities grew with more bank stocks and newly formed insurance companies, a need for an organized market developed.

By early 1792, Wall Street was enjoying its first bull market. Several merchants, encouraged by the increased activity, kept a small inventory of securities on hand that would be sold over the counter like any other of their wares. Today's over-the-counter market got its name from this early form of trading. Business was booming. Some days as many as 100 bank shares would be traded.

Wall Street businessmen began to schedule stock and bond auctions, as they had for commodities. Soon, several leading merchants organized a central auction at 22 Wall Street where securities were traded every day at noon. Customers of the newly formed "Stock Exchange Office," or their

agents, left securities with the auctioneers who received a commission for each stock or bond sold. A customer's agent, or broker, would also receive a commission for shares purchased.

With predictable ingenuity, some businessmen came to the auction only to listen. They noted the prices and, after the auction, would offer the same securities but at reduced commission rates. Even auction members traded in this after-hours market.

On March 21, 1792, concerned Wall Street leaders met at Corre's Hotel to establish an improved auction market that would also better serve their own interests. On May 17, 1792, twenty-four men signed a document they called "The Buttonwood Agreement" in which they agreed to trade securities only among themselves, to maintain fixed commission rates, and to avoid other auctions. These men are considered to be the original members of the New York Stock Exchange.

For a while, the new broker's union met under the aging buttonwood tree that faced 68 Wall Street, but they soon moved indoors when the Tontine Coffee House was completed in 1793 at the northwest corner of Wall and William Streets. They prospered and moved to larger quarters in what is now 40 Wall Street. On March 8, 1817, the

members adopted a formal constitution, creating the New York Stock and Exchange Board. Every morning a list of all the stocks to be auctioned was read to the assembled board members who would then make bids and offers while seated. Only members were allowed to trade and the privilege to sit at the auctions cost $25. The fee was later raised to $400. To this day, a member of the NYSE is said to own a "seat," although he is never seated while trading.

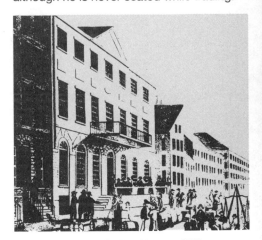

Tontine Coffee House, 1793

The Board moved several times until it took space in a building located at the present NYSE site in 1863. Also that year its present name was adopted. In 1865, NYSE members were prohibited from trading at the "Evening Exchange." The building occupied by the New York Stock Exchange today was completed in 1903.

Brokers not able to afford a seat on the Board or who were simply refused membership often found it difficult to make a living. In poor markets, many went bankrupt. Others drifted away to take odd jobs elsewhere only to return for another try when business improved.

By 1850, Wall Street was throbbing with activity. Gold had been discovered in California and the country turned its attention to the West. Mining stocks and railroad shares were especially popular. Many issues, considered too speculative by the Board, were eagerly traded by non-members. Few could afford office space so they traded in the street. By the late 1870s, the corner of William and Beaver Streets filled daily with brokers shouting out orders to buy and sell. They were called "curbstone brokers" and their market was known as The Curb.

In the early 1890s, when The Curb was moved to Broad Street for more room, many brokers used offices in the nearby Mills Building. There, telephone clerks took orders and shouted them to the brokers below. But with several hundred brokers being called, more or less simultaneously, shouting soon proved futile. A system of hand signaling was developed (parts of which are still used today) to convey price and volume information to the waiting brokers. Clerks would lean out the windows of the Mills Building or balance precariously on an outside ledge working their fingers furiously. The brokers below often wore brightly colored or otherwise distinctive clothing, allowing the clerks to spot them in the crowd. Although it looked like pandemonium, the brokers knew that certain stocks were traded at specific landmarks, usually lampposts. Action was brisk in any kind of weather.

In 1908, Emanuel S. Mendels, Jr., a leading curbstone broker, organized the Curb Market Agency, which developed appropriate trading rules but had little enforcement power. In 1911, Mendels and his advisors drew up a constitution and formed the New York Curb Market Association.

One of the most colorful spectacles in American business ended on the morning of June 27, 1921. Edward McCormick, the Curb Market's chairman, led the curbstone brokers in a march up Wall Street to their newly completed building on Trinity Place behind Trinity Church. They sang the "Star Spangled Banner" and went inside to begin their first session on the new trading floor. Inside, each trading post was marked by a lamppost which, interestingly, resembled those left behind on the street.

In 1953, the New York Curb Exchange, as it was called after 1928, adopted its present name: the American Stock Exchange.

The Primary Market The investment process begins with a primary market. Its focal point is the "investment banker," an important member of Wall Street who specializes in raising the capital business requires for long term growth. He guides a company into the public marketplace and generally helps the company in its dealings with Wall Street.

Assume, for example, that a company has enjoyed several years of business success and is now ready to expand. The firm's management has determined that several million dollars are needed for plant expansion. An investment banker is contacted to explore financing alternatives, including the possibility of going public.

Before recommending a specific method of financing, the investment banker must consider several factors such as general economic conditions, the Wall Street market environment, and the company's particular circumstances including its financial condition, earnings history within its industry, and business prospects. These and other factors would also be used to establish an offering price.

In this case, it is decided that a public offering of common stock would be appropriate as opposed to a form of debt obligation.

The investment banker agrees to "underwrite" the issue by buying all the shares for resale at a pre-established price per share. If the issue were larger, the risk could be spread by inviting other investment bankers to join in an underwriting group or "syndicate." At the time of sale, the syndicate usually invites other security dealers to join them in a selling group, and together they sell the new shares to the public at a set price. Before a new issue can be sold, however, the company must comply with the full disclosure requirements of the Securities and Exchange Commission.

In a registration statement filed with the SEC, the company lists the essential facts of its financial condition and operations. These facts must also be printed in a "red herring," later called a "prospectus," that members of the selling group must give to every buyer or potential buyer.

The company pays all underwriting costs allowing the buyer to purchase the stock free of any commissions or other charges. In general, this is the only time a stock price is ever fixed — when the price is temporarily supported by the investment banker. After that, the shares are traded as usual, according to supply and demand, in the secondary market.

The Secondary Market Just as a corporate treasurer works closely with an investment banker in the primary market, the investor's main contact in the secondary market is the registered representative.

This title means that this individual is "registered" with the SEC and "represents" the firm's brokers and dealers who actually execute a customer's order on the trading floor of an exchange or in the OTC market. The representative does not buy from or sell to the customer, but rather acts on the customer's behalf as an agent.

The registered representative, also known as a "stockbroker" or "account executive," and the brokerage firm are compensated by a "brokerage commission," which is charged each time a stock is bought or sold. In the OTC market, a customer may pay a "mark-up" or a "mark-down" or a commission depending on how the order is handled. A mark-up is an amount added to the purchase price while a mark-down is subtracted from the sales price by the OTC broker/dealer. The actual mark-up or mark-down must conform to National Association of Security Dealers (NASD) regulations limiting the amount that may be charged. The NASD regulates the over-the-counter market under the supervision of the SEC.

Prior to 1975, an investor could expect to pay a predetermined minimum commission depending upon the number of shares involved and the price, for any stock listed on an exchange. This system of minimum fixed commission rates was abandoned on May 1 ("May Day") of that year, ending a practice that began when the first members of the NYSE agreed to charge fixed rates in 1792. At the SEC's direction, commission charges on all orders were made fully negotiable. Thus, it is now possible for an investor, who would have had no choice but to pay a fixed commission under a set schedule, to bargain with brokers for the lowest commission rate, although competition tends to keeps the rates low.

Of course, major financial institutions, such as pension funds, banks, insurance companies, and mutual funds have the greatest bargaining power due to the large amounts of stock in each order. If the transaction is for 10,000 shares or more, it is referred to as a "block" trade and has an even lower per-share transaction cost. Orders of this type account for the majority of activity on the NYSE today.

In addition to varying commission rates, brokerage firms, also called "brokerage houses," differ by the types of services offered. The main office of a large NYSE member firm, for example, usually includes trading departments for exchange-listed

The New York Stock Exchange
in session just after the Civil War
and 100 years later

25

stocks, OTC stocks, and various types of bonds; a research department where security analysts appraise the investment potential of securities; an underwriting department for new issues; a corporate finance department for investment banking; and appropriate record-keeping departments for account maintenance and securities safekeeping. Other firms may offer only a few of these services and still others specialize strictly in order execution. All firms must, however, conform to extensive SEC requirements as well as additional exchange or OTC rules. Cash and securities held in custody are usually insured by the Security Investors Protection Corporation (a federal corporation) and by other insurance companies.

Finally, a brokerage firm can be differentiated on the basis of exchange memberships and by the source of their commission income. Only an exchange member is allowed to execute orders on the exchange trading floor. To become a member, a brokerage firm must buy a "seat," an expression that recalls the days when brokers paid $25 for the privilege to be seated during the stock auctions.

The number of NYSE members who own seats (1,366) has remained unchanged since 1953. Since there is a limited number available, seats, like stocks, have their own auction market. By 1929, the price of a seat rose to $625,000, dropped to $17,000 in 1942, and later hit a record $2,650,000 in 1999. Recently, the price was quoted at almost $2 million.

Firms not owning seats are called "non-member" firms. Their orders for exchange-listed stocks must be processed through a member firm or be executed in the so-called "Third Market" (buying and selling exchange-listed stocks in the OTC market).

A brokerage firm doing most of its commission business with individual investors is referred to as a "retail house" while a firm emphasizing institutional business by servicing mutual funds, pension funds, insurance companies, and banks is called an "institutional house." This distinction is less clear today than it was years ago due to cross-over functions and similar capabilities via the internet.

Just as brokerage firms differ, the markets are also different in terms of both listing requirements and methods of execution.

When a stock is "listed" on an exchange, it means that the stock has been accepted for trading there. The term recalls the "list" of stocks that was read to the assembled brokers at the daily auctions more than a century ago. Before its stock can be listed, the company must meet certain minimum listing requirements.

Each exchange has its own minimums. For a company to be among the 2,800 listed on the NYSE, for example, it must have pretax earnings of $2.5 million, a total of 1.1 million shares publicly held, net tangible assets of $40 million, and at least 2,000 holders of 100 share units. The NASD imposes similar, but less stringent, requirements before a company is accepted for quotation in the computerized National Association of Security Dealers Automatic Quotation System (abbreviated NASDAQ and pronounced "nazdak") of the OTC market. In general, the company must have $30 million of equity and $18 million of market value with an operating history of two years, and at least 400 round lot shareholders. Like the NYSE, a company can be "de-listed" if it falls below certain minimum requirements.

The net effect of the various listing requirements has been to attract the oldest, largest, and best-known companies to the NYSE; smaller and younger companies to the Amex; and the newest, least-seasoned companies to the OTC market. But there are some important exceptions. Many large, well-known companies such as Microsoft, Apple Computer, Intel Corporation, and others, have not sought NYSE listing by their own choice. No longer is a NASDAQ-listed company regarded as a low-priced "penny stock" selling for less than $1 each. Also, today, many of the NYSE's most actively traded stocks are quoted on NASDAQ and are thus traded in the Third Market.

A company can be listed on more than one exchange. Dual listings are common on the regional exchanges where transactions in dually traded issues are usually based on current NYSE or Amex prices. Typically, many companies listed on the regional exchanges are local or regional businesses. Finally, today's markets are global in scope and many companies are listed on overseas exchanges just as many foreign companies are listed here.

There are currently ten regional exchanges. Nine, including the three largest (the Midwest Stock Exchange, the Pacific Stock Exchange, and Philadelphia Stock Exchange), are registered with the SEC. In general, the regional exchanges increase the liquidity of the marketplace.

Now, six markets (the NASD, Boston, Cincinnati, Pacific, Midwest, and Philadelphia exchanges) are linked by computer through the Inter-market Trading System (ITS) with the New York and American exchanges. This has led to a truly national listing for many stocks.

One major difference between the exchanges and the OTC is the method of order execution. Trading on an exchange is accomplished by a two-way auction process while OTC trading is by negotiation.

The old Edison "dome" stock ticker is now a relic of the past.

How the System Works

After opening an account with a brokerage firm, similar in many ways to opening a bank account, the investor is free to buy or sell stocks through any exchange or in the over-the-counter market.

The following example of a NYSE transaction represents the traditional way stocks have been bought and sold for more than a century. Actually, the system has changed dramatically in recent years, which will be described in detail shortly. But visualize how the important forces of supply and demand influence the price with this interactive specialist system.

A shopkeeper in Atlanta, Georgia goes to his local brokerage firm, one of 336 NYSE members, and places a "market order" to buy 100 shares (the standard unit of trading, commonly called a "round lot") of the XYZ Company. A market order is an order to be executed as soon as possible at the best price available. At about the same time, a teacher in Denver, Colorado places a market order with her local broker, also a member firm, to sell 100 shares of XYZ stock. The orders are quickly sent to the trading departments of the respective firms and then transmitted directly to the floor of the NYSE. The firms' "floor brokers," employees located on the trading floor, receive the orders and proceed immediately to the "trading post" where XYZ is bought and sold.

Each listed stock is traded at one of 17 "posts," and each stock has a "specialist" assigned to it. The specialist's primary function is "to insure a fair and orderly market" in each assigned stock by buying and selling for his own account in the absence of competing bids and offers. There are roughly 450 specialists, each responsible for about six stocks, employed by seven firms. Some very big stocks have specialists devoted solely to them.

At the post, the brokers enter the "crowd," a group of two or more brokers who also have orders for XYZ. "How's XYZ?" asks the broker representing the Atlanta shopkeeper. "Thirty and forty to thirty-fifty" someone – usually the specialist — responds. This is the current "bid and asked" quotation. This means that $30.40 is the best bid, the most anyone in the crowd is then willing to pay; and $30.50 is the best offer, the lowest price at which anyone will sell. The difference between the two is called the "spread."

The shopkeeper's broker would try to get a better price than the offer by saying "30 and 45 for one hundred." If there is no response, the broker could raise the bid, but also risk losing the best asking price. Perhaps at $30.45, the teacher's broker hollers "sold" feeling it is the best price he can expect at that time. The transaction has been completed. The customers are notified by their registered representatives often within a minute or two after the order was first sent to the floor. The company's stock symbol, usually an abbreviation of the name, and the execution price of the trade are both printed immediately on the consolidated ticker tape which is displayed electronically in brokerage offices throughout the country.

If there had been no offers to sell stock when the floor broker representing the Atlanta customer arrived at the post, the specialist would have filled the order himself by selling stock from his own account. Similarly, if the broker had a sell order, the specialist would have bought the stock for his own account. The specialist's bid and asked quotation reflects the orders in his "specialist's book," a notebook containing special types of customer orders for each assigned stock. Orders in the specialist's book cannot be executed immediately because they are "away from the market," that is, they are above or below the price at which that stock is currently being traded. The specialist, or his specialist firm, must always have enough capital on hand to buy 2,000 shares of any stock he has been assigned. In discharging his responsibility to preserve a fair and orderly market, the specialist attempts to keep the spread narrow and minimize any sharp price fluctuation either up or down.

When the specialist trades for his own account, he is said to be acting as a "dealer," much like the dealers in the OTC market. A dealer acts as a principal in a transaction, buying from and selling stock to a customer. A broker, on the other hand, only represents a customer as a middleman or agent.

In early 2001, as an SEC directive, the exchanges ended the quaint pricing system of quoting stocks in "eighths" of a dollar. Since then, stocks have been quoted in decimals (pennies) with narrower spreads as a result.

Moreover, this traditional system utilizing the specialist has changed considerably in recent years. In 1976, the New York Stock Exchange introduced the Designated Order Turnaround (DOT) system. DOT, which has since been improved and renamed "SuperDOT," is an electronic order-routing system allowing member firms to transmit orders directly to the specialist post. Thus, member firms' market and day limit orders up to specified sizes are transmitted by SuperDOT. With the narrow spreads today, orders can be filled almost immediately and at prices in line with customer expectations. Presently, SuperDOT is capable of a daily volume exceeding two billion shares.

Before the opening bell to begin the day's trading, SuperDOT continuously pairs buy and sell orders and presents the pre-opening balance to the specialist who then uses the imbalance to determine the opening price. In addition, the specialist's book is no longer a pencil and pad, but a touch-screen electronic display book. The specialist activates a computer by simply touching the display screen at the appropriate places.

Today three out of four orders on the NYSE take place between customers without any capital participation of the specialist. Also, nearly all trades take place at less than $0.05 from the last sale.

The specialist would act as a dealer if an investor wants to buy or sell from 1 to 99 shares, called an "odd-lot." On the NYSE, an odd-lot order with a price limit is processed by computer and is executed automatically at the next round-lot price struck at the post. The specialist receives periodic reports indicating how many odd-lot shares have been added to or subtracted from his inventory. For this service, the specialist charges the customer a small fraction (1/8 point, typically) per share, traditionally called the "odd-lot differential." Odd-lot orders without a price limit are otherwise immediately executed on the NYSE bid or offer prices without any odd-lot differential.

If the Atlanta shopkeeper wanted to buy 100 shares of an OTC stock rather than an exchange-listed stock, the order would have been sent to the firm's OTC trading desk.

The individuals at the desk are referred to as "broker/dealers" because they can act in either capacity depending on the circumstances.

The shopkeeper's order may be filled directly from the firm's inventory if the broker/dealer "makes a market" in the stock. In this case, the broker/dealer acts as a principal, or, in other words, as a dealer. As a market maker, the dealer maintains an inventory of the stock, must be prepared to buy or sell at least 100 shares at any time, and must announce bid and asked prices continuously. The OTC trading department, through the registered representative, quotes a single "net price" to the customer, which includes the dealer's mark-up. The customer is free to negotiate for a lower price. The order is completed as soon as the customer and the dealer agree.

If the broker/dealer does not make a market in the stock and the stock is quoted in the NASDAQ System, the broker/dealer interrogates the system's computer by typing the trading symbol of the stock onto a keyboard attached to an electronic display screen. The names and bid and asked quotations of all market makers in that stock instantly appear on the screen.

The broker/dealer then calls the market maker offering the best quote, negotiates a price, and buys the stock for the customer. The broker/dealer has acted as a broker or agent and charges the customer a commission.

If the stock is not among the 4,000 stocks currently being quoted on NASDAQ, the broker/dealer will have to negotiate a price with one of the market makers listed in the "pink sheets," a daily list of all OTC market makers and their quotes published by the National Quotation Service. The process takes longer but is otherwise identical to a NASDAQ System trade.

The OTC Market is the largest securities market in the country. Although it does not meet in any one central place, OTC broker/dealers are connected by the computer of the NASDAQ System and by telephone. Traded in the OTC market are almost all federal, state, municipal, and corporate bonds; almost all new issues; most mutual funds; several foreign stocks; and nearly 30,000 domestic stocks. The aggregate dollar volume of the OTC market greatly exceeds the dollar volume executed on all stock exchanges combined.

In terms of average monthly equity volume reported, NASDAQ surpassed the New York Stock Exchange several years ago. However, most observers agree that NASDAQ's volume could be overstated by as much as 40% due to trading mechanics and their reporting procedures. Moreover, the average price of a share traded on the New York Stock Exchange is nearly twice that of a NASDAQ share.

Program Trading

Computerized "program trading" has increased in recent years and now represents more than one-third of NYSE daily volume. A program trade, which typically involves a computer-directed trade of a basket of stocks, immediately and automatically executed, has been a controversial subject. In general, the net result of this activity tends to increase the volatility of stocks overall, but also adds to their liquidity. And there are some controls.

Collars and Circuit Breakers

The stock market crash in 1987 was a rude awakening for Wall Street. Given the numerous economic "safety nets" installed since the Depression years, many believed a crash similar in magnitude to 1929 would be an unlikely event. This proved false in October, 1987. So, following the lead of the Tokyo exchange, a series of rules were adopted to allow the markets to "take a breath" during a highly-emotional period.

"Collars" and "circuit breakers" were set according to the price levels of the Dow

Jones Industrial Average and these rules will change with higher or lower prices.

The collar, which suspends program trading activity whenever the specified DJIA limit is reached, is calculated quarterly. Collars are set as 2% of the average closing value for the last month of the previous quarter. For example, if that calculation shows the DJIA figure to be 9,000, the collar would be established at 180 points and can go into affect whether the market is rising or falling.

The "circuit breakers," which apply under more extreme conditions, can halt all trading when the Dow average declines by 10%, 20%, and 30%.

Under circuit breaker limits, trading can be halted for one hour if the Dow declines 10% before 2 PM (30 minutes if it occurs between 2-2:30 PM) and there would be no trading halt after 2:30.

If the Dow declines by 20% before 1 PM, trading will be halted for two hours (one hour between 1-2:00 PM) and for the remainder of the day if the drop occurs after 2 PM.

A 30% drop will halt trading for the day regardless of when it occurs.

These rules do not change marketplace emotions but they are a calming factor.

Who Buys Stock? Common stock ownership is broadly separated into two categories, individual and institutional, even though institutions invest on behalf of individuals through pensions, trusts, profit-sharing, and mutual funds.

In 1952, an early industry census revealed that shareholder ownership was under 10 million. Ten years later a similar census indicated the number of shareowners to be close to 17 million.

In recent years, investor surveys have placed the number of individuals who own shares, either directly or indirectly, at approximately 84 million, divided almost equally between men and women.

Although stockholder characteristics vary widely, it is generally believed the average shareowner has a median age in the mid to upper-40's and that about two-thirds have had education beyond high school.

To the surprise of some, according to recent surveys, not more than 20% of all shareowners have a family income above $100,000. Also, a majority of shareholders have investments in IRA-type accounts, 401(k)'s, or Keogh accounts.

The internet currently accounts for nearly half of all retail trades and this activity has been increasing. Yet the number of very active traders is still relatively small.

Today, billions of shares change hands daily on the New York Stock Exchange and NASDAQ.

During the past several decades, institutional investors have steadily replaced individuals as the most important factor in the stock market. Overall, U.S. institutional investors now own $5.5 trillion or nearly 50% of outstanding equities. The holdings of foreign institutions, private funds, and certain other funds are also considerable. The largest institutional investors, judged by the market value of their holdings, have been: uninsured pension funds, investment firms, nonprofit institutions, insurance companies, common trust funds, and mutual savings banks.

One of the most important developments in recent years has been the introduction of exchange-traded funds (ETFs) pioneered by the American Stock Exchange. These new investment instruments, explained later, have become very popular and now represent a significant portion of Amex daily volume.

The Future In the years ahead, as we move further into the twenty-first century, a global market network will be operating that will encompass all of the world's major stock markets including those in the United States, Japan, Europe, as well as other countries. It will be possible to buy or sell securities twenty-four hours a day.

The technological developments of the past forty years and the organizational efforts that began as far back as the 1970's will one day be in place. The markets will be efficient, with minimal duplication, and worldwide orders to buy and sell will be routed and filled on a timely basis. Investors will be able to locate the best bid and asked prices, no matter where they might be.

This process of change is continuing and should reach fruition within the next eight to ten years. Eventually, Wall Street may once again hear the words spoken in 1921 by Edward McCormick. Just before the curbstone brokers went inside for the first time, he said: "The die is cast. The old order is gone forever."

Analyzing
your company

3

Introduction The company with the best performing stock over the long run – ten or twenty years – almost always has a superior record of earnings, dividends, and improved financial condition. An individual investor will find it easier to identify such a company once the rudiments of security analysis are mastered.

The unfortunate situations that investors encountered a few years ago, such as illegal accounting gimmicks, temporarily placed a dark cloud over all fundamental analysis. This was, indeed, discouraging because such activity does not represent typical corporate behavior.

This chapter will show how to read corporate financial statements and will highlight the most important analytical concepts used by successful long term investors.

Johnson & Johnson Drug Backed by FDA

Getting to Know the Company

"What is this company's business?" is the first question an investor should ask. The president of a diversified company might answer, "Oh, we're in business to make money" or "We make motorbikes, golf clubs, tennis balls, and football helmets." Yet, like a ship, a company must have a charted course to follow. An answer such as: "We manufacture and sell quality sporting goods to the leisure-time market" would indicate that the company has a corporate strategy. Before anything else, an investor should know the corporate purpose and have confidence that management also knows.

There are various ways an investor can become acquainted with a company. First, and most important, is through the firm's literature: past annual reports and 10-K's, quarterly interim reports, management speeches, and press releases. This information can be obtained free of charge by writing to the secretary of the corporation or visiting the company's website on the internet. In most cases, the company's mailing address is available online, or at many brokerage offices, or in research books in the public library.

Research reports written by securities analysts of brokerage firms provide another way to learn about a company. The typical brokerage report ordinarily deals with an analysis of current earnings prospects, but rarely provides the necessary insight into the industry, the competition, or management. However, these reports can help an investor better understand current operations and problems. The investor should read the reports, extract factual information, and avoid unsubstantiated assumptions. The investment decision should be made by the investor alone after studying all the information available.

The development of the internet in recent years has created yet one more excellent way prospective shareholders can become "tuned in" to the company. Immediately after an earnings release many companies sponsor an online conference call. Usually only analysts and current stockholders are permitted to ask questions during this management presentation, but the details and information, as well as officer candor, can be very valuable at times.

A fourth way to learn about a corporation is by attending its annual meeting. Depending on company policy, it is sometimes possible to attend without being a stockholder – that is, as a "guest." A phone call or letter to the company's secretary will answer this question.

Annual meetings can be interesting because the corporate executives want to make a favorable impression. At the same time, investors are trying to look beneath smooth

AT&T Slates Plan
Of Stock Ownership

or clumsy presentations for any indication of management talent or weakness. Company presentations become increasingly valuable as the investor gains experience through exposure to different companies.

The meeting is usually held at or near the corporate headquarters, although many large, widely-held firms accommodate stockholders by holding the meeting in a different city each year.

In most cases, the annual meeting is scheduled for the same day every year according to the company's bylaws. The date, time, and location of the annual meeting normally can be found on the inside cover of the annual report or in a variety of other places, including online or at the public library.

One major order of business at the annual meeting is the election of the company's directors by the stockholders. A few weeks prior to the meeting the company will mail a "proxy statement" to each stockholder. The stockholder reviews the proxy material, decides how to vote on the election and other proposals, fills out the proxy, and returns it to the company to be counted like any other election ballot.

The business portion of the meeting usually takes a few minutes but can continue for an hour or so, depending on the length of

the stockholders' question and answer period. Sometimes the annual meeting also includes a tour of the company's offices or factories. In fact, several companies such as General Motors and others are well known for holding stimulating annual meetings. If it is possible to attend, an investor will find a well-organized annual meeting an interesting and worthwhile experience.

Financial Statements The annual report, usually published a few months after the company's fiscal year ends, is the best place to begin the analysis of a company. The typical report contains the President's Letter to Stockholders, which outlines the events of the past year and the present status of the corporation. The body of the report explains the company's business operations in greater detail. Located in the back is the financial section, the most revealing part of any annual report. This section contains three important financial statements:

- The Income Statement
- The Balance Sheet
- The Statement of Cash Flows

The *Income Statement* presents the company's business results for the year. It shows, in dollar terms, the company's sales, costs, and earnings (profits) over the past twelve months compared with the preceding twelve-month period.

The *Balance Sheet* presents the company's financial condition at the end of the year by listing: (1) What the company owns (assets such as cash, inventory, factories, equipment, etc.); (2) What the company owes (liabilities such as short term bank borrowings and long-term debt); and (3) The "stockholders' equity," which is the difference between the assets and liabilities. Said another way . . . On every balance sheet, the Total Assets figure is always equal to the sum of the company's *Total Liabilities* figure and the *Stockholders' Equity* figure.

The *Statement of Cash Flows,* also called the "Source and Application of Funds Statement," is best described as a bridge between the Income Statement and the Balance Sheet. It explains exactly how the company's financial position changed during the year. In short, the Statement of Cash Flows outlines how the company financed its growth during the year (i.e., the "source," where the money came from, and the "applications," where the money went).

All three statements are accompanied by a series of footnotes that explain the figures in greater detail. Sometimes these footnotes contain significant information and are worth reading. In addition, there is a table showing several years of financial history. This table generally includes income data, balance sheet data, and supplementary statistics that can further help an investor understand the company and its background.

Finally, the financial section contains a report submitted by an independent accounting expert indicating that the statements were prepared in accordance with generally accepted accounting principles and that the financial statements present, fairly and on a consistent basis, the financial position of the company for the years noted. The investor should read it to check for any "qualifications" the auditors considered important and be wary of the company if its financial reports have any.

To better understand the example to follow, an investor should be familiar with several terms:

On the Income Statement

The term Sales is used to describe the total dollar amount received for the products sold to customers during the period. Cost of Products Sold, or sometimes called Cost of Sales, represents the cost of manufacturing these products. These costs include raw materials, wages, salaries, fuel, and other direct production costs. The difference between the company's sales and cost of sales is called "gross profit." Selling, General and Administrative Expenses include officers' salaries, sales commissions, advertising spending, research and development expenses, and other general expenses. The term Depreciation is often used to describe the gradual decline in the value of assets such as buildings and equipment. Depreciation is not a cash outlay. Nevertheless, it is another cost of operating the business due to the reduction in service life of the property. These assets are typically in use for more than a year and, therefore, an estimated portion of their original cost is recognized as they are "used up." The Operating Profit is calculated by deducting cost of sales, SG&A expenses, and depreciation from the sales figure.

Once all costs and expenses are deducted from all revenues, the profit that a company achieves before paying taxes (federal, state, local, and foreign) is called Profit Before Taxes. The profit that a company earns after deducting taxes is referred to as Net Earnings.

On the Balance Sheet

The Balance Sheet is divided into three major parts: Assets, or what the company owns, *Liabilities,* or what the company owes, and the difference between them, known as *Stockholders' Equity.* The company's assets and liabilities can be either "current" or "long term." "Current" refers to any time within twelve months

from the date of the balance sheet, whereas "long term" refers to any time period beyond twelve months.

Current Assets are assets that are expected to be converted to cash within twelve months. Current Liabilities are obligations that will be paid within twelve months. Among the important items included in current assets besides cash and securities are Accounts Receivable (money owed to the company primarily by customers) and Inventories (raw materials, work in process, supplies, and finished products ready to be sold).

Current Liabilities include an Accounts Payable figure that represents money the company owes to raw material suppliers and others in the normal course of business. A Notes Payable figure in the current liability section indicates the company is obligated to pay a debt, often to a bank or a supplier, within 12 months.

One important term used frequently is "working capital," which is simply the excess of current assets over current liabilities. In the example to follow, the working capital of the XYZ Company is $630 ($946 current assets less $316 current liabilities). Sometimes current liabilities exceed current assets, although this rarely happens with good companies. When this does occur, it is said that the company has "negative working capital."

Long Term Debt is debt the company will have to repay sometime beyond twelve months after the date of the balance sheet. The footnotes of the annual report explain in greater detail the types of obligations and exactly when the debt is due for repayment. The company's long-term debt could be in the form of bank debt, mortgage bonds, debenture bonds (issued solely on the credit of the company rather than secured by property), or other types of obligations.

Stockholders' Equity, sometimes called Net Worth, represents a value of the stockholders' ownership in the company and is defined as total assets less total liabilities. Included in the Stockholders' Equity figure would be the amount of money that has been invested directly into the company and all earnings reinvested back into the business up to the date of the balance sheet.

When a stockholder calculates the amount of equity behind each share, the result is called "book value." This figure is determined by dividing the amount of stockholders' equity by the number of shares outstanding.

In addition to common stock, many companies have preferred stock outstanding. As the name implies, these shares have preference over common stock in the payment of dividends and in

the event of corporate liquidation. If preferred stock is outstanding, any amount to which preferred shareholders are entitled must first be deducted from total stockholders' equity before calculating book value of the common.

Frequently an investor will see the term "par value" applied to common stock. Par value is an arbitrary amount put on the certificate having no relation to the market price of the stock or its liquidation value. The term is used principally for bookkeeping purposes. To avoid confusion, many companies simply place an arbitrary stated value on the stock and call it "no-par value stock."

When reading financial statements expect to see three additional terms used often:

First is "Generally Accepted Accounting Principles," or "GAAP," which refers to a list of reporting standards that have been established by the Financial Accounting Standards Board, an oversight group for the accounting profession.

Another is "pro forma." This term refers to financial statements that have one or more assumptions or hypothetical conditions built into the data.

A third popular term is "restructuring," which refers to the reorganization of a company's operations or organization.

The Basics of Analysis How the three financial statements are constructed, how they relate to one another, and how the company's fundamental story is told can be seen in the example of the hypothetical, well-managed XYZ Company on the next two pages.

The most effective means of analyzing a company is to study its record over the past few years and to compare it to other well-managed companies, preferably of the same industry or having the same financial characteristics. Companies and industries are very different. A retailer will differ from a pharmaceutical company or an airline. An electric utility will differ from a computer manufacturer or a fast food company. *However, each company and its management have one thing in common with every other company: An obligation to achieve the best possible investment return for the owners of the business* (the stockholders).

When one individual buys a share of stock from another individual, the investor is acquiring a share of ownership in the business and a part ownership of the company's equity. This equity, belonging to the stockholders, is entrusted to the management. They have an obligation to invest this money wisely, taking into consideration the company's opportunities, its expertise, and the degree of risk the stockholders are willing to assume.

One of the most important calculations in security analysis is figuring the company's "return on equity" ("ROE"). This ratio indicates the rate of investment return the company's executives have been able to achieve on the equity entrusted to them. A return of much less than 10% is generally regarded as unsatisfactory.

Using the example of the XYZ Company, as shown, the return on equity is calculated by dividing the net earnings figure ($184 located on the income statement) by the stockholders' equity figure ($1,150 located on the balance sheet). The return on equity of the XYZ Company is, therefore, 16%. To be more precise, it is preferable, when calculating return on equity, to use the average equity over the past year since the company's $184 income was earned over the prior twelve months, whereas the equity figure on the balance sheet is a year-end figure. Average equity is calculated by averaging the year-beginning and year-ending stockholders' equity figures. Nevertheless, the idea is the same.

Another important calculation is the "retention rate" or, in other words, the percent of net earnings reinvested back into the business rather than being paid out as dividends. The retention rate is easily calculated from the Statement of Cash Flows by dividing the amount of net earnings reinvested back into the business

XYZ Company
Income Statement
For the Year Ended December 31

REVENUES

Sales to Customers	$2,225
Interest Income	12
Royalty and Other Income	15
Total Revenues	2,252

COSTS AND EXPENSES

Cost of Products Sold	1,100
Selling, General and Administrative Expenses	755
Depreciation	69
Other Expenses	18
TOTAL COSTS AND EXPENSES	1,942

PROFIT BEFORE TAXES	310
Less:	
Federal, State and Foreign Taxes	126
NET EARNINGS	$184

XYZ
Balance Sheet

ASSETS

Current Assets

Cash	$ 38
Marketable Securities	200
Accounts Receivable	288
Inventories	397
Other Current Assets	23
Total Current Assets	946

Long Term Assets

Property, Plant and Equipment	528
Other Assets	77
Total Long Term Assets	605
TOTAL ASSETS	$1,551

Return on Equity

Net earnings divided by stockholders' equity

pany
f December 31

LIABILITIES		
Current Liabilities		
Accounts Payable	$ 99	
Loans and Notes Payable	88	
Other Current Liabilities	129	
Total Current Liabilities		316
Long Term Debt		85
STOCKHOLDERS' EQUITY		
Common Stock	145	
Retained Earnings	1,005	
Total Stockholders' Equity		1,150
TOTAL LIABILITIES & EQUITY		**$1,551**

XYZ Company
Source and Application
of Funds Statement

SOURCE OF FUNDS		
Net Earnings	$184	
Depreciation of Property	69	
Other Sources	7	
Provided by Operations		260
Increase In		
Long Term Debt	13	
Proceeds from Employee's		
Stock Options	4	
Proceeds from the		
Sale of Property	3	
Provided by Outside Sources		20
TOTAL		280
APPLICATION OF FUNDS		
Additions to Property, Plant		
and Equipment	$136	
Cash Dividends Paid	49	
Decrease in		
Long Term Debt	10	
Other Applications	10	
TOTAL		205
INCREASE IN		
WORKING CAPITAL	$ 75	

Retention Rate

Net earnings less
dividends divided by
net earnings

(net earnings less dividends) by the net earnings figure. Last year the retention rate of XYZ Company, for example, was 73% or $184 less $49 divided by $184.

Of course, the retention rate can also be found in the same manner by using the earnings per share and dividend per share figures. Most analysts do it this way.

A company that grows entirely by reinvesting its earnings back into the business is said to be self-financing. Generally speaking, the most successful companies today are self-financing, which can be particularly important during inflationary or deflationary periods.

Both the "return on equity" and the "retention rate" calculations are very important to an analyst because they provide a clue to the company's internal growth rate potential for earnings (analysts refer to this growth potential as the "reinvestment rate"). A company can only grow either: (1) By plowing earnings back into the business, or (2) By obtaining new debt or equity capital from outside the company.

The reinvestment rate is simply the product of the return on equity and the retention rate as shown in the formula above.

The internal growth potential for the XYZ Company is, therefore:

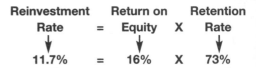

Reinvestment Rate		Return on Equity	X	Retention Rate
11.7%	=	16%	X	73%

It can be seen from the formula that a company can improve its reinvestment rate by either increasing its return on equity or expanding its retention rate or a combination of both.

The retention rate is influenced directly by the dividend policy of the company and can be adjusted at will by management, while improving the return on equity is a more complex task, as illustrated later.

Any substantial enhancement or deterioration of a company's reinvestment rate can influence the market performance of its stock. Consequently, every serious investor should understand this formula and recognize its limitations.

At certain times the formula can be misleading. For instance, a low-quality company can achieve a high return on equity by simply showing a profit with a small amount of equity (perhaps the result of many unprofitable years). For this reason, it is also advisable to calculate the company's "return on total assets" (net income divided by the total assets).

When both return on equity and return on assets are high, the reinvestment rate can be used with greater confidence.

In addition to the reinvestment rate formula, there are many other statistical calculations that can be applied when analyzing companies. Here are a few using the figures of the XYZ Company:

Operating Profit Margin
(Income Statement)

$$\text{Operating Profit Margin} = \frac{\text{Operating Profits}}{\text{Sales}}$$

$$13.5\% = \frac{\$301}{\$2,225}$$

This calculation tells an investor how profitable the company's products are to manufacture and sell. An operating profit margin of less than 8% is usually regarded to be unsatisfactory for manufacturing companies.

Pretax Profit Margin
(Income Statement)

$$\text{Pretax Profit Margin} = \frac{\text{Profit Before Taxes}}{\text{Total Revenues}}$$

$$13.8\% = \frac{\$310}{\$2,252}$$

The pretax profit margin, or pretax margin as it is often called, shows how profitable the company's operations have been, taking into account all sources of income and all costs, before paying income taxes.

Tax Rate (Income Statement)

$$\text{TaxRate} = \frac{\text{Taxes}}{\text{Profit Before Taxes}}$$

$$40.6\% = \frac{\$126}{\$310}$$

The tax rate calculation shows the percent of profits paid to federal, state, local, and foreign governments – usually in the form of income taxes. Most often a company's tax rate will be in the 30% to 45% range. However, the tax rate could be lower for several reasons. Perhaps the company has a plant in a foreign country with an extremely low tax rate or perhaps the company has taken advantage of various tax credits (allowances for unprofitable operations in previous years or incentives established by the government for one reason or another).

Net Profit Margin (Income Statement)

$$\text{Net Profit Margin} = \frac{\text{Net Earnings}}{\text{Total Revenues}}$$

$$8.2\% = \frac{\$184}{\$2,252}$$

The net profit margin measures a company's profitability after all costs, expenses, and taxes have been paid. For many U.S. companies, 8% is typical.

Current Ratio (Balance Sheet)

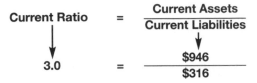

$$\text{Current Ratio} = \frac{\text{Current Assets}}{\text{Current Liabilities}}$$

$$3.0 = \frac{\$946}{\$316}$$

The current ratio is one measure of financial strength. A ratio of 2.0 or higher is desirable, although a somewhat lower current ratio might still be considered healthy if current assets are mostly cash or the business is cash-oriented. A ratio of more than 5.0 could indicate that business volume is not meeting expectations or that the company's assets are not being employed to their best advantage.

Another current relationship is the ratio of cash and equivalents (e.g., marketable securities) to current liabilities. This is sometimes called the "acid test ratio." The acid test ratio of XYZ Company last year was 75% ($38 + $200 divided by $316).

Capital Structure

The capital structure, frequently called "capitalization," is the total money invested in a company, including both bonds (long-term debt) and equity. The capital structure of the XYZ Company, for example, appears as follows:

Capitalization (Balance Sheet)

Long Term Debt	$ 85	7%
Stockholders' Equity	1,150	93%
Total Capitalization	$1,235	100%

The XYZ Company is conservatively managed, judging by the low amount of debt within the total capital structure. This is a desirable quality since it permits management greater flexibility during difficult economic times. Unless the company is a utility or in a finance-oriented business, the general rule is: the greater the proportion of debt, the greater the risk to the stockholder.

One of the notable trends in years past was the so-called "Leveraged Buyout." Typically, management would have the company assume substantial debt and the money would be used to buy stock from the shareholders, often for the benefit of management. It is best to avoid becoming a creditor in a leveraged buyout.

The trend in more recent years has been the repurchase of shares in the open market. This, of course, will reduce the number of outstanding shares and can be good for stockholders in many ways – but not always. Everything depends on the amount of money involved, the source of the funds and, most importantly, the purchase price. Regarding buy-backs, there are many questions stockholders should be asking.

Here are just a few:

- Are the buy-backs for the benefit of ALL the shareholders or just to benefit the executives holding stock options?
- What is the source? Is this the best use of the money, or should the cash be re-invested back into the business?
- How many shares are outstanding and what is the average daily trading volume? Once in a while buy-backs can benefit a stock's price markedly.

By judging the amount of money involved, the likely price range for the purchases, and by comparing the buy-back price with the per share book value, the investor can answer many of these key questions.

Cash Flow (Statement of Cash Flows)

Cash Flow = Net Income + Depreciation

$$\$253 \quad = \quad \$184 \quad + \quad \$69$$

Cash flow can be helpful in the analysis of profit trends and in measuring a firm's ability to finance its construction programs. It is especially meaningful when comparing companies because not all depreciate their assets at the same rate. It can be seen from the Statement of Cash Flows how important the cash flow items of net income and depreciation can be. Depreciation is regarded as a source of capital because it is a non-cash expense on the Income Statement.

Free Cash Flow (FCF) is an alternative and similar way to view the health of a company. Security analysts frequently use "Discounted Cash Flow" and "Discounted Free Cash Flow" models to estimate the current market value of the stock. Applying this approach, however, depends on the many assumptions that go into the model as well as the type of company being analyzed. See the table in the Growth Stocks chapter to better understand and appreciate this "discounting" approach.

The definition of free cash flow is: Profits after taxes, *plus* depreciation/amortization, *less* the total of dividends, capital expenditures, required debt repayments, and any other scheduled cash outlays. It is also sometimes loosely defined as "cash flow, plus after-tax interest, plus any non-cash decrease in net working capital."

The *earnings per share* figure is watched more closely by the financial community than any other company statistic. It is calculated by dividing net earnings by the average number of shares outstanding.

Using the XYZ Company as an example, if net earnings last year happened to be $184 million and the company had 40 million shares outstanding, the earnings per share of the XYZ Company would be $4.60 per share. Sometimes the number of shares outstanding changes during the year. When this occurs, the earnings per share calculation is usually based on the average number of shares outstanding during the year rather than the number of shares outstanding at year end.

The earnings per share figure can be calculated another way, which, once more, illustrates a relationship between the company's financial statements:

Earnings Per Share	=	Return on Equity	X	Book Value Per Share
↓		↓		↓
$4.60	=	16%	X	$28.75

As this section and the next illustrate, there are many ways to analyze a company and to value its shares.

Other Analytical Concepts The importance of management attaining a high profit return on the stockholders' investment cannot be overemphasized. As additional money is invested into the business, either as new capital or reinvested earnings, sales should increase. Sales growth is important, but loses its meaning if each incremental sales dollar does not produce the profit to justify the new investment. For these reasons, an investor should watch for trends in sales, profitability (including return on equity), and earnings growth.

Sales Growth

A sales increase or decline can occur in any or all of these three ways: (1) An increase or decline in the absolute number of units sold; (2) Higher or lower selling prices of each unit; (3) If a company's products are sold overseas, an increase or decline in the values of currencies between countries. These factors should be recognized when sales growth is being monitored or estimated.

Another effective method of measuring a company's sales progress is watching for a trend in "equity turnover" (sales divided by average stockholders' equity). The level of equity turnover often reflects the type of business in which the company is engaged. As a general rule, companies with high profit margins usually have a low equity turnover while companies with low profitability usually have a high equity turnover. A trend, either up or down, could be important.

Profitability

Sales growth loses significance if it is not translated into earnings "at the bottom line." Growing net earnings is, of course, the primary means of increasing stockholders' equity. When sales advance more rapidly than costs and expenses, profit margins expand and vice versa. As explained earlier, profit margins can be analyzed many ways – among the most popular: the *operating profit margin,* the *pretax profit margin,* and *net profit margin.*

The Profitability of Selected Industries

Industry	ROE%				
Aerospace	16%	Conglomerates	12%	Office Equipment	17%
Airline	NIL	Drugs	19%	Paper	16%
Automotive	15%	Electronics	15%	Railroads	8%
Banks	11%	Food Processing	16%	Retailing (non food)	13%
Beverages	15%	Food Retailing	13%	Steels	8%
Broadcasting	20%	Machinery	14%	Textiles & Apparel	13%
Building Materials	12%	Metals & Mining	7%	Tire & Rubber	9%
Chemicals	15%	Natural Resources	14%	Utilities	11%

EBITDA (earnings before interest, taxes, depreciation and amortization) gained a measure of fame when analysts, unable to justify equity valuations during the internet craze, used it to measure of a stock's value because the companies were not profitable. While EBITDA is a valuable analytical tool, it cannot be a substitution for net earnings. After all, the investor's objective is to identify companies that grow their ability to pay dividends. EBITDA is only a small step in that direction.

Many Wall Street Analysts apply a "rule of thumb" that has proven to be very useful. They compare the company's P/E multiple to its long term growth rate (this calculation is called "Price-to-earnings-growth" or just simply "PEG"). Thus, the stock that sells at a P/E ratio of 18 with annual EPS growth rate of 15% has a PEG of 1.2, which is not too far above the desirable 1.0 figure. A PEG of more than 2.0 is considered high.

Return on Equity

A company can improve its return on equity by either increasing its equity turnover or its profitability or both, as the following formula demonstrates, again using the XYZ Company as an example:

Return on Equity		Net Profit Margin	X	Equity Turnover
↓		↓		↓
16%	=	8%	X	2.0

For the XYZ Company to improve its return on equity from 16% to, say, 18%, management would either have to attain a net profit margin closer to 9% or increase the equity turnover to more than 2.2, or a combination of both.

Return on equity is not the same for every industry as the table above illustrates. In recent years, the average return on equity for the major industries in the U.S. has been just over 14%.

Some industries are regarded as "growth" industries while others are referred to as "basic" industries. Generally speaking, growth companies have consistently superior profitability, usually require less money to build a new plant (i.e., they are less capital-intensive), and usually have a better return on the money invested. But within each industry, some companies are consistently more profitable and have more promising futures than others.

Regardless of the industry, for long term success in the stock market, it is always better to buy shares of a company in which financial progress can be expected. That is, the company should be enjoying steady improvement in revenues, as well as healthy and expanding profit margins. It should also hold the promise of higher dividends in the future, and it should have a financial condition that can support these expectations.

Conclusion Statistical analytical concepts are important, to be sure, but there are many questions that must also be answered in the selection process:

• What is the company's primary business and is it THE leader in its industry?

• Will there be good demand for the company's products or services in the years ahead?

• Who are the principal competitors and can the company compete?

• Will product prices be under pressure?

• What are the strengths and weaknesses of management? And do they have a good record of accomplishments and what are their goals?

• Does management recognize its responsibilities to the stockholders of the company?

Here is one good rule to follow: If the story and the numbers that go with it appear "too good to be true" ... use extreme care.

In recent years, there have been many questions regarding accounting and the earnings produced by various accounting procedures. Lock six accountants into one room and they will later emerge with ten correct answers. For example, employee stock options and how they are recorded could be a point of discussion. The added expense for options could be greater for a technology stock, for instance, than for a consumer products stock. Also, pension funding is a continuing controversy. Thus, security analysis should be approached with a modest degree of common sense.

Despite these shortcomings, once the statistical methods outlined in this chapter become routine, the investor should find security analysis an enjoyable challenge. Success in the stock market will come more easily if you take the time to analyze your company.

Reading
the financial
pages

Introduction Reading the financial section of a newspaper is much like watching a baseball game. Neither one can be fully appreciated unless you know the rules, understand the objectives, and can at least identify a few players.

Some readers may even quit before they begin, discouraged by what appear to be endless columns of meaningless numbers and equally unintelligible graphs.

But the financial pages, although they seem confusing at first, are not difficult to comprehend. Once mastered, this section of the newspaper can be read quickly and easily.

This chapter will help explain why many people open directly to the business section before any other and why they consider reading the financial pages to be an important part of their day.

30 Stocks in the Dow Jones Industrial Average

AmerIntlGr (AIG)	ExxonMobil (XOM)	McDonalds (MCD)
Alcoa (AA)	GenlElect (GE)	Merck (MRK)
AltriaGrp (MO)	GenlMotors (GM)	Microsoft (MSFT)
AmerExp (AXP)	HewlettPk (HPQ)	Pfizer (PFE)
Boeing (BA)	HomeDepot (HD)	ProctGamb (PG)
Caterpillar (CAT)	Honeywell (HON)	SBC Comm (SBC)
CitiGroup (C)	IBM (IBM	3M Co (MMM)
CocaCola (KO)	Intel (INTC)	UnitedTech (UTX)
Disney (DIS)	JohnsJohns (JNJ)	Verizon (VZ)
DuPont (DD)	JPMorgan (JPM)	WalMart (WMT)

The Dow Jones Averages The Dow Jones Industrial Average is, by far, the most popular single indicator of day-to-day market direction. Charles H. Dow, one of the founders of Dow Jones Company and first editor of *The Wall Street Journal*, is credited with the original 1884 calculations of what are still, to this day, the most widely followed stock market averages in the world. It was his intention to express the general level and trend of the stock market by using the average prices of a few representative stocks.

In 1896, there were two Dow Jones averages. Most important at the time was the Dow Jones Railroad Average comprised of 20 rail stocks. The other average, containing 12 stocks representing all other types of businesses, was called the Dow Jones Industrial Average (DJIA). In 1916 the Industrial Average was increased to 20 stocks. Twelve years later, in 1928, it was increased to 30 stocks, the same number used today.

A third average, the Dow Jones Utility Average, was established as a 20 stock average in 1929 – later reduced to 15 stocks, as it is today. The three averages, the 30 Industrials, now regarded as the most important; the 20 Transportations, revised and renamed to include airlines and trucking stocks; and the 15 Utilities together comprise the fourth average, the 65 Dow Jones Composite.

Over the years, the widely followed Dow Jones Industrial Average has changed considerably with many substitutions. Fewer than twenty of the thirty stocks in 1928 remain, and only General Electric of the present Industrial Average was included in Dow's original computation. The 30 stocks currently used to compute the Dow Jones Industrial Average appear above.

The Industrial Average is simply an average of the prices of these thirty stocks. However, when one of the companies in the group declares a stock split or a stock dividend, explained later, the divisor has to be decreased accordingly to maintain comparability. Today, the divisor, instead of being 30, is about 0.1458. This means that for every one dollar that each DJIA stock advances or declines, the average moves about seven points.

With the passing of time, the level of the Industrial Average has increased, mainly reflecting the growth of the companies in the average. From 1915 to about 1925, the Industrials fluctuated around the 100 mark. During the economic boom of the late 1920s, the Dow Industrials rose to a 1929 peak of 386.10.

The sharp stock market plunge in late 1929 and the steep decline of the Great Depression took the DJIA back to below

The Dow Jones Industrial Average, comprised of thirty major companies, is recognized and quoted worldwide.

57

50 in 1932. It remained in the 100-200 range throughout the late 1930s and during the decade of the 1940s. The Dow Jones Industrials advanced in the post-World War II bull market from under 200 to above 700. Following a sharp setback in 1962, the index continued to climb to the "magic 1,000" mark, reached for the first time in early 1966. It is interesting to note that IBM was replaced by American Telephone within the Dow Jones Industrial Average in 1939. Had this substitution not been made, the DJIA would have crossed the 1,000 mark four years before it did.

The 1966-1982 period brought several sharp swings in the stock market, taking the Dow Industrials on a roller coaster ride few investors will ever forget. The most dramatic experience occurred in the two-year period 1972-1974. In only twenty-two months, the DJIA dropped 45% from 1,067 to 570, one of the steepest declines in its history.

Beginning in 1982, the Dow began a climb that pushed the average to 2,747 in 1987. The crash that year resembled the panic in 1929, but the economic climates were very different. In both cases, a great many stocks lost more than 40% of their market value in only a matter of days. The rapid recovery after the 1987 Stock Market Crash was but one more reminder of Wall Street's famous quote: "The stock market will

fluctuate." In 1988 the Dow resumed its advance and the average reached almost 12,000 in January, 2000 before encountering the most substantial multi-year bear market since 1974. But for those who invest for the longer term, bear markets such as these represent nothing more than an opportunity to buy shares in superior companies at attractive prices.

Once the Dow Jones Industrial Average is calculated, the result is expressed in terms of "points" rather than "dollars."

When the news commentator announces: "The market was up 72 points today to close at 8985," what is really being said is: "the Dow Jones 30 Industrial stocks averaged 8,985 when calculated at 4 PM today (the end of the NYSE trading session), which is an increase of 72 points from the 8,913 calculation at the close of the session yesterday."

The DJIA is frequently criticized because a higher-priced stock such as 3M tends to have a greater influence on the average than a lower-priced stock such as Disney. In addition, some people would prefer a broader list than just 30 or 65 stocks. As a result, other market barometers are also watched closely. One is the Standard & Poor's 500 Index, which was first calculated in 1957. Weighted according to the market value of each security in it, the S&P 500 accounts for about 85% of the dollar market value of all stocks listed on the New York Stock Exchange. However, the DJIA stocks are its most important top issues. Another, the New York Stock Exchange Index, was initiated in 1966. It includes all listed stocks on the Big Board and, like the Dow Jones Averages and the S&P 500, it is, like the others, calculated by computers continuously throughout the trading day.

The Dow Jones Industrial Average is an important benchmark for investors in more than one way. Not only does it provide a means of indicating overall direction of stock prices, but the average can also be used as a guide to relative values. The DJIA has its own earnings and dividends, which are averages of the earnings and dividends of the component companies. These statistics are readily available and can be used by investors as a basis for comparison with individual stocks. Similar calculations are also available for the other Dow averages as well as the Standard & Poor's indexes.

For investors who want to "buy or sell shares" in the broad market such as the S&P 500, there are Exchange Traded Funds (or ETFs) which are discussed later. Anyone who wants to invest directly in the Dow Jones Industrial Average can do so through an ETF called "Diamonds" (Amex symbol DIA). The *Journal* now has a few columns devoted just to ETFs.

The Stock Tables In years past, just as a minute is divided into sixty seconds, a foot into twelve inches, or a gallon into four quarts, Wall Street once used the quaint Spanish system of dividing a stock dollar into fractions of eight or, as they say, "eighths of a point" with each eighth of a dollar having a value of 12.5 cents. For example, a share of stock priced between $30 and $31 was quoted as 30 1/8, 30 1/4, 30 3/8, 30 1/2, 30 5/8, 30 3/4 or 30 7/8, which is another way of saying $30.125, $30.25, $30.375, $30.50, $30.625, $30.75 or $30.875. Since April, 2001, however, stocks have been traded with the fractions of shares quoted in cents.

An individual can buy one share or many shares, although the broker's commission charge is proportionately lower when a greater number of shares is bought or sold. An investor who buys 100 shares of stock at $48.75 per share pays $4,875.00 total, before a brokerage commission is added for executing the order. (The fee is calculated the same way, and deducted from the total, when the stock is sold.) This fee can vary widely, from $10 to $100, depending upon the brokerage firm's commission table.

If this company's stock were listed on the New York Stock Exchange, the transaction or "trade" would appear next to the company's name on the NYSE table for that day. If the stock were listed on the

| YTD | 52-WEEK | | | | Yield | | VOL. | | NET |
% CHG.	High	Low	STOCK (Symbol)	DIV	%	PE	100's	CLOSE	CHG.
-18.1	42.78	21.05	Thor Ind (THO)	0.04	0.1	12	4012	28.35	0.29
-0.2	21.33	16.20	Thornburg Mtg (TMA)	2.32	11.6	8	2362	20.18	-0.37
-30.3	16.42	3.47	Three-Five (TFS)		...	def	1078	5.15	-0.18
2.1	131.55	105.50	3M (MMM)	2.48	2.0	25	18019	125.83	0.75
-8.9	45.70	23.38	Tidewater (TDW)	0.60	2.1	16	5478	28.03	-0.29
-1.7	41.00	19.40	Tiffany (TIF)	0.16	0.7	19	2943	23.22	0.40
-8.4	45.95	25.80	Timberland (TBL)		...	13	3467	32.28	-0.25

American Stock Exchange, or one of the regional exchanges, or traded in the over-the-counter markets (the NASDAQ Market, or not listed on an exchange), the transaction would be recorded in either a composite table or in the appropriate table elsewhere in the business section.

Each line of the daily stock table tells a different story. As an example, assume a long-term stockholder of the 3M Company is reading a copy of *The Wall Street Journal*, or any other major daily newspaper. 3M is the well-known manufacturer of "Scotch Tape" and thousands of other products. Its stock is listed on the New York Stock Exchange and can be found alphabetically in the "T" section of the stock table with the heading "New York Stock Exchange Composite Transactions." Since this shareholder has been watching 3M's stock for many years, its exact location on the stock table can be found very quickly. Today's paper reports the transactions that occurred yesterday, as illustrated above.

The three columns to the left of the company's name show the price range of the stock over the preceding fifty-two weeks and its percent change (+2.1%) since the beginning of the current year. On this day, 3M closed at $125.83, up $0.75 from the close of the preceding day. During the session, 1,801,900 shares (referred to as "volume") were bought and sold. And with every trade there was a buyer and a seller.

The "MMM" notation immediately to the right of the company's name is the stock's ticker symbol. The figure to the right of the symbol is the company's estimated annual dividend per share (based on the last quarterly or semi-annual payment rate). This expected dividend of $2.48 is higher than the $2.40 per share that 3M holders received twelve months earlier, and about 50% greater than the dividend that was paid to this shareholder when the stock was first purchased nine years earlier. Fortunately, 3M's earnings have improved over the years and the company's directors have increased the dividend periodically – which explains why the stock has more than doubled in value during this period.

The stock's current 2.0% dividend "yield" is indicated on the stock table. Although a 2.0% yield does not appear especially exciting right now, this long-term shareholder is satisfied. Due to increased earnings and dividends over the years, the stock price is much higher now and today's $2.48 dividend represents an annual return of more than 5% on the original investment made nine years ago. This investor is also encouraged by the fact that 3M has paid dividends every year, continuously, since 1916. Management is obviously conscious of this enviable record.

The price/earnings ratio, also called the P/E multiple, measures the relationship between the current price of the stock and 3M's earnings per share. The company recently reported $4.99 per share for the past twelve months. The P/E is calculated by dividing the current price of the stock by the earnings per share. Based on the closing price of 3M yesterday ($125.83) and the most recent four quarters of earnings reported by the company (not shown on the table), 3M's P/E ratio is 25.2, as it appears, rounded to 25, in the middle column. In this case, it can be said that 3M is selling at roughly 25 times earnings.

It should be noted that this P/E ratio will fluctuate whenever the stock's price (or earnings per share) rises or declines.

Investors can see quickly, too, that 3M is currently paying its shareholders just under half of its earnings (i.e., a 49.7% "payout") in the form of a cash dividend.

The stock of 3M is listed not only on the New York Stock Exchange, but also on the Boston, Midwest, Cincinnati, Chicago, Pacific, and Philadelphia exchanges as well. As indicated earlier, 1.8 million shares were traded yesterday. Because the New York Stock Exchange is the largest exchange, most of these shares were probably traded on the trading floor in New York, but from these figures the reader cannot be sure.

Stock Market Activity On the first or second page of most daily newspapers that have a financial section, a special market activity segment appears. It shows total shares traded, the "volume," and highlights the ten or fifteen most active stocks of the day and those that have gained or lost the most during the session. Volume is important, but investors should not be concerned if a particular stock is on, or not on, the most active list. A stock can rise or fall on high or low volume.

The number of shares traded during the day is totaled by each exchange after it closes. However, the total volume reported by the New York Stock Exchange is the figure used most often by commentators to describe the day's market activity.

In the early 1920s a very active day on the New York exchange was a total of 1,500,000 shares traded. By the late 1920s daily volume of 4,000,000 shares was not unusual. The panic in October, 1929 produced several days of high volume (the record 16,410,000 shares of October 30, 1929 was not surpassed for nearly forty years). Since the 1950's, volume has steadily increased due principally to a larger number of companies and shares, not to mention greater activity by institutions (mutual funds, pension funds, insurance companies, and banks). The single-day

Most Active Issues

	Volume	Close	Chg
AT&T Wrlss	40,621,500	7.23	+0.22
Pfizer	38,935,400	31.12	+0.88
GenlElec	34,672,100	33.01	-1.11
ExxonMobl	33,783,300	34.66	+0.55
Wyeth	28,229,800	37.70	+1.03
Citigroup	24,325,100	35.46	-0.42
Xerox	22,812,100	9.43	-0.15
NortelNtwks	20,114,700	3.18	+0.03
LucentTch	18,311,200	2.10	-0.05
EMC Corp	14,328,900	8.98	-0.22
TX Instr	12,983,400	18.18	+1.07
Sprint PCS	12,266,700	4.68	+0.29

Diaries

	Tues	Mon	Wk Ago
Issues traded	3,442	3,421	3,451
Advances	2,185	650	1,093
Declines	1,097	2,633	2,197
Unchanged	160	138	161
New highs	53	47	101
New lows	44	23	34
Adv vol (000)	983,564	743,006	332,912
Decl vol (000)	360,234	500,535	929,865
Total vol (000)	1,345,897	1,245,649	1,324,872
Closing Tick	+83	-77	+22
Closing Arms (trin)	0.65	1.43	1.89
Block trades	23,453	21,651	20,443

record of 608 million shares traded on October 20, 1987 is no longer viewed with awe. In October, 1997, only ten years later, the record was set at 1.2 billion shares. Today, 1.5 billion is common.

Market Breadth In addition to using stock market averages, the general market trend can be seen by glancing at the "market breadth" figures usually found in the "Market Diary" column near the stock tables. These figures, available for the NYSE as well as the other markets, show the number of stocks that advanced or declined for the day, the number of shares that advanced or declined, as well as the number of stocks that reached new high or low prices in the past 12 months.

When the ratio between advancing and declining issues is compared to the ratio of advancing and declining volume, an "ARMS Ratio" is created. As a general rule, an ARMS reading of less than 1.00 indicates buying demand and above 1.00 suggests selling pressure.

These statistics have only limited value on a day-to-day basis. But they become more significant as trends are established over a period of time. For more on this, see the "Principles of Technical Analysis" chapter.

Seasoned observers like to see the market breadth figures improve whenever the more widely followed averages move higher. To have most stocks participate in the advancing market trend is regarded as a "confirmation" and a "healthy sign" that the upward trend will continue.

Wall Street professionals often say "it is a market of stocks rather than a stock market" and, to a great extent, this is true. The company's business prospects will always be the most powerful influence on a stock's price action. And it is not unusual to see a stock or a group of stocks contrarily hit new highs in a bear market or sink to new lows in a bull market.

However, a broad stock market advance or decline can have an important effect on an individual stock. For this reason, it pays to keep abreast of the technical condition and trend of the overall market.

Earnings Reports Over the long term – a few years or longer – the price of a stock will most likely rise or fall in line with the company's earnings, dividends, and financial condition. Consequently, there is a tendency for investors to anticipate future earnings reports which, in turn, places some importance on earnings announcements and how these figures are perceived by investors.

A company usually reports its sales and earnings results every three months. In most cases, the figures are available a few weeks after the quarter ends. A majority,

3M Beats Q4 Views, Raises Q1

but not all, of the companies end their business year on December 31, the end of the regular calendar year. If December 31 is used (rather than a "fiscal year" that ends on another month), the first quarter would close on March 31, the second quarter on June 30, and the third quarter on September 30. These quarterlies are referred to as "interim reports." A company's year is comprised of three interim reports and one annual report.

A quarterly interim report is mailed to each shareholder almost immediately. However, many of the pertinent figures will frequently appear over the news wires and in the newspaper a few days before the report is actually received by the shareholder. Sometimes the earnings report is better or worse than Wall Street expects, and this can produce an immediate positive or negative price change in the stock. Although most long term investors do not buy or sell stocks based solely on quarterly results, short term traders are oftentimes influenced by these reports.

Most major newspapers publish company sales and earnings announcements. *The Wall Street Journal* devotes considerable space to these reports in a daily column entitled "Digest of Corporate Earnings Reports," usually found near the middle of the paper. The reporting formats between newspapers can differ – and some tables are easier to interpret than others.

The fourth quarter announcement for the 3M Company is a good example. The story that appeared in *The Wall Street Journal* is shown to the right, along with the *Journal's* earnings digest figures.

This brief report tells the reader that, in the three-month period ending December 31, 3M's revenues increased 7.3% to just over $4.13 billion compared with about $3.85 billion in the same quarter a year earlier. It also shows that 3M enjoyed profits of $511 million in the quarter, or $1.29 per share, comparing favorably with $381 million, or $0.96 per share, last year. 3M's numbers were also published by other business dailies. That earnings table appears below:

THREE M COMPANY		MMM 125.64
Diversified Operations		Eps 87 Rel 61
Qtr. Dec 31:	2002	(NYSE) 2001
Sales +7%	4,138,000,000	3,856,000,000
Income	511,000,000	387,000,000
Extrd loss	. . . .	k-6,000,000
Net Income	511,000,000	381,000,000
Avg shares	390,300,000	391,500,000
Earn/shr +32%	1.31	0.99
Net earn/shr	1.31	0.97
Share earns (diluted):		
Earn per share	1.29	0.98
Net earn per shr	1.29	0.96
12 mo.		
Sales	16,332,000,000	16,054,000,000
Income	2,082,000,000	1,742,000,000
Extrd loss	k-108,000,000	k-312,000,000
Net Income	1,974,000,000	1,430,000,000
Avg shares	390,000,000	394,300,000
Earn per share	5.34	4.42
Net earn per shr	5.06	3.63
Share earns (diluted):		
Earn per share	5.26	4.36
Net earn per shr	4.99	3.58
k Non-recurring items.		

Fourth-Period Earnings at 3M Rose 34%, Helped by Solid Sales

Dow Jones Newswires

ST. PAUL, Minn.—Manufacturer 3M Co. said fourth-quarter earnings rose 34% from a year earlier, helped by solid overall sales and cost-cutting measures.

The company said it had net income of $511 million, or $1.29 a share, compared with $381 million, or 96 cents a share, a year earlier.

In October, 3M said it expected to earn between $1.25 and $1.30 a share for the period.

The company, a component of the Dow Jones Industrial Average, has a product line that includes such consumer products as household tape and Post-it notes, as well as industrial abrasives and adhesives. The company's results often are viewed as an indicator of economic trends because other manufacturers buy many 3M products.

In 4 p.m. New York Stock Exchange composite trading, 3M shares fell 68 cents to $125.64.

3M's sales for the quarter increased 7.3% to $4.14 billion from $3.86 billion a year earlier. The company said sales volumes increased 14% in its transportation, graphics and safety businesses; 4.6% in industrial products; 4.5% in consumer and office supplies; 3.6% in health care; and 2.2% in electronics and communications operations. U.S. sales rose 1.8% to $1.84 billion, the company said.

For the year, 3M said net rose 38% to $1.97 billion, or $4.99 per share, compared with $1.43 billion, or $3.58 a share. Sales for the year rose 1.7% to $16.33 billion from $16.05 billion for 2001.

The company invested more than $1 billion in research and development in 2002, said Chairman and Chief Executive W. James McNerney Jr.

The company said it expects earnings of between $1.38 and $1.43 a share for the first quarter and full-year earnings of between $5.80 and $6.00 a share.

DIGEST OF CORPORATE EARNINGS REPORTS

COMPANY	PERIOD	REV (mill)	% CHG	INC CT OP (mill)	NET (mill)	% CHG	PER SHARE CURR	PREV	% CHG
Thornburg Mtge	Q12/31	...	...	...	35.2	64	.67	.65	3.1
TMA (N) ▲	Yr	...	...	120.0	120.0	105	2.59	2.09	24
3M Co	Q12/31	4,138	7.3	...	511.0	34	1.29	.96	34
MMM (N) ▲	Yr	16,332	1.7	...	a1,974	38	4.99	3.58	39
a-Includes nonrecurring net charges of $108,000,000.									
Tidewater Inc	Q12/31	163.1	-10	...	23.6	-30	.42	.60	-30
TDW (N) ▼	9 mo	482.0	-14	...	a70.0	-35	1.24	1.92	-35
a-Includes one-time gain of $4,875,000.									
Tredegar Corp	Q12/31	176.9	-1.4	a1.98	1.98	...	.05	(.12)	...
TG (N) P	Yr	737.4	-3.4	a6.20	(2.53)	...	(.07)	.25	...
a-Includes nonrecurring gains of $3,705,000 in the quarter and $2,263,000 in the year.									
Tropical Sprtswre	13wk12/28	99.0	-10	...	(5.02)	...	(.45)	.38	...
TSIC (Nq) L									

3M reported a sharp improvement in the fourth quarter in line with its guidance a few months earlier.

The company's annual numbers (earnings of $4.99 per share on revenues of $16.3 billion) were, of course, also part of this announcement. And, as many better-managed companies do, 3M released rough guidelines for the next quarter and for the year to come.

Once in a while it is necessary for a company's management to revise its projections, either up or down, as the year progresses. If it is negative, this so-called "earnings warning" could hurt the stock price temporarily. However, as a rule, long term investors should not make rash portfolio decisions based solely on interim reports, though they should be monitored.

Of course, not all companies have the benefit of publicity with each quarterly report, but 3M is a widely held blue chip. Investors frequently interpret a company's interim report positively when the quarterly comparison is better than the preceding quarterly comparison and view it negatively when the reverse occurs. Stated a little differently, investors like to see earnings improve – especially at an increasing rate. Also, at the same time, much depends on what the analysts were expecting.

Finding Well-managed Companies

Earnings growth, although desirable, does not alone define a well-managed company. Equally important are *revenue growth* and the many management decisions required to attain it. The earnings report can be one clue in finding a well-managed company.

Firing thousands of top-notch workers in the name of "productivity" in order to maintain a dividend or to meet a quarterly profit target is not necessarily superior management. This is especially true if the company should be investing in research, developing new products, modernizing its production facilities, or hiring new salespeople. Long term holders become familiar with their company over time and can recognize the possibility of important fundamental changes when they occur.

In the fourteen years, 1988 to 2002, 3M has effectively doubled earnings (EPS growth of only 5% annually) by introducing new and innovative products. Also, 3M improved profitability through greater productivity. The company's revenue growth has been a meager 3% per year. This timeframe included the recession in 1990-1991 as well as the recession in 2001-2002 – plus a negative currency. So, informed 3M Company shareowners found this quarterly report very encouraging and they will almost certainly be monitoring the company's progress very closely.

Dividend Announcements

Dividends Reported

COMPANY	PERIOD	AMT	PAYABLE DATE	RECORD DATE
REGULAR				
AGL Resources Inc	Q	.27	3-01-03	2-14
BankcorpRhodeIsl	Q	.14	3-11-03	2-18
BectonDickinson	Q	.10	3-31-03	3-10
BostonFed Bancorp	Q	.16	2-20-03	2-06
CNB Florida Bcshs	Q	.05	2-07-03	1-28
Carrollton Bcp	Q	.09	3-03-03	2-13
Crane Co	Q	.10	3-12-03	3-03
DPL Inc	Q	.235	3-01-03	2-14
Diamond Offshore	Q	.125	3-03-03	2-03
Eastern Co	Q	.11	3-14-03	2-21
ElkCorp	Q	.05	2-27-03	2-10
Ethan Allen Inter	Q	.06	4-25-03	4-10
Fahnestock Viner A	Q	b.09	2-28-03	2-14
FarmersCapBank	Q	.32	4-01-03	3-01
FstCitznBncshrs A	Q	.25	4-07-03	3-17
FirstBank CorpMI	Q	.19	3-14-03	2-28
HF Fin'l	Q	.115	2-18-03	2-04
Hibernia Corp A	Q	.15	2-20-03	2-07
HsehldInt'l$4.30pf	S	2.15	3-31-03	2-28
IntlBusMach	Q	.15	3-10-03	2-10
KanCityLifeIns	Q	.27	2-24-03	2-10
Knight-Ridder	Q	.27	2-24-03	2-12
MeadWestvaco Corp	Q	.23	3-03-03	2-07
Neub&Berm Inc	Q	.075	2-19-03	2-07
NJ Resources	Q	.31	4-01-03	3-14
NiagMohawk 3.60%pf	Q	.90	3-31-03	3-10
NiagMohawk 3.90%pf	Q	.975	3-31-03	3-10
NiagMohawk adjpfl	Q	.863125	3-31-03	3-10
Norfolk Southern	Q	.07	3-10-03	2-07
Oregon Trail Finl	Q	.11	2-28-03	2-14
Peabody Energy	Q	.10	3-05-03	2-11
Pennichuck Corp	Q	.195	3-03-03	2-14
Potash Corp Saskat	Q	.25	5-15-03	4-17
Schering-Plough	Q	.17	2-28-03	2-07
Sthn Missouri Bcp	Q	.14	2-28-03	2-14
Sun Bancorp-PA	Q	.165	3-07-03	2-21
TECO Energy	Q	.355	2-15-03	2-07
Teletlex Inc	Q	.18	3-14-03	2-25
UnitedStates Steel	Q	.05	3-10-03	2-19
WVS Finl Corp	Q	.16	2-20-03	2-10
Weis Markets	Q	.27	2-21-03	2-07
IRREGULAR				
Chesterfield Finl	Q	.06	3-03-03	2-14
Guaranty Financial	-	.075	2-10-03	1-29
Health Mgmt Assc A	Q	.02	3-03-03	2-07
FUNDS, REITS, INVESTMENT COS, LPS				
Correctional Props	Q	.40	3-04-03	2-14
Cousins Properties	Q	.37	2-24-03	2-10
DreyfusStratMunlBd	M	.051	2-28-03	2-13
Hancock(J)PatGlbDv	M	.081	2-28-03	2-07
HealthCarePropInv	Q	.83	2-20-03	2-06
Hlth CarePrp pfA	Q	.492188	3-31-03	3-17
Hlth CarePrp pfB	Q	.54375	3-31-03	3-17
Hlth CarePrp pfC	Q	.5375	3-31-03	3-17
HealthcareRltyTr	Q	.61	3-06-03	2-14
Highwoods Props	Q	.585	2-24-03	2-10
Highwoods Props B	Q	.50	3-17-03	3-03
Highwoods Props D	Q	.50	4-30-03	4-01
Oil ServiceHOLDRs	-	.01375	3-05-03	2-03

COMPANY	PERIOD	AMT	PAYABLE DATE	RECORD DATE
MerLyUtilHGi DRs	-	.002	4-02-03	3-14
Penn VA ResLP	Q	.50	2-14-03	2-04
Plum Creek Co Inc	Q	.35	2-28-03	2-14
TCW/DW Trm2003	M	.047	2-21-03	2-07
STOCKS				
Central Coast Bncp		10%	2-28-03	2-14

INCREASED

COMPANY	PERIOD	AMOUNTS		PAYABLE DATE	RECORD DATE
		NEW	OLD		
AmerHomeMtge	Q	.10	.05	4-17-03	4-03
Bank of Montreal	Q	b.33	b.30	2-27-03	2-12
City National Corp	Q	.205	.195	2-18-03	2-05
Comerica Inc	Q	.50	.48	4-01-03	3-15
CommunityBkNrtVA	Q	.07	.06	3-01-03	2-15
McClatchy Co	Q	.11	.10	4-01-03	3-12
NASB Financial	Q	.17	.15	2-28-03	2-07
Port Fin'l Corp	Q	.20	.18	2-21-03	2-07
Praxair Inc	Q	.215	.19	3-17-03	3-07
R&G Fin'l pfB	Q	.0985	.092	3-27-03	3-21
SterlingBcsh TX	Q	.045	.04	2-21-03	2-07
TransCanada Pipins	Q	b.27	b.25	4-30-03	3-31
WA Banking Company	Q	.07	.065	2-26-03	2-10
Wells Fargo Co	Q	.30	.28	3-01-03	2-07
Woodward Governor	Q	.24	.2325	3-03-03	2-17
Wrigley(Wm) Jr	Q	.22	.205	5-01-03	4-15

SPECIAL

COMPANY	PERIOD	AMT	PAYABLE DATE	RECORD DATE
Methanex Corp	Q	b.25	2-14-03	2-06

EXTRA

COMPANY	PERIOD	AMT	PAYABLE DATE	RECORD DATE
SouthwestGasCorp	Q	v.215	3-03-03	2-18

v Amount has been changed. Reflects $.01 from redemption of rights.
A-Annual, M-Monthly, Q-Quarterly, S-Semi-annual.
b-Payable in Canadian funds. c-Corrected. h-From income. k-From capital gains.
r-Revised. t-Approximate U.S. dollar amount per American Depository Receipt/Share before adjustment for foreign taxes.

Stocks Ex-Dividend

COMPANY	AMOUNT	COMPANY	AMOUNT
AT&T CapPINES8.125	.50781	MerLynAmgen7%	.7966
AbbeyNatl7.25%Nts	t.453125	NY Community Bncp	.25
AffiliatedMgrPRIDE	.375	NewfieldFinIquipsA	.8125
Alberto CulverA	.105	ONEOK	.155
Alberto CulverB	.105	PNM Resources	.22
BNP Resident Prop	.25	Pall Corp	.09
Banco BradescoADS	t.019582	Pengrowth Engy Un	b.20
Borg-Warner Inc	.18	Pinnacle West Cap	.425
Citigrp Inc	.20	Russell Corp	.04
Cleco Corp	.225	Southern Co	.3425
ColgatePalm	.18	Sovereign Bcp	.025
CntySanDiegoPINES	.561458	Staten Island Bncp	.13
Diamond Offshore	.125	Sussex Bancorp	.07
Dow Jones & Co	.25	Toys R Us EqUn	.781
Eaton Corp	.44	Union Planters	.3334
EqtyOfficeProp pfB	.65625	Vornado Rlty Tr	.68
Everest ReCapTRUPS	.496076	Wausau-Mosinee Pap	.085
HartfordFinlCorpUn	.75	Wilmington Trust	.255
Mkt2000+ HOLDRs	.006	Winn-Dixie Stores	.05
Oil ServiceHOLDRs	.01375	Wireless Telecom	.02
MerLyUtilHOLDRs	.099325	t-Approximate U.S. dollar amount per	
Horton (DR) Inc	.07	American Depository Receipt/Share be-	
Kimco Rlty depshsA	.484375	fore adjustment for foreign taxes.	

					— H—H—H —				
36	27⅛	Hack W	2.48	7	1	32⅝	32⅝	32⅝ —	⅛
18⅝	14¾	HallFB	.60	13	74	17⅝	17⅜	17½ +	⅛
17¼	13¾	HallPrt	.80a	7	5	15¼	15⅛	15¼ —	⅛
166	133½	Hallibtn	1.68	13	373	155½	153	153⅜ +	¾

Before the "when issued" period 3/24

					— H—H—H —				
36	27⅛	Hack W	2.48	7	3	32⅞	32½	32½ —	⅛
18⅝	14¾	HallFB	.60	13	40	17½	17¼	17½	
17¼	13¾	HallPrt	.80a	7	18	15½	15⅛	15¼	
166	133½	Hallibtn	1.68	13	230	152½	150¾	151½ —	1⅞
.....	.....	Hallibrtn	wi	...	1	51⅛	51⅛	51⅛	

The new stock's first day of trading 3/25

Dividends and Stock Splits

Each quarter a company's board of directors meets to decide how much, if any, earnings will be paid to stockholders as a cash dividend. If a dividend is "declared," the directors will also set a "date of record." This means stockholders on record on or before that date are entitled to this dividend. Anybody buying the stock after that date would have to wait for the next declaration to receive a dividend. As a result, the stock's market price is reduced by the amount of the dividend on the day after the date of record. To say it another way, the stock is "ex-dividend" after that date.

When a company's earnings improve, the directors might raise the regular dividend rate or, perhaps, declare an "extra dividend." This term is not to be confused with the term "ex-dividend." On the other hand, if the company's earnings trend is unfavorable, the dividend could be reduced or omitted entirely. Dividend announcements, good or bad, can be found in a special dividend section of the newspaper.

Sometimes the directors of a corporation will want to conserve cash but still reward the stockholders. In this instance, the directors might declare a "stock dividend." As an example, a stockholder who owns 100 shares of a company declaring a 10% stock dividend would receive another 10 shares from the company – although the value of all 110 shares would be the same as the 100 shares held initially. The pie is simply being divided into eleven pieces rather than ten. If the company's per-share cash dividend rate remains the same, the stockholder has, in effect, been given increased future dividend income. However, if the dividend rate is cut to adjust for the stock dividend or if the company does not pay a regular cash dividend and has no intention of doing so, then the stockholder has received absolutely nothing new. In this case, the directors of the company should explain their action to the stockholders.

Much the same can be said about a "stock split," regardless of how the stock is divided – 2 for 1, 3 for 1, 3 for 2, or whatever. For example, if XYZ Company has 20,000,000 shares outstanding and the directors declare a 2 for 1 stock split, there would be 40,000,000 shares or twice as many outstanding after the split. If the stock price happened to be $50 before, it would be $25 after. At the same time, the earnings per share figure is also halved. A stockholder owning 100 shares before the split would, of course, own 200 shares after, but the total value would be the same (similar to holding two nickels instead of one dime). In other words, unless the dividend is increased, the stockholder receives nothing new when a company's stock is split.

There is, however, a school of thought that a lower priced stock becomes more "marketable" or more attractive to the investing public. To a certain degree, this is true. For psychological reasons primarily, some investors prefer owning stock in denominations of 100 shares, called "round lots," rather than any amount less than 100 shares, called "odd lots." It is a common belief by many investors that 600 shares of a $5 stock will appreciate in value more rapidly than 200 shares of a $15 stock or 10 shares of a $300 stock. While it is true that a lower-priced stock is often more volatile, the company's earnings progress is, by far, a more important influence on the future value of the stock.

Inexperienced investors can be misled by stock splits or, for that matter, by low-priced stocks in general. A $20 stock is not necessarily a better buy than a $40 stock. In fact, higher priced stocks are frequently among the leading companies in their industries.

For example, there is IBM in the office equipment field, GM among the auto companies, Alcoa Aluminum, Johnson & Johnson, and so on. While all of these stocks have split at one time or another, the managements of these and other leading companies are probably fully aware of the informal status of having their shares appear at a "respectable" price.

Normally, when a company – especially an important company – announces a stock split, the newspapers reveal the necessary details. *The Wall Street Journal* places an "s" after the company's stock symbol to denote "split" and then an "n" once the new shares trade on a split basis. Note on the next page how the *Journal* presented Microsoft's latest 2 for 1 split.

Years ago, a split rarely went undetected. There was a transitional period of at least a week or so between the time "old" shares were being traded and the new, split shares were trading. During this transition, the split stock would be trading on a "when-issued" basis, which meant the shares were authorized by the corporation but not yet issued or delivered.

The illustrations above show how a split used to appear in the newspaper using the sequence of Halliburton Company's 3 for 1 stock split of many years ago as an example. Today, the stock split ceremony is fast and less formal but the behind-the-scenes process remains the exactly same.

As the NYSE explains it: "Ordinarily, the date fixed for settlement of when-issued contracts is the fourth business day after the mailing of split shares. When-issued trading itself terminates on the mail date."

In Wall Street parlance, a "stock dividend" involves the distribution of less than 25%

5.8	29.75	18.32+MicrosSys MCRS		...	26 z82802	23.72	0.97
26.4	21.78	4.66+Microsemi MSCC		...	dd 1731	7.70	-0.18
-6.6	65	41.41 Microsoft MSFT	.16p	...	28 401698	48.30	1.31
2.0	24.30	23.10 Microsoft wi MSFTV n		...	... z3550	23.98	0.56
37.9	32.40	4.20 MicroStrat MSTR		...	10 3695	20.83	1.27
-33.3	2.32	0.01 MicroStratw n		...	... 14	0.04	...
-13.9	3.55	0.88 MicrotekMed MTMD		...	16 156	2.05	-0.03
-39.9	16.69	1.52 Microtune TUNE		...	dd 2122	1.88	0.03
8.5	13.68	2.64 Micrvisn MVIS		...	dd 624	5.77	-0.11

February 18

4.8	29.75	18.32+MicrosSys MCRS		...	25 1332	23.50	-0.22
29.9	21.78	4.66+Microsemi MSCC		...	dd 1174	7.91	0.21
-3.4	32.50	20.71 Microsoft MSFT s	.08p	...	29 560722	24.96	0.81
39.1	31.80	4.20 MicroStrat MSTR		...	10 3784	21	0.17
33.3	2.32	0.01 MicroStratw n		...	... 18	0.08	0.04
-13.1	3.55	0.88 MicrotekMed MTMD		...	16 368	2.07	0.02
-39.6	16.69	1.52 Microtune TUNE		...	dd 3573	1.89	0.01
9.4	13.68	2.64 Micrvisn MVIS		...	dd z54265	5.82	0.05

February 19

of the outstanding shares. A "partial stock split" is the distribution of 25% or more, but less than 100% of the outstanding shares. A "stock split" involves the distribution of 100% or more of the outstanding stock.

After a nasty bear market the price of a stock can be taken to an unacceptable level. The board of directors might declare a "reverse stock split." Shares that have fallen to penny-stock status could face delisting procedures or simply be shunned by the investment community. Thus, a reverse split might be appropriate. For example, a 1-for-10 reverse split would raise the share price of a $1.25 stock to $12.50. The effect is just the reverse of a stock split, as explained earlier. However, because the circumstances are not entirely positive, reverse splits rarely help stocks regain upside momentum immediately.

Short Interest One popular Wall Street trading technique is "short selling" or "selling a stock short." When an investor expects a stock to rise, it is purchased with an intention of selling it later at a higher price. On the other hand, if the price is expected to decline, the shares can legally be "sold short" by borrowing them from a broker and then immediately selling them on the open market. The short seller must buy an equivalent number of shares back later, hopefully at a lower price. Once repurchased, the same number of shares is repaid to the broker. The profit, or the

difference between the price at which the stock was sold and the price at which it was later purchased, belongs to the short seller (less commissions and taxes, of course).

At mid-month, each exchange announces its short-interest figures. This is a list of companies showing, individually, the number of shares that had been sold short and were still short as of the indicated date, usually the 14th or 15th. For the most part, these are shares that must be repurchased in the future. It can be said that a high short interest is both bearish (because many believe stock prices will be declining) and bullish (because these shares must be repurchased at some future date and, thus, represent potential buying power).

Mutual Funds Today there is a greater number of mutual funds than there are stocks so finding the mutual fund tables does not present a difficult task. Due to the diversification of their portfolios, mutual funds are much less volatile than individual stocks, so reviewing their prices every day may not be necessary – but reading the table is easy.

Because there are so many, *The Wall Street Journal* lists only those funds with $100 million or more of total net assets. The next page illustrates a small portion of a typical daily table.

T. Rowe Price Associates, the high-quality investment firm in Baltimore, has a family of no-load mutual funds and its offerings are typically found under the heading "Price Funds." For example, an investor who owns two TRP funds, the Capital Appreciation Fund and the New Era Fund, will see the following in the newspaper …

FUND	NAV	NET CHG	YTD %RET	3-YR %RET
P Q				
PBHG Funds				
CliprFoc	12.97	0.21	-1.9	14.3
EmgGro	8.44	0.13	0.6	-35.5
Growth	13.90	0.18	-2.0	-30.6
IRACapPres	10.00	...	0.3	5.7
LrgCpGr	14.67	0.17	-0.9	-20.8
LrgCpVl	9.90	0.15	-2.7	-2.2
LrgCp20	10.97	0.12	-1.8	-29.2
MidCpVal	12.43	0.18	-2.7	3.8
SelEq	15.43	0.15	-4.2	-36.1
SmtCpVl	13.63	0.07	-2.9	-2.7
TechCom	7.52	0.10	0.8	-51.2
PIMCO Fds Admin MMS				
CapAppAd p	12.38	0.18	-1.3	-9.9
PIMCO Fds Admin PIMS				
HiYldAd p	8.67	0.02	2.4	1.9
LDurAd p	10.27	0.01	0.2	7.6
LTrmGvt n	10.92	-0.01	-1.0	13.7
RealRetAd p	11.30	-0.03	0.5	NS
ShortTrmAd p	10.00	...	0.3	5.0
StockPlAd p	7.60	0.09	-2.1	-12.0
TotlRtAd p	10.67	...	0.3	10.5
TRII Ad p	10.27	...	0.2	10.3
PIMCO Fds Instl MMS				
CapApp	12.57	0.18	-1.2	-9.7
EmgComps	15.68	0.19	-1.0	1.4
MdCp	15.33	0.19	-1.6	-5.8
Renaissance	13.74	0.14	-6.5	6.4
RCM LCGwth	9.84	0.13	-2.6	-17.4
RCM MidCap	1.83	0.03	-1.1	-17.7
PIMCO Fds Instl PIMS				
EmMktsBd	9.33	0.03	1.4	19.6
FrgnBd	10.69	...	1.3	9.7
GlblBd	10.03	0.01	2.5	9.7
HiYld	8.67	0.02	2.4	2.1
LowDur	10.27	0.01	0.2	7.9
LowDurII	9.99	...	0.2	7.8
LTUSG	10.92	-0.01	-1.0	13.9
ModDur	10.33	0.01	0.3	10.3
MuniRd	10.17	...	-0.3	8.9
RealRtnl	11.30	-0.03	0.5	13.1
ShortT	10.00	...	0.3	5.2
Stk<PLS	7.74	0.09	-2.0	-11.7
TotRt	10.67	...	0.3	10.8

FUND	NAV	NET CHG	YTD %RET	3-YR %RET
PionFdC p	28.62	0.32	-4.1	-10.8
Pitcairn Funds				
DivValue	8.23	0.10	-2.9	NS
TaxFxRd	10.70	-0.01	-0.3	NS
Preferred Group				
AssetA	9.97	0.11	-2.3	-6.1
FxdIn	10.59	...	0.3	9.2
IntlVal	9.99	-0.03	-3.9	-7.2
LgCpGwth	8.44	0.13	-1.5	-21.6
ST Gov	10.12	...	...	7.1
Value	14.48	0.18	-3.0	-4.7
Price Funds				
Balanced	15.24	0.09	-1.7	-2.9
BlChip	21.57	0.32	-1.7	-13.2
CA Bond	11.01	-0.02	-0.8	8.3
CapApp	14.11	0.13	-0.7	11.4
DivGro	16.20	0.20	-3.3	-4.4
EmgMktB	10.45	0.01	0.9	12.1
EmMktS	10.10	0.04	-1.2	-33.9
EqInc	19.15	0.25	-3.2	1.3
EqIndex	23.11	0.30	-2.4	-13.2
Europe	11.93	0.01	-7.4	-16.6
FinSvcs	16.32	0.17	-2.6	6.4
FL Inter	11.11	-0.01	-0.5	7.3
ForEq	9.99	...	-6.1	-19.2
GNMA	9.87	-0.01	0.1	9.5
Growth	18.28	0.27	-1.6	-10.3
GrdIn	16.70	0.20	-2.4	-5.7
HelScl	14.52	0.20	0.1	-2.3
HiYield	6.34	-0.01	1.8	2.7
InstHiYld	9.98x	-0.02	1.6	NS
N Inc	8.90	-0.01	0.4	9.1
IntlBond	9.54	-0.01	2.9	6.8
IntlDis	15.99	-0.06	-0.4	-20.6
IntlStk	8.33	...	-6.2	-19.6
InstSmCap	9.12	0.09	-3.9	NS
Lat Am	6.98	0.02	-7.1	-11.0
MCapGro	30.48	0.41	-1.8	-5.0
MCapVal	14.70	0.12	-2.0	10.3
MCEqGr	14.94	0.20	-2.0	-5.1
MD Short	5.29	...	0.2	5.1
MD Bond	10.79	-0.02	-0.6	8.6
MediaTel	14.48	0.18	0.3	-19.1
N Amer	21.77	0.30	-1.3	-16.0
N Asia	5.74	0.03	2.7	-17.3
New Era	19.57	0.25	-5.1	2.8
N Horiz	16.17	0.16	-2.6	-12.3

On this day the Capital Appreciation Fund had a Net Asset Value of $14.11 which was $0.13 above the NAV for the previous day and down 0.8% since the beginning of the year. The New Era Fund reported a Net Asset Value of $19.57, a $0.25 gain from the prior day, and down 5.1% since the beginning of the year. For these funds, the trailing three-year annualized returns were 11.4% and 2.8%, respectively.

Business News In addition to the most popular *Wall Street Journal*, there are many newspapers that offer business news in detail. One of these is *Investor's Business Daily*. Although this paper is directed more to traders than to investors, and its stock tables are arranged in a very awkward manner, the additional statistics and analytical insights make the newspaper worth its competitive price.

The social, economic, and political circumstances of each market are never exactly the same, although "old-timers" occasionally cite similarities. Nevertheless, an investor can be well informed on the financial events of the day by focusing on two principal subjects: *The Business Cycle* and the status of *Inflation* or *Deflation*.

The Business Cycle

Described as the expansion or contraction of the economy as a whole, the business cycle has an important influence on the

Jobless Rate Jumped to 6.8% During March

profit trends of most companies. To keep abreast, there are eight key items the investor should watch:

(1) Trends in consumer confidence and spending.

(2) Actions by the Federal Reserve Board (FRB) to tighten or ease the supply of money.

(3) The trend of interest rates (the "treasury bill rate" or the "prime lending rate" are good benchmarks).

(4) The Government's Index of Leading Indicators.

(5) Tax increases or tax cuts.

(6) The accumulation or liquidation of business inventories.

(7) Capital expenditure plans of businesses for new plant and equipment.

(8) Government spending for defense and social needs.

Today, business is more global than ever before. The business cycle in the U.S. will be influenced to an ever-increasing extent by international trade opportunities, currency exchange rates between countries, and competing products and services from abroad.

Inflation or Deflation

Inflation, the declining value of money due to rising prices, is caused, many economists believe, by excessive Government spending. This subject should be closely monitored because it influences, and is influenced by, the business cycle. Moreover, and most importantly, inflation has a direct impact on the investment environment. A rising or declining inflation rate can shift the balance of investment returns between stocks, bonds and other alternatives.

In this regard, investors should watch the Consumer Price Index (see Appendix) and the Producer Price Index. The government announces the monthly figures for each on or about the middle of the month to follow. In addition, the Commodity Research Bureau (CRB) Index, along with the prices of gold, silver, and oil, are all good indicators for measuring inflation.

The effect of deflation, or declining prices mostly due to excessive competition or lack of demand, is best exemplified by the economic conditions of the early 1930's. As a general rule, the operating results of most companies can be hurt badly in an environment of high inflation OR steep deflation, especially if the company has little or no ability to control its prices.

House Approves Compromise Bill

Historically, the most positive environment for equities has been during periods of a declining rate of inflation (economists call this "disinflation"). The three periods in U.S. history when this environment was most prevalent (measured by year-to-year changes in CPI) were in the decade of the 1920's, the 1981 to 1986 period, and the 1991 to 2001 period.

Over the long term, investors can probably assume that inflation will persist ... to be held in check only temporarily by a slowdown or decline in business activity or by tough Fed policies (i.e., sharply higher interest rates). In its present form, the U.S. political system promotes inflation.

Politics and the Stock Market

Harry Truman once said: "the buck stops here." Not so with Congress. Under present circumstances, a responsible fiscal policy is nearly impossible because members of Congress will always find new programs on which to spend our fiat currency "for the benefit of their constituents." Politicians, of course, are motivated by re-election and are more apt to be elected if they deliver what they promised on the campaign trail.

There are two political measures that could help solve this problem – although neither is likely without a crisis to force the issue:

(1) Some means of restraining pork barrel legislation now that the line-item veto has been struck down by the Supreme Court; and

(2) A constitutional amendment that requires the Federal Budget to be balanced every year, including limits on spending, with exceptions only in cases of dire economic circumstances.

Unfortunately, both solutions are remote. If history is a guide, politicians never relinquish power willingly and, given a choice, they would prefer not to be held accountable for budget decisions.

When it comes to politics and the stock market, there is a general misconception regarding "the party in power." The U.S. Constitution places the burden of finance on Congress: "All Bills for raising Revenue shall originate in the House of Representatives; but the Senate may propose or concur with Amendments as on other Bills." The President can propose legislation, but can only temporarily halt Congressional spending. Therefore, the direction of the stock market depends mostly on the party that controls Congress.

Among other times, Republicans controlled both houses of Congress during the entire decade of the 1920's and from November, 1994 until May, 2001. And Republican control returned with the 2002 election.

LINDBERGH IS IN PARIS
PROHIBITION ENDED
THE WAR IS OVER
Astronauts Walk On The Moon

For more related discussions, see the later sections on the Federal Reserve Board as well as the chapter on Gold & Silver.

Conclusion Long term shareholders must continuously maintain a steady perspective and beware of excessive "news minutiae." Between the promotional financial channels on TV, the internet, magazines, and daily newspapers, investors can be misled by unimportant news items and can be "whipsawed" attempting to catch every short term cycle. When each so-called "critical financial story" breaks, the long term implications of its details will need to be weighed.

To benefit from this new input, it will be necessary to first develop a long-term economic picture on which an investment strategy should be based. Then, each day, decide how this new information relates to it. This personal scenario will change only gradually – and rarely will it be altered dramatically from one month to the next. But without this framework, it will be easy for the investor to "miss the forest for the trees," as they say, making success in the stock market that much more elusive.

Finally, the investor should be alert for unusual opportunities. History contains many examples of how unexpected events can affect stock prices. By definition, unexpected events cannot be predicted, but they sometimes present an opportunity to profitably buy or sell against the emotions of the crowd.

Beyond the emotions of the day, however, the keys to investment success are often found between the lines of the financial pages.

Investing
and trading

Introduction Noted financier Bernard M. Baruch once said "there is no investment which does not involve some risk and is not something of a gamble." Indeed, most experienced investors can immediately recognize the relationship between the risk level of a security and the reward it promises.

Because individuals' investment needs and objectives are different, their risk and reward expectations are different and their approaches to the stock market are different.

This chapter will help the new investor enter the Wall Street arena. It will aid in the selection of a stockbroker and provide guidelines to help the investor establish a realistic investment objective. In addition, it examines many market details serious investors should know. Explanations of the margin account, bear market strategies, hedges, arbitraging, a preliminary look at taxes, investment clubs, mutual funds, and the more-recent popular vehicles, ETFs, are among the topics discussed.

Family Financial Planning Financial advisors unanimously recommend against buying common stocks, preferred stocks, or long-term bonds at least until:

(1) Some money has been set aside to meet emergency family needs for a few months or longer.

(2) An adequate property, health, and life insurance plan has been established.

(3) Provisions have been made for other obvious needs such as a home and education.

Any money earmarked for investing (even including a retirement nest-egg) should be referred to as "risk capital" – no matter how conservative the intended investment program might be. Although the degree of risk can be controlled to a great extent, an investor should use only that capital that can be called "discretionary." Moreover, advisors often recommend against committing the entire amount at any one time or in any single investment. A flexible investment program provides considerable peace of mind.

Besides money, time is also a factor. Managing a portfolio properly requires a certain amount of time and effort. Surveys have shown that dedicated investors can spend six to twelve hours, or more, each month on investment work.

Tax-free retirement programs can be administered in various ways. Here, most individuals will require some honest and practical advice. There is no better time to begin than now.

For specific, personal advice on family financial planning, one approach might be to consult an attorney or an accountant, both being somewhat impartial observers. But, the fact is, nearly everyone today is trying to sell something financial.

A well-organized financial plan will reveal exactly how much risk capital can or should be made available. With this family program complete, a personalized "investment objective" can then be established to determine the types of investments most suitable under the circumstances. Here, a good stockbroker, sometimes called an "account executive," can be worth his or her weight in gold.

The Stockbroker Except for the folks in the oil patch in Texas many years ago, and Silicon Valley's boom & bust cycle recently, none have seen a greater change to their industry in such a short span of time than the stockbroker of just a few years ago.

At the highs of the bull market in 2000, there was also a peak in the number of stockbrokers in the United States. Several large NYSE member firms each have

10,000 or more registered representatives and at least 650,000 were registered with the NASD. With the bear market that followed, not to mention the growing acceptance of the internet and what it has to offer, the numbers have been dropping sharply. Also, their roles have been changing. Today's stockbroker places much greater emphasis on fee-based financial services. So now they are moving into the 21st century with a professional title that is antiquated, but with a broader financial perspective. Today, they can affectionately be called "stockbrokers," but they are more accurately defined as "financial consultants."

Searching for a good stockbroker is much like looking for a family doctor. Expertise, personality, and reputation are all important qualifications.

Ordinarily, a broker is referred by family, friends, or business associates. It is best to begin the search with a candidate list of two or three people. The choice would be made following individual "interviews" (really nothing more than friendly conversations).

The person selected should be employed by a reputable brokerage firm, preferably a New York Stock Exchange member firm, and have the necessary experience or access to it. As a stockbroker for a member firm, the individual is most likely a graduate of an extensive training course and has passed a comprehensive test prepared by the New York Stock Exchange and the National Association of Securities Dealers before being approved by the Securities and Exchange Commission.

The rules and code of ethics are strict. Among the many regulations, a broker is forbidden to guarantee any customer against a loss and cannot share in the profits or losses of any customer's account or rebate compensation to secure business.

Every broker interviewed will most likely appear as a friendly person in a busy, almost hectic environment. The choice might be difficult. It is not unusual for a broker to have two hundred customers, although probably no more than ten or fifteen might be considered extremely active. A broker is obviously on the phone often and cannot devote too much time to only one client, so the interview should be brief – perhaps in the evening.

Other items to consider during the interviews are personality, investment philosophy, quality of the firm's research, other services, and, of course, the level of commission rates and fees. Often, brokers have areas of special interests or investment talents. It is particularly beneficial when the broker/client relationship is compatible in this regard.

Sometimes, but not often, paperwork in the "back office" of a well-managed brokerage firm can result in clerical errors. Discussions with others who use the brokerage firm being considered could be one way to check the frequency of this possible inconvenience.

Once all interviews have been completed and the selection has been made, a conference should be held between the customer and the broker to review the client's investment objective. If personal finances are discussed, the topics might include age and family circumstances, income, personal debt, interest payments, insurance coverage, and inheritance, if any. As suggested earlier, it is advisable to have all family financial planning completed beforehand.

The brokerage firm charges a commission each time stock is bought and sold. The stockbroker, an employee of the firm, will receive a portion of that fee. For example, the commission on the purchase or sale of 200 shares of a $25 stock, a $5,000 investment, is typically about $75 to $100 (1.5% to 2%) – or much less using the internet – and, depending on the firm's policy, the stockbroker's share would be roughly $20-$40. A stockbroker's income obviously increases if stock is bought and sold more frequently which is, for the customer, usually counterproductive. This practice, taken to an extreme, is called "churning" and can result in severe penalties to the broker and to the firm if they encourage it. This is not usually a problem, however. Stockbrokers know it is to their own advantage in the long run for each customer to be a successful investor.

Stockbrokers should not be judged by the short-term price action of stocks recommended or not recommended (they can neither control stock prices nor consistently predict them). They should be judged primarily by the type and quality of service they provide for the commission dollars they are being paid.

To use a stockbroker most effectively, the investor should:

• Be considerate and call only when necessary rather than just to "chat." As a result, the stockbroker will return a call more promptly thinking it must be important. To be fair, a small-commission customer should not demand a large slice of the broker's time.

• Listen to the stockbroker's advice. The ultimate decision to buy or sell, however, should rest entirely with the customer – the same person assuming the credit or the blame for each decision.

• Be explicit when placing an order or giving instructions to minimize any "misunderstandings." This is important

*"Let me put it this way. It's five years from now. What am I
kicking myself for not having bought?"*

because most business is conducted over the telephone.

• Look to the stockbroker as a valuable information source. The customer should feel free to ask for research reports and other investment data. In most cases, this information, along with account access, is available via the brokerage firm's internet website. The broker can help here, too.

• Build a research library at home. Old stock guides, investment handbooks, annual reports, and other research material kept in home files will make the job of searching later for background information much easier.

Discount Brokers Most investors do not have the time. They also want or need the extra assistance and the stockbroker relationship the so-called "full-service" brokerage firm can provide. However, firms that offer cut-rate commissions, referred to as "discount brokers," are worth considering if the investor expects to be independent and active and figures that commission costs could be high.

An individual who trades only a few times each year might not find the substantially lower cost worthwhile considering all the services required. Also, in most cases, discount brokers post a minimum level of activity below which there could be an account maintenance fee. But for an active, independent investor trading fifteen or twenty times or more each year, the savings could be sizeable.

Ever since fixed commission rates have been abolished – and now with internet access – the selection of a discount broker has been made very easy. They are in every city. And as with other aspects of investing, if a discount broker is being considered, it would be wise to investigate the firm and its background.

Opening an Account Opening a brokerage account is no more difficult than initiating a charge account at a local store or a checking account with a bank. In fact, they are similar in many ways. The client must demonstrate a satisfactory credit rating, certain financial responsibilities must be met, the account can be personal or joint, and a monthly statement is usually mailed to the customer.

The typical stock brokerage office is a large room with ten to twenty desks for the brokers and a designated "gallery" area where customers can stand or sit to watch the ticker tape(s) on the wall that display stock prices. In addition, there is often a small library containing reference books, research reports, and other investment material, plus a quotation terminal, once called a "Quotron," available for customers who want real-time quotes and a "broad tape" for up-to-the-minute news items.

An artist's rendering of trading on the New York Stock Exchange in 1850

Depending upon the policies of the firm or office manager, it is usually not necessary to have an account with the brokerage firm to visit the office. However, it is considered discourteous to be in the way of the firm's regular customers.

For more about opening an online account, see the Internet chapter.

The day on which a share of stock is bought or sold is called the "trade date." The customer (and the brokerage firm) must deposit the required cash and/or securities into the account on or before the third business day after the transaction takes place. This deadline is known as the "settlement date." Saturdays, Sundays, and holidays are not included.

Once the brokerage firm has been paid in full for stock purchased, the new stockholder can request any one of three procedures:

(1) The stock can be "transferred and shipped." This means the name of the owner is transferred onto the stock certificate that is mailed to the designated address. This process, usually involving a transfer agent (e.g., a bank), normally takes about two weeks. The stockholder must then find a safe place to keep the certificate. If it is lost or destroyed it can, with some effort, be replaced.

(2) The stock can be "transferred and held." This means the certificate is prepared, as in the first case, but is kept for the owner in the brokerage firm's vault. If the stock is sold later, the owner must sign a "stock power" permitting transferal to the new owner.

(3) The stock can be held in "street name." In this instance, the stock is safely held by the broker in the broker's name for the customer's convenience. All dividends, otherwise mailed directly from the company to the stockholder, are credited to the account or forwarded as the customer directs. Corporate reports and proxy statements (used for voting) are forwarded to the customer.

The monthly statement mailed to the customer is similar to a bank statement in appearance. It shows, in addition to other data, a beginning balance, all transactions made during the period, a final cash balance, and stock positions at the end of the period. Stock held in the account at the date of the statement is said to be "long"; stock owed to the account by the customer is said to be "short."

There are two basic types of accounts – a cash account and a margin account. Many brokerage customers have both.

The cash account, by far the most popular, is used when securities are bought or sold in a direct cash transaction. In a cash account, every transaction is concluded on or before the settlement date. If stock has been purchased, the customer has paid for it in full, the customer's broker has paid the seller's broker, and the shares have been credited to the buyer's account ... all within three business days.

A margin account, which will be explained in greater detail later, allows the customer to borrow from the broker part of the amount needed to purchase or sell securities. The minimum New York Stock Exchange requirement is $2,000 to open a margin account in which most types of securities can be bought and sold. The margin account, like the cash account, demands that all transactions be concluded by a settlement date, but a customer buying or selling "on margin" need not deposit more than the required amount by that time. The broker will extend some credit to the customer based on the amount of cash and/or securities in the account. For this service, the customer pays an interest charge to the broker.

Because a minor does not have the legal power to contract in his or her own name, opening a brokerage account is limited to adults. Until the mid-1950s, giving securities to minors and having shares registered in a minor's name presented complications. Since then, to deal with this problem, all states have adopted laws similar in most cases to the 1956 Uniform Gifts to Minors Act sponsored by the brokerage industry. Under these laws, minors can own securities in special "custodial accounts" if the minor also has an adult custodian (most likely an adult family member). The laws are different in many states. It is, therefore, advisable to know the legalities and their possible disadvantages before a custodial account is opened.

Professional Counsel A professional investment advisor is worth considering if an individual has a large sum of money to invest, say $100,000 or more, and has neither an interest in mutual funds (explained later) nor the time to devote to personal portfolio management. Advisory fees, which are usually tax-deductible, vary. The fee is typically 1% to 1.5% annually on portfolios up to about $200,000. Thereafter, the cost declines proportionately. The investor must still pay brokerage commissions but may designate a stockbroker, give the counselor freedom to select the broker, or instruct that orders be executed at the lowest possible commission rate.

Most investment counselors work closely with several stockbrokers and a few banks to obtain their services. Commissions directed to brokers (typically for research services) are referred to as "soft dollars." In addition to investment counselors, trust departments of many banks also offer professional services. These services frequently include both portfolio management and custodial functions, for essentially the same 1% to 1.5% fee structure. Most investment counselors and banks either have in-house investment research or the ability to obtain it elsewhere. Custodial functions, such as safekeeping of securities, dividend or interest collection and disbursements, and other accounting tasks, are handled primarily by banks.

The recommended approach, at least initially, for persons employing professional money management services is a "nondiscretionary" account with an understanding that the advisor has some freedom in managing the portfolio. In this way, the investor will be involved, can learn more about the investment process, and be in a better position to evaluate the style and talents of the portfolio manager.

Investment Objectives Selecting an objective that best meets an individual's personal financial needs is difficult. There are often many confusing alternatives.

Generally speaking, portfolios are managed for income, capital appreciation, or safety, or some combination thereof.

Risk and Reward

Perhaps the most basic of all Wall Street concepts is: "The greater the expected return, the greater the investment risk." In effect, the "risk/reward ratio," as it is often called, places a desire to preserve capital at one end of the spectrum and a desire to maximize return at the other end. Evidence of this principle has been documented in several thorough studies of historic rates of investment return. The table presented on the next page is based on these findings. It shows, in very general terms, the approximate risk/reward choices investors have had over the past several decades. Throughout this period, the rate of inflation averaged 2-4% annually.

It is important to note that this risk/reward table can change dramatically from one month to the next as investors respond to changes in interest rates or inflation. For example, given an inflation rate of 5.5%, U. S. Treasury Bills 4.5%, Savings Accounts 5.0%, and Corporate Bonds 7.5%, one might conclude that a share of stock should provide a return of at least 10% to be competitive for the investor's dollar. Today, it might be less than that.

With the higher interest and inflation rates experienced in past years, it is easy to see why investors have become more sensitive to these relationships.

Investment	Degree of Risk	Annual Return (Reward)
Treasury Bill	*Smallest degree of risk. Only the government has the power to print money. The return is usually just enough to offset inflation.*	2.5–3.5%
Government Bond	*High degree of safety. Adjusted for inflation, the return is modest.*	3.0–4.0%
Savings Account	*Greater risk than government bonds, although funds are insured by the government. Little protection against higher rates of inflation.*	3.5–4.5%
Corporate Bond	*More risk than a savings account. Priority over common stock if there is a business failure. Adjusted for inflation, the return is modest.*	4.0–5.0%
Share of Stock	*The highest degree of risk due to possible business failure. The return includes about 4% from dividends. Some protection from inflation.*	7.0–9.0%

In addition, each category on the table obviously has its own risk/reward scale—and all opportunities relate to one another. There are, for example, many low-quality bonds that provide a better return (also with greater risk) than the typical high-quality stock.

Selection and Timing

To be successful on Wall Street, every investor must find a satisfactory combination of two key variables ... *Investment selection* and *timing*. While it may sound elementary and trite, an investor must make the proper selection at the proper time to obtain the best possible results. A wrong selection at the wrong time can be costly and mixed results can be obtained with any other combination.

As a general rule, investment selection and investment timing are inversely important. When the investment horizon is longer, selection becomes more important than timing. But timing is far more critical when the horizon is shorter. For example, the common stock of Deere, the leading manufacturer of farm equipment, was quoted well off its high at $42 per share in 2002. Had the stock been purchased at $18 (adjusted for splits) in 1991, an investor would have been disappointed that it was selling 25% lower a mere twelve months later. Yet it was just a good opportunity to buy more. A trader in 1992 would have

viewed the situation differently and may have sold it. If the company is growing, it can be said that time works in favor of the long term investor.

Total Return

Securities analysts often compare investment opportunities by estimating the total capital appreciation, plus dividend (or interest) return, each investment provides annually. This calculation, expressed as a total annual percentage figure, is referred to as "total return."

Done properly, total return takes into account possible tax consequences – especially when tax-free investments are under consideration. Because taxes are personal and unique to each investor, they are excluded in the examples to follow, however.

Future capital appreciation of a stock is difficult to estimate. To make the calculation easier, analysts assume in their total return assumptions that today's price/earnings ratios will not be changing in the future. This means the estimated growth rate of earnings per share can be used in place of the capital appreciation estimate. Thus, a stock with a projected earnings per share growth rate of 8% and a current dividend yield of 3% is offering a total return of 11% before taxes.

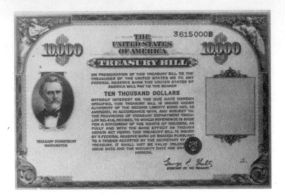

The Treasury Bill is an investment benchmark, although the certificates are no longer in use.

Using this total return approach, an investor can immediately see what each investment offers. A hypothetical comparison is illustrated below.

	Possible Capital Appreciation	Dividend or Interest Yield	Total Return
"X" Growth Stock (Earnings Per Share Growth + Div. Yield)	10%	2%	12%
"Y" Income Stock (Earnings Per Share Growth + Div. Yield)	7%	5%	12%
"Z" Corporate Bond (Bond Discount to Maturity + Int. Yield)	2%	7%	9%*
Savings Account	0%	5%	5%
Treasury Bill	4%	0%	4%

* Also called "yield to maturity."

In this case, an investor comparing total return opportunities must make a value judgment between the highly-assured 4% return of the treasury bill, a reasonably safe 5% return of the savings account, a less certain 9% return of the bond, and a much less certain 12% return from either stock. To repeat, taxes must also be taken into consideration.

Finally, when comparing individual stocks of similar quality that offer the same total return investors should realize that a growth stock probably represents higher initial market risk and greater reward over time than a slower-growing, higher-yielding stock. In the preceding example, both stocks promise the same total return of 12% but, based on the "bird-in-the-hand" argument, there might be greater assurance obtaining 12% from the income stock initially than from the growth stock. However, patient investors will find that future earnings increases of the growth stock will, within a few years, produce superior investment results overall.

The Margin Account In a land of credit cards and financial conveniences and more than 80 million investors, it is somewhat surprising there are only a few million margin accounts in use. While it is true the margin account is sometimes complex and definitely not for everybody, its application extends well beyond the simple function of buying securities on credit. The margin account is a tool that provides flexibility for the serious investor.

Upon opening a margin account and submitting the normal credit information, the investor will be asked to sign a margin agreement and loan consent which will permit the brokerage firm to pledge or lend securities carried for the account. In addition, the margin account will be subject to various rules including, as mentioned earlier, an initial minimum requirement of the NYSE, an initial margin requirement established by Regulation T of the Federal Reserve Board (FRB), and maintenance requirements enforced by the brokerage firm.

The initial margin requirement is the minimum percent of total value investors must deposit to purchase or sell securities in a margin account. The initial margin requirement for stocks (not all stocks qualify) has been raised twelve times and lowered ten times since the FRB was given power to regulate security credit under the Securities Exchange Act of 1934. The margin requirement since 1934 has been as low as 40% (1937) and as high as 100% (1946). The most recent Board action was in January 1974 when the initial margin requirement was lowered from 65% to 50%. In other words, to make a $10,000 stock purchase in a margin account today, an investor must put up, within five days, at least $5,000 collateral rather than $6,500 as it was before.

There is an easy way to calculate the amount that can be bought with a specific amount of cash available:

*Add two zeros and divide
by the margin number.*

By applying this simple formula, an investor can quickly see that $6,000 cash will buy $8,571 worth of marginable securities when the margin requirement is 70% ($6,000 + 00 divided by 70); or $10,000 when the margin is 60% ($6,000 + 00 divided by 60); or $12,000 when the margin is 50% ($6,000 + 00 divided by 50).

Using the figures in the last case as an example, if the margin requirement is 50% and the investor deposits $6,000 cash collateral, a decision to purchase, say, $9,000 of marginable stock would be recorded in the margin account in this manner:

$9,000 Current Market Value
  3,000 Debit Balance
  _____

$6,000 Current Equity
  4,500 Required Margin (50% x $9,000)
  _____

$1,500 Excess Margin (can be withdrawn
          or invested)

The $1,500 excess margin, if invested, has a "buying power" of $3,000 (i.e., $1,500 + 00 divided by 50) which, with the $9,000 already invested, would take the account up to its marginable limit of $12,000.

"Debit balance" is money the investor owes to the brokerage firm. For this service, the investor is charged an interest rate somewhat above the prime rate charged by banks. This cost should not be disregarded. Normally based on a daily average of the debit balance, the interest cost can fluctuate from month-to-month as interest rates swing. For example, several years ago, when the prime rate rose to about 12%, an investor's annual cost of carrying a debit balance could have been 14% or more. This is a high price to pay for stock market capital.

A margin account provides leverage that can expand or contract an investor's equity position quickly as the figures below demonstrate.

Continuing the earlier example, if the market value of the portfolio climbed 22% from $9,000 to $11,000, the investor's equity would increase 33% and buying power would be 67% greater.

$11,000 Current Market Value
   3,000 Debit Balance
  _____

$ 8,000 Current Equity
    500 Required Margin (50% x $11,000)
  _____

$ 2,500 Excess Margin ($5,000 buying
           power)

If, instead of rising, the value of the portfolio declined 22% to $7,000, the results would be quite different. In this Case, equity declines 33% and buying power drops 67%.

$7,000 Current Market Value
  3,000 Debit Balance
  _____

$4,000 Current Equity
  3,500 Required Margin (50% x $7,000)
  _____

   500 Excess Margin ($1,000 buying
          power)

At most brokerage firms, the margin account is the responsibility of a centralized back office department, called the margin department. With the help of computers, these people review every account daily to

The curbstone brokers filling orders during a blizzard in the early 1900's

keep the firm's stockbrokers and customers informed regarding certain guidelines. The first is a check to see whether a margin customer's equity is above or below the current Federal initial margin requirement, as explained earlier. If it has fallen below, the account is considered "restricted." In a restricted account, the investor has no additional buying power and cannot withdraw more than 30% of any sale proceeds. The remaining 70% would be retained to reduce the debit balance.

Another guideline closely watched is the maintenance requirement set by the New York Stock Exchange (NYSE) or by the brokerage firm itself, which sometimes has a requirement that is more strict than that of the exchange. The NYSE maintenance requirement states that a customer's equity may at no time be less than 25% of the market value of securities carried (brokerage firms often set a 30% or 35% limit). If equity does drop below this level, the account is said to be "under-margined" and the customer will be asked to put up more margin. This is known as a "margin call." If more collateral is not deposited, the securities are sold by the broker.

The margin department will establish more than one type of margin account for a customer who uses margin for other specific reasons such as selling stock short, buying or selling convertible bonds, buying or selling nonconvertible bonds,

and so on. Moreover, margin requirements often vary for different types of securities. There are, in other words, many details investors should learn before using a margin account extensively. This information can be obtained from most brokerage firms or by writing to:

The New York Stock Exchange
11 Wall Street
New York, New York 10005

"Playing the Market" There are several tools and strategies that can lend versatility to an investment program and, in some cases, make stock market investing more profitable. While many of these techniques are not appropriate for conservative long-term portfolios, all serious investors should at least be aware of the alternatives available.

Types of Orders

The *market order* to buy or sell is the most widely used type. It is simply an instruction to the stockbroker and others involved to buy or sell stock at the best possible price once the order reaches the trading post or trading desk. Normally, a market order is executed at a price reasonably close to the quote obtained before the order was entered. If the stock is volatile, however, the final price could be better or worse than expected. It normally takes only a few minutes to complete a market order transaction and report back to the stockbroker. In most cases, a confirmation is mailed to the investor within 24 hours.

The *limit order* is an instruction to buy or sell a stated amount of stock at a specific price (or better). When the target price is not within the current market quote, it is said to be "away from the market" and will be entered on the specialist's book beneath any similar orders received earlier. Therefore, if there are, as they say, "shares ahead of you," the limit order may not be executed immediately or maybe not at all at that price.

The *stop order*, called a stop-loss order many years ago, is a trading tool designed to protect a profit or prevent further loss if the stock begins to move in the wrong direction. This idea is based on the ageless Wall Street advice: "Let your profits run; cut your losses short." The stop order becomes a market order once the stock trades at or through a certain price, known as the "stop price." If the stop price is reached, there is no guarantee the executed price will be as favorable. It is possible, for example, to place an order to sell 100 shares of XYZ at 54 "stop" and later receive notice that your stock was sold at 53 1/2. Except in technical analysis situations, the stop price should not be placed too close to the current market price since many stocks can randomly fluctuate 15% or more in a brief period of time. Long term investors will probably not need the stop order in the normal course of investing.

The *stop limit order* is a stop order and limit order combination. Like the stop order, it is a trading tool that requires extreme care. A stop limit order to *buy* means, "as soon as a trade occurs at this top price or higher the order becomes a limit order to buy." A stop limit order to *sell* works the same way. As soon as a trade occurs at the stop price or lower, the order becomes a limit order to sell.

Each order to buy or sell may be entered for a single trading day, week, or month, or it may be an "open order" – also called a "good 'til canceled (GTC) order." An open order will remain in force until it is canceled by the investor. However, the investor does have an obligation to keep the broker informed on the status of every open order because the exchange specialist must receive confirmation at regular intervals. Not all brokerage firms accept stop orders or GTC orders for unlisted stocks.

Dollar Cost Averaging

There are no magic formulas to stock market investing, but one widely used and frequently successful approach is dollar cost averaging. Dollar cost averaging involves

Year	Annual Price Range	Shares Bought	Shares Owned at Year End	Average Price	Estimated Annual Dividend Check
1	$29.63–20.38	80	80	$25.00	$ 25
2	26.50–19.25	90	170	23.50	106
3	30.25–23.13	75	245	24.50	251
4	38.25–26.13	63	308	26.00	422
5	37.50–22.63	70	378	26.50	594
6	32.75–21.88	77	455	26.38	664
7	47.75–29.25	52	507	27.63	571
8	48.63–30.75	57	564	28.38	633
9	40.75–29.75	57	621	29.00	702
10	46.38–32.63	56	677	29.50	770

purchasing the same dollar amount of stock at regular intervals regardless of price. As a result, more shares are bought at low prices than at high prices. Dollar cost averaging usually works well when the investor:

(1) Has an investment horizon of at least several years.

(2) Selects a company that has favorable growth prospects that could lead to a rising stock price over the long term.

(3) Selects a high-quality stock that, preferably, pays a dividend.

(4) Is willing to continue the program relentlessly – barring any major change in the company's long term outlook.

As a real-life example of dollar cost averaging, the table above shows the result of a ten-year investment program. The name is not important. This stock's price performance was especially disappointing in this specific time frame and it was selected for this reason.

During the period, the company's earnings record was erratic but profits did grow from $2.79 per share in year ONE to $3.08 per share in year TEN. At the same time, the dividend was increased from $0.69 per share to $1.20 per share. In the beginning the stock price was $29. At the end it was just above $32.

The table above illustrates the result of investing $500 quarterly throughout the ten-year period. The program was accomplished by buying the rounded number of shares $500 would purchase each time. After ten years, the total capital invested was $20,000 before commissions (probably not more than $800).

If profits grow, dividends can become more important as time passes. Had the investor continued the program shown above, nearly half of the annual $2,000 investment would have been contributed by dividends five years later.

Better still, today many companies offer direct dividend reinvestment plans (called "DRIPS"). By reinvesting dividends without transaction costs an investor can enjoy the huge benefit of compounding values. See the Growth Stocks chapter for even more dramatic dividend examples.

Exchange Traded Funds (ETFs)

Perhaps the most attractive investment vehicle created in recent years is the Exchange Traded Fund, known as an ETF. It is a basket of securities designed to track an index, whether it is a broad market, an industry sector, or an international stock. However, an ETF trades almost exactly like a stock.

This clever idea was pioneered by the American Stock Exchange in early 1993 with the introduction of the Standard & Poor's Depositary Receipt (SPDR, and pronounced "spider"). It trades on the Amex with the ticker symbol SPY. On its tenth anniversary, SPY assets totaled $35 billion and had an average daily trading volume of 34 million. The Amex now offers more than 120 different ETFs with assets totaling over $100 billion.

One of the most notable of Amex's ETFs is the Dow Jones Industrial Average fund known as "Diamonds" with the symbol DIA. Another, and even more popular, is QQQ which tracks the value of the Nasdaq-100 Index (about 1/40 value).

Over the years, most mutual fund portfolio managers have been unable to match the performance of the S&P 500 and the DJIA. So, introducing an investment that moves in lock-step with each average can be a compelling alternative to a managed fund. An ETF offers diversification, lower costs (regular brokerage commissions apply), all day trading (most mutual funds can only be purchased or redeemed at day-end prices), tax efficiency, and dividend opportunities. As with mutual funds, ETFs also offer hedging possibilities. One disadvantage: A slight market premium can develop when the market's trend is obvious to all. Prospectuses can be obtained from the Amex and NYSE.

Bear Market Strategies

Stock prices will tend to rise over the very long term. They always have. Yet, since World War I, there have been no fewer than ten major bear markets in which stocks declined dramatically. In the bear markets of 1929-1932, of 1973-1974, in 1987, and, of course, in the early 2000's the market values of a great many stocks were sliced by more than half. Moreover, as a general rule, prices often drop faster than they rise. Experienced investors realize that the "disasters" that occur frequently in bear markets can be devastating to the long-term performance of any portfolio. While most people are merely trying to preserve capital or hedge in a bear market, the risk-oriented trader regards severe market weakness as an opportunity to make a substantial profit.

There are several ways to make money in a bear market:

Buying Special Purpose Funds There are mutual funds to meet this need, as explained shortly. It can be a good tool.

Buying Contra-market Stocks When the market (measured by the averages or any broad list) is advancing or declining, the contra-market stock will be moving in the opposite direction. It is usually among an industry group that has attracted special attention for one reason or another. A

The SPX pit . . . options trading on the Chicago Board Options Exchange in Chicago

contra-market stock is especially noticeable during a bear market when everything else is dropping. Each bear market is different. In years past, the groups that outperformed the market were oil and gas in 1946; pharmaceuticals, food, and tobacco in 1957; gold briefly in 1962; and coal and automobile replacement parts in 1969-1970. One of the worst bear markets since the 1930s occurred in 1973-1974 when gold, sugar, steel, and fertilizer stocks were in favor. During the bear market of the early 2000's, gold stocks performed very well.

Once a bear market has ended, contra-market stocks do not follow a definite pattern. Sometimes they continue rising, sometimes they turn down immediately. In any case, the investor should investigate the industry and company before buying. It is not advisable to buy a stock simply because it is going up when other stocks are declining.

Buying Put Options A put option is a contract to sell 100 shares at a definite price within a specified time limit. The put option buyer (who expects the stock price to decline in the short term) purchases the right to "put" the stock to someone else under the terms of the contract.

There are two primary reasons for buying a put option in a bear market: (1) As a leveraged, high-risk vehicle to obtain a quick capital gain; or (2) As a defensive hedge against a stock the investor does not want to sell for various reasons – usually taxes.

Writing Call Options A call option is a contract to buy 100 shares at a definite price within a specified time limit. A call option buyer (who expects the stock price to rise in the short term) purchases the right to "call" the stock from someone else under the terms of the contract. Thus, an investor who owns 100 shares of stock and believes its price might be going down can write a call option against those shares and sell the option to someone who believes the stock price will be going up.

Writing a call option when the stock is not owned is referred to as "writing a naked call option." The writer of a naked call option can only profit by the amount received from the option buyer, but much more can be lost. In other words, the writer is a speculator willing to bet the stock will not be rising within the time limit of the contract. Writing a naked call option is, obviously, a very high-risk undertaking and is *not* recommended for most investors.

Short Selling Selling a stock (or an ETF) short is one of the best ways for investors to profit in a bear market. Of course, this approach is not appropriate for everyone and there is an additional risk involved.

In effect, the normal sequence of the purchase and sale is reversed. When stock is sold short, the brokerage firm either lends the stock to the customer or borrows it for the customer, who then sells it in the open market. Eventually the same number of shares will have to be repurchased (this is referred to as "short covering") and be returned to the lender. If the repurchase price is lower because the stock dropped as expected, the short seller will make a profit. If the price is higher, more money will be needed to cover the same number of shares and the short seller will suffer a loss.

There is a special risk to short selling. Stock that is bought "long" in the regular way cannot drop below zero and, therefore, does not involve a loss greater than the total investment. But a stock sold short could, theoretically, produce unlimited losses. There is no ceiling to a stock's appreciation potential. For this reason, the fear of being "squeezed" can make the short seller a more restless investor. To limit this potential loss, the short seller can use a stop order or, preferably, purchase a call option as a hedge against the short position.

Unless the investor is experienced with short selling, it is best not to short a stock that (1) has a favorable fundamental outlook (i.e., having earnings gains or an improving profit trend); (2) has already suffered a price decline of 60% or more; (3) has been strong technically (e.g., the price should not be above its average price of the prior 200 days); or (4) is a candidate for a merger.

Note that ETFs, unlike stocks, are not subject to the up-tick rule (i.e., for stocks, there must be an up-tick trade before the shares are sold during the short sale).

In the discussion of margin earlier, short selling was not explained to avoid confusion. It is more complicated. A short seller must know three things to calculate the current equity figure in the margin account:

(1) The initial credit (deposit).
(2) The stock's current market value.
(3) The net proceeds of the short sale.

Current equity can be found by using the two-step formula shown above.

As an example, assume an investor sells short 100 shares of Baltimore Buggy Whip at $70 after depositing $5,000 cash into the margin account. The formula would read:

$$.714 = \frac{\$7,000 + \$5,000}{\$7,000} - 1.000$$
$$\$5,000 = .714 \times \$7,000$$

Step 1.

$$\text{Current Margin} = \frac{\text{Proceeds} + \text{Deposit}}{\text{Market Value}} - 1.000$$

Step 2.

$$\text{Current Equity} = \text{Current Margin} \times \text{Market Value}$$

If the stock declines to $55, the short sale becomes profitable and current equity increases:

$$1.182 = \frac{\$7,000 + \$5,000}{\$5,500} - 1.000$$
$$\$6,500 = 1.182 \times \$5,500$$

On the other hand, if Baltimore Buggy Whip had advanced to $85, the short seller's equity would have been reduced:

$$.412 = \frac{\$7,000 + \$5,000}{\$8,500} - 1.000$$
$$\$3,500 = .412 \times \$8,500$$

As the stock rises, the current margin drops, which, in turn, reduces current equity. At $85 and a current margin of 41%, the investor is probably unhappy, but still safe from a margin call. If the brokerage firm's maintenance requirement happens to be 35% on short sale transactions, a margin call for an additional deposit would be issued if the stock advances to $89.

Taxes

Tax laws are complicated. To make matters worse, they are always changing. When tax problems are encountered, it is advisable to seek the help of a qualified accountant. In fact, a few of the strategies suggested in this book will require professional tax guidance.

Active investors are constantly faced with tax decisions. It is now especially true, because tax reforms in 1986 and later in 1997 changed the way investors must treat capital gains when filing income taxes. The 60% capital gain deduction for individuals, estates, and trusts has been eliminated. Under these laws, all capital gains, whether short-term or long-term, are now being treated as ordinary income. While it is possible for tax rates to be higher than the 15% and 28% brackets into which most families will fall, the tax rate for capital gains cannot, by law, exceed 20% (or 10% if the taxpayer is in the 15% tax bracket).

If an individual would like to continue investing in the stock market and wants to establish a tax loss, there are basically three things that can be done:

(1) Sell the stock outright and repurchase it 31 days or later.

(2) Purchase an equal number of shares (called "doubling up") and sell the original holdings 31 days later.

(3) Sell the stock and immediately replace it with another stock.

Before 1997, investors who wanted to postpone profits from one year to the next could use a technique called "shorting against the box." This transaction was essentially the same as normal short selling except the short position would be covered by similar shares already in the account rather than borrowing them from the broker. But it is no longer allowed. Still, investors should avoid waiting until December to work out a tax strategy.

Arbitrage

On Wall Street, the term "arbitrage" refers to the simultaneous purchase and sale of two different securities which have a close relationship (e.g., a convertibility of one security into the other) to take advantage of a disparity in their prices. This activity can apply to equivalent securities trading in different markets, securities with convertible features, or securities involved in mergers, tender offers, recapitalizations, or corporate divestitures.

A "merger arbitrageur," sometimes known as the riverboat gambler of Wall Street, will risk a substantial loss in an attempt to make a small, quick profit. Purchasing one stock and short selling the other eliminates all risk, except a possible change in the agreement that reduces the terms of the merger – an unusual situation – or a termination of the proposal – a much more likely event. In other words, if the proposed merger is completed, a smart merger arbitrageur will almost always make a profit. If the marriage is not consummated, however, the purchased stock could decline sharply and the short stock could rise, producing a substantial loss.

Hundreds of viable arbitrage opportunities arise each year. Therefore, anyone entering this arena can afford to be patient and should select and research the situation carefully.

There are several brokerage firms that specialize in arbitrage activity and make a point of being well-informed. The spreads, therefore, tend to be fairly representative of the risk involved.

An individual willing to assume the risks of merger arbitrage should establish a list of personal criteria and concentrate on only the mergers that meet those standards. For example, it might be advisable for the acquired company to be high quality, medium-sized, and in a growing field that is different from the acquiring company. As such, there could easily be other suitors and the chance of government intervention would be less.

Because the risks in merger arbitrage are high, the investor should either make an effort to become knowledgeable about the companies involved, or simply avoid merger arbitrage altogether.

Investment Clubs An individual seeking fun, education, and profit can join or start an investment club. Typically, it is a group of 10 to 15 friends who meet once a month to manage their collective investment portfolio. The monthly contribution from each member, a modest sum that is convenient to the membership, is pooled and usually invested in growth stocks using a dollar cost averaging approach. Dividends and capital gains are reinvested in most cases.

About 28,000 investment clubs (only a fraction of the large, unknown number established in the United States) belong to the National Association of Investors Corporation (NAIC), founded in 1951.

The NAIC is a nonprofit organization that provides guidance and literature to its membership. Individuals may be NAIC members for a $39 annual fee, or clubs may belong for an annual payment of $40 plus $14 per member. Further information on investment clubs or on the NAIC may be obtained by contacting:

The National Association
of Investors Corporation
P.O. Box 220
Royal Oak, Michigan 48068

Toll-free (877) 275-6242
www.better-investing.org

Investment Companies Being part owner of a portfolio that is managed by professionals is a good alternative for individuals who:

(1) Neither have an interest in security analysis nor the time for their own portfolios;

(2) Do not want to pay an investment advisor;

(3) Are willing to forego some capital appreciation potential to obtain a professionally-managed diversified portfolio.

There are two kinds of funds that investment companies manage: open-end funds, also called mutual funds, and closed-end funds.

An open-end fund deals directly with investors and always stands ready to sell or buy its shares at current net asset value. Stated differently, an investor can buy shares from a mutual fund (subscribe) or sell shares to the fund (redeem) at any time. As a result, money flows in or out of a mutual fund when investors subscribe for or redeem shares. A closed-end fund, on the other hand, has a fixed number of shares outstanding and investors buy or sell them in the open market like any other stock. Because the market price rises or falls according to supply and demand, the

98

price of a closed-end fund share can be at a premium or, most likely, at a discount to its net asset value at any time.

Therefore, if the investor wants the market value of each share to directly reflect the net asset value of the fund's portfolio, an open-end fund is preferable to a closed-end fund.

A mutual fund can be either a "load fund" or a "no-load fund." When an investor buys a load fund, a sales charge (called the "load") is normally deducted immediately from the investment to compensate the salesman who sold the fund. This fee is typically 6% or more and is usually charged one time, up front. However, a no-load fund is bought directly from the investment company, and the investor is not charged a fee, although both also charge operational expenses. Otherwise, load funds and no-load funds are comparable in terms of their operations and investment performances.

At least once a year, *Business Week*, among other business publications, reviews the performances of load and no-load mutual funds. These articles frequently provide extensive data and other background information as well. Furthermore, many public libraries subscribe to services that also cover this subject in great detail and there many additional sources on the internet.

Unless there is a strong reason to prefer a particular load fund management, no-load funds should always be considered first. A load fund portfolio must grow annually about 2% faster than a no-load fund portfolio for investors in each just to be even at the end of a five-year period.

Mutual Funds A mutual fund is an investment company, usually organized by an advisory firm, for the purpose of offering the fund's shareholders a specific investment objective. Anyone buying shares in the fund becomes a part owner and, agreeing with the fund's investment objective, wants to participate.

To manage the company, the shareholders elect a board of directors to oversee the operations of the business and the portfolio. Normally, the advisory firm that organized the company is selected as the investment advisor and operations manager. For this service, the firm is paid an annual fee (typically about one-half of one percent of net assets) that will vary according to the size of the fund.

It is often assumed that the investment advisory firm is the "owner" of the fund. Actually, the shareholders own it and may decide to hire another investment advisor if the fund's performance is unsatisfactory.

Many advisory firms manage more than one mutual fund and each fund in this "family"

Some Funds Gain From Falling Dollar

usually has a different investment objective. Often, with just a quick telephone call, an investor can switch money from one fund to another to achieve a different investment objective or to pursue a new investment strategy. In fact, this is one big reason to prefer mutual funds over ETFs. The biggest question otherwise: How talented is the manager?

All mutual funds are closely regulated by the SEC. A "prospectus," which explains the fund, its investment objectives, and the risks, must be made available to all potential investors.

Aside from the sales fee, or "load," as discussed earlier, mutual fund investors should be aware of any special charges against the fund's assets for marketing and advertising (sometimes referred to as "12b-1" plans). The ratio is excessive whenever 12b-1 expenses exceed 0.5% of assets.

As stated earlier, the mutual fund will stand ready to buy back (redeem) or sell shares at their net asset value (NAV) at any time. If it is a well-known or popular fund, its per-share value is most likely quoted daily in the financial section of any major newspaper. The value of each share is entirely dependent upon the value of the securities in the portfolio. For this reason, become familiar with the largest holdings.

There are six basic types of mutual funds:

• **Common Stock Funds** invest almost entirely in equities (common stocks), although their objectives vary considerably. *Growth funds* are seeking capital appreciation by selecting companies that should grow more rapidly than the general economy. *Aggressive growth funds* buy shares in small or more speculative growth companies for maximum capital appreciation. *Growth and income funds* seek long term capital appreciation with income. *Index funds*, a popular type in recent years, buy representative stocks to simply match the market indices.

• **Special Purpose Funds** attempt to satisfy certain investment interests such as participation in technology, gold, or energy. These funds can also use futures and options and short selling to meet more aggressive objectives. In addition, funds of this type can be used as a method for hedging portfolios in bear markets.

• **Income Funds** are portfolios consisting of bonds and common stocks as well as preferred stocks. Income fund managers try to obtain satisfactory interest and dividend income for the shareholders.

• **Bond Funds** seek high income and preservation of capital by investing primarily in bonds and selecting the proper mix between short-term, intermediate-term, and long-term bond maturities. In recent years, tax-free municipal bond funds have been popular.

• **Balanced Funds** buy both common stocks and bonds based on a popular belief that conditions unfavorable to common stocks are oftentimes favorable to bonds and vice versa.

• **Money Market Funds** offer their shareholders a means of participating in the high-quality, short-term instruments of the money market including CDs, treasury bills, and commercial paper.

The Investment Company Institute classifies mutual fund objectives into sixteen categories:

—Aggressive Growth Funds
—Growth Funds
—Growth and Income Funds
—International Funds
—Global Funds
—Precious Metals/Gold Funds
—Balanced Funds
—Income Funds
—Option/Income Funds
—Corporate Bond Funds
—U.S. Government Income Funds
—GNMA or Ginnie Mae Funds
—Long-Term Municipal Bond Funds
—Single State Municipal Bond Funds
—Money Market Mutual Funds
—Short-Term Municipal Bond Funds

Clearly, mutual funds can be classified in many ways and there is really no limit. New and different funds are being formed almost every day, and the way they do business will also become more imaginative.

Where to Begin

As a general rule, the larger the mutual fund, the less capital appreciation one should expect relative to the market. For the more aggressive investor, the optimum size of a common stock fund is $100 million to $2 billion. Of course, there have been a few notable exceptions to the size rule. Two management companies, Wellington and Fidelity, for example, have managed sizable portfolios with great success. Nevertheless, history does show that the larger the fund, the more difficult it is to manage.

As it is with an individual security, management is an important consideration, and the process of identifying a well-managed mutual fund is much the same. First, look at the fund's performance over the last five or ten years and compare it to other funds with similar objectives. Become familiar with the people on the investment committee and how long they have been with the fund.

Then consider what management is doing today: What are the fund's largest areas of investment? What holdings are being increased or reduced? And what percent of the fund is in cash, considering the current state of the market? Remember, portfolio managers, like most investors, are subject to emotions and can be notoriously poor market timers.

Finally, what has management been saying in its reports and to the press? And have their comments been consistent with the fund's stated longer term objectives?

The challenge to the mutual fund investor is selecting an investment company capable of superior performance taking into consideration the fund's investment objectives.

For investors who have a limited amount of time to spend on their portfolios and who want greater diversification, mutual funds are worth considering. But, as with individual stocks, the old Wall Street saying still holds true: "Investigate before you invest."

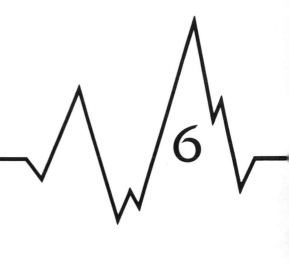

Growth
stocks

6

Introduction The "Growth Stock Theory" of investing is not new; it can be traced at least back to the 1930s. Simply stated, this investment concept involves the purchase of shares in companies that, over the years, increase earnings and dividends faster than the growth rate of the general economy. A true growth company has some control over its own destiny because it has the ability to finance itself internally by reinvesting earnings back into the business.

Growth stocks, appropriate for most but not all portfolios, require patience and usually possess somewhat greater short term market risk due to their higher P/E ratios. But if the investor has a time horizon of at least four or five years and knows how to select and value them, growth stocks can be, by far, the best method of profiting from the stock market over the long term.

Many of the examples in this section continue the work presented in the first edition of this book nearly thirty years ago. They are not merely included for the obvious benefit of hindsight.

This chapter further defines the Growth Stock Theory and shows how companies grow. Most importantly, the chapter will help investors identify growth stocks and determine how much to pay for them.

Why a Growth Stock? The power of compounding values, which is frequently overlooked and usually underestimated, is brought to light by growth stock investing. A company that grows at a compound rate of 15% per year, for example, doubles its size in five years, triples in eight years, and grows to ten times its original size in seventeen years.

Perhaps the best single definition of a growth stock is: "A company that, by growing earnings over time, improves its *ability* to pay dividends." One of the best examples of this definition is Microsoft, a growing firm that increased its profits to billions of dollars before declaring its first dividend ever in 2003. Over the years, Microsoft's ABILITY to pay dividends improved substantially as its earnings soared. And, to the delight of its holders, the stock price reflected its growth. See the discussion on Microsoft later in this chapter.

How does the growth stock investor benefit? Here is a highly simplified explanation:

Assume the following ...

• A growth company earning $1.00 per share today increases its earnings at an average growth rate of 15% per year for twelve years.

• Each year the company pays out 30% of earnings as a cash dividend to its stockholders.

• The price/earnings ratio of the stock today is twenty times earnings.

• The price earnings ratio in the twelfth year is fifteen times earnings (a lower P/E ratio reflects the probability of a slower growth rate in later years).

	Today	Year Twelve
Earnings Per Share	$1.00	$5.35
Dividend Per Share	$0.30	$1.60
P/E Ratio	20 times	15 times
Stock Price	$20.00	$80.25
Current Yield	1.5%	2.0%
Dividend Yield on the Original Investment	1.5%	8.0%

A buyer of 100 shares today would be investing $2,000. The initial $30 dividend from the company, representing a yield of only 1.5%, is small compared with higher returns other investments offer.

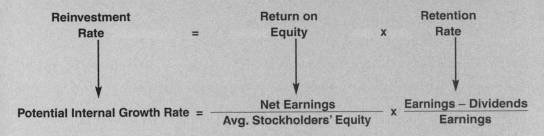

Reinvestment Rate = Return on Equity × Retention Rate

Potential Internal Growth Rate = $\dfrac{\text{Net Earnings}}{\text{Avg. Stockholders' Equity}}$ × $\dfrac{\text{Earnings} - \text{Dividends}}{\text{Earnings}}$

But, by the twelfth year, the market value of the 100 shares becomes $8,025 and more than $800 in dividends has been received over the years. The twelfth-year dividend check, $160, is not 1.5%, but is now 8% of the original investment! If the company continues to grow beyond the twelfth year and the dividend is further increased in line with earnings, the annual return becomes even greater.

It is not uncommon for a long-term growth stock investor to be receiving a large return on the original investment in the form of an annual dividend check. As an example, a stockholder in Wal-Mart Stores during its most rapid-growth phase could have cashed an annual dividend check (every year!) larger than the entire original investment of several years earlier. This is the power of compounding values and the advantage of growth stocks. And this is despite the fact that Wal-Mart's stock periodically declined sharply from one year to the next. Any politician in favor of a double taxation of dividends does not understand this concept.

Today, Wal-Mart Stores is the world's largest retailer. Was this phenomenal growth impossible to anticipate or forecast years ago? Not at all! For many years, well before gaining recognition on Wall Street, WMT was the largest holding in the well-known T. Rowe Price New Horizons Fund portfolio.

Measuring Growth For a growth company to be successful, it must earn a high return on stockholders' equity and a significant portion of that return must be reinvested into the business. In the calculations to follow, "return on equity" is based on the average of a given year's beginning and ending stockholders' equity. Many successful growth companies, such as General Electric, have increased their growth rates through the skillful addition of outside capital. When interest rates are low, this strategy works well. But the ability to grow internally is crucial in the long run.

A company's internal growth rate potential is best measured by the "reinvestment rate" formula illustrated above.

For instance, if a company has a return on average equity of 16%, earns $4.00 per share, and pays an annual dividend of $1.00 per share, the reinvestment rate would be calculated in this manner:

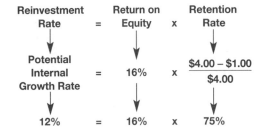

Reinvestment Rate = Return on Equity × Retention Rate

Potential Internal Growth Rate = 16% × $\dfrac{\$4.00 - \$1.00}{\$4.00}$

12% = 16% × 75%

Johnson & Johnson Posts Increase of 18%

In other words, unless this company improves its return on equity or pays out proportionately less to stockholders, it could not grow faster than 12% per year without assuming additional debt or selling new stock.

The reinvestment rate formula, as valuable as it is, should be used with care. A low-quality company can attain a high return on equity if stockholders' equity is small in relation to profits (perhaps the result of many unprofitable years). When a company's return on equity and return on assets are both high, the reinvestment rate formula can be used with greater confidence.

Learning from the Past As the following examples indicate, growth stock investing can produce favorable results if the investor is patient and owns the right stocks. And finding the right stocks is not an impossible task! Below is a table from the third edition of this book. In 1960, Merck & Company, General Mills, and Procter & Gamble were already recognized growth companies. A $1,000 investment in each of these growth stocks at the end of 1960 would have produced the following results three decades later without the benefit of reinvesting dividends.

	Cost 12/31/60	Market Value on 12/31/90	Dividend Paid in 1990
Merck	$1,000	$41,420	$ 894
General Mills	$1,000	$24,575	$ 609
P&G	$1,000	$10,320	$ 222
Total	$3,000	$76,315	$1,725*

* 58% of the original investment

Again, this real-life example illustrates "the power of compounding values" referred to earlier. Between 1960 and 1990, the market value of this small portfolio advanced an average of almost 11.5%, not including the benefit of dividends. The difference between Merck's 1990 market value and that of Procter & Gamble is accounted for by Merck's higher market appreciation (about 13% per year) compared with that of P&G (about 8%). Why? During that period, Merck's earnings per share advanced 14.8% per year, while P&G's per-share growth averaged 9.5% annually.

How important are dividends to growth stock investors? Merck has proudly paid a dividend every year since 1935. General Mills has paid one every year since 1898; and Procter & Gamble every year since 1891. This portfolio alone demonstrates how important dividends can become to patient growth stock investors.

George Eastman (1854–1932) performed early photographic experiments in his mother's kitchen. In 1881, he and a family friend founded The Eastman Dry Plate Company, later known as Eastman Kodak Company.

By year end 2002, twelve years since the table was published, Merck's market value increased to $156,527 and its annual dividend check had grown to $3,982. General Mills' value was $62,429 with a dividend check of $1,163. P&G was $40,993 with a dividend check of $728. As a whole, our modest portfolio had reached a total value of $259,949 (an average gain of 10.8% per year) and its annual income from the three companies rose to $5,873, nearly twice the original 1960 investment. It is also worth noting that all three stocks were well below their previous 2000-01 bull market highs.

Note: The General Mills figures included the 1995 spin-off of Darden Restaurants.

So, what will the value of this portfolio be in the year 2014? No one can say for sure, but if the earnings and dividends of these mature businesses continue to grow, even at an expected slower rate (9-10% yearly), this portfolio should continue to outpace the rising cost of living during the period.

Below is a classic case study of two very similar companies operating in the same industry at the same time to illustrate this thought process. It is especially important for the investor to see the big picture and watch PROFITABILITY and PROGRESS. An improving trend in profitability can help investment performance markedly.

—Air Products vs. Airco Inc.—

AIRCO INC.
(formerly Air Reduction Co.)

	Sales	Operating Margin %	Net Income	Long Term Debt	Return on Equity	Earnings Per Share	Avg. 10-Year EPS Growth	Dividend Per Share
1965	$376.8mm	12.8%	$25.7mm	$124.6mm	12.6%	$2.50	4.5%	$1.25
1975	$765.7mm	12.1%	$42.7mm	$187.7mm	14.0%	$3.76	4.2%	$0.95

Ten Year (1965–75) Investment Performance –25%

AIR PRODUCTS & CHEMICALS

	Sales	Operating Margin %	Net Income	Long Term Debt	Return on Equity	Earnings Per Share	Avg. 10-Year EPS Growth	Dividend Per Share
1965	$121.1mm	13.7%	$ 7.4mm	$ 94.0mm	11.0%	$0.70	12.4%	$0.04
1975	$699.0mm	17.0%	$54.2mm	$184.1mm	19.7%	$4.02	19.1%	$0.20

Ten Year (1965–75) Investment Performance +328%

NOTE: Per share figures have been adjusted for splits and stock dividends for comparability.

Bill Gates (r.) and Paul Allen in 1981 just after signing their landmark contract with IBM for the DOS program

Air Products was much more aggressive than Airco in its pursuit of growth during those years. The importance of internal and external financing, and profitability, is very obvious in this case.

Air Products amplified the impact of its improving profitability and high earnings retention with additional debt to finance long-term gas sales contracts. This strategy produced superior growth for Air Products during the period. As a result, Air Products' stockholders enjoyed a far better investment performance.

Two stocks highlighted in the third edition of this book provided exceptional results in the twelve-year period, 1990 to 2002 – Microsoft Corporation and Dell Computer. Neither stock was an unknown entity at the time they were mentioned. In fact, the products of both companies were actually being used to create those written words.

The story of Bill Gates, today the world's richest man, and Microsoft is well known. Microsoft's revenues in FY 1990 totaled $1,183 million while earnings rose 55% to $2.34 per share that year. The estimate for the June, 1991 year was $3.70. On December 31, 1990 the stock was $75.25, 24.9 times its latest 12-months earnings and 20.3 times the earnings projection. The P/E multiple was well below the growth rate of the company at the time.

It was Microsoft's policy to reinvest all of its profits back into the company rather than pay dividends. In effect, the company was building its ability to pay dividends at a later date. In the twelve-year period since 1990 Microsoft's earnings increased at a rate exceeding 31% annually.

A growth stock investor in 1990 who shared that vision would have seen 100 shares increase after seven stock splits to 7,200 shares by early 2003 and then finally enjoy a first-ever dividend check of $576.

By 2003, Microsoft's revenues climbed to roughly $32 billion and the company's net profit was being estimated at near $0.95 per share – from which, that first $0.08 per share dividend would be declared. Twelve years earlier the company employed 5,600 workers and had $450 million cash in its coffers. By 2003, the workforce surpassed 50,000 and the company's cash on the balance sheet was close to $43 billion.

No less amazing is the tale of college dropout Michael Dell. In the early '80s, he was filling orders for custom-built personal computers from his college dormitory. By early 1991 Dell was selling $546 million in computers, $397 million in the U.S. and in other parts of the hemisphere, plus $149 million into the European market.

On December 31, 1990 Dell shares were $18.50 with an earnings estimate of $1.36

3M's first plant located on the shore of Lake Superior at Crystal Bay, Minnesota

per share for fiscal year 1990-91 and a P/E multiple of 13.6 times. Moreover, the rough estimate for FY 1991-92 was $2.10. Like Microsoft, the P/E multiple was not out of line with the firm's expected growth rate.

Twelve years later, in fiscal year 2002-03, Dell's revenues reached $35 billion, $24.9 billion from the Americas, $6.7 billion from Europe, and $3.4 billion from the Far East. During this period, the company's profits compounded at a 39.9% annual rate to about $0.80 per share (a purchase of 100 shares in late 1990 became 9,600 shares, after seven stock splits, having a value of close to $257,000).

On December 31, 2002 Dell's stock price was $26.74, or 33 times current earnings, but down sharply from its $56.68 peak hit in March, 2000. At the highs of the stock market bubble, Dell sold at a P/E multiple of nearly 100 times earnings!

The Growth Cycle Almost every company faces a so-called "growth cycle" which can be even more pronounced with growth stocks. That is, a company is *born*, it *expands* (and sometimes at a very rapid pace for growth stocks), it *matures*, and then *declines*. If management fails to act by entering new markets and developing new products before the company goes into its decline phase, the firm can die.

The single best example of this necessary "re-birth" process is the 3M Company. Minnesota Mining & Manufacturing was founded in 1902 in Minnesota as a venture to quarry a mineral called Corundum. It was to be sold to eastern manufacturers as a new, improved abrasive. The product failed. However, in the meantime, the company converted an old flour mill into a sandpaper manufacturing facility. From that point on, 3M's growth has been the result of nothing less than a research & development engine, producing a constant stream of new products from discoveries developed, either internally, or acquired.

A dramatic example of how a fundamental picture can change and affect an industry adversely came in the late 1990's with the photographic companies, Eastman Kodak and Polaroid Corporation. Decades ago, both were growth stocks.

In the early years of the 21st century we find Polaroid in bankruptcy and Eastman Kodak in a struggle to keep profits from sinking further. Kodak has been firing its workers and transferring its manufacturing overseas in an effort to stay afloat. Digital photography, which requires no film, has been taking a greater share of total photo images in a shift that began in 1996 or 1997. No alert growth stock investor should have been surprised. Will Eastman Kodak be able to "re-invent itself" and flourish? Only time will tell.

Dr. Edwin H. Land (1909–1991) founder of Polaroid Corporation in 1937, unveiled his instant photographic process before the Optical Society of America in 1947.

These exercises, as well as other past experiences, show that successful growth companies have several characteristics in common. The investor should, therefore, be looking for a company that has:

• A product or service gaining in customer demand and profitable enough to finance most or all future growth internally (that is, capable of a high reinvestment rate).

• A positive trend in profitability so that, by growing earnings over time, the company improves its ability to pay dividends.

• A capable, imaginative management team that can turn promise into reality.

There are other related factors to consider. Does the company also have:

• A growth record over the past few years? Look at revenue, facilities, and employees.

• A solid balance sheet with ample cash, little debt, and/or the management talent to use debt skillfully?

• Competitive marketing and strong service capabilities?

• A position in the marketplace that allows some product pricing flexibility? Often, it is or will become the leader in its industry.

• Good labor relations?

• An ability to pursue new markets and add new, improved products to its line? If not, the company will most likely face maturity and, eventually, a decline.

Perspective To be successful, growth stock investors must learn to look beyond a stock's short-term price swings. Growth stocks require both patience and a long term perspective. This is why periodic accumulation and dollar-cost-averaging is the best way to build a growth portfolio. The following explains what is meant by "long-term perspective."

Imagine that it is June, 1990 and you are looking at a chart in Trendline's *Current Market Perspectives* of a stock that you just purchased. The company, Wal-Mart Stores, reported a 28.6% increase in earnings in the first quarter, following a similar gain in fiscal year 1989 … and a spectacular 33% gain in the prior year.

Before you bought the shares at $58, you estimated 1990 earnings to be roughly $2.28 per share, an increase of about 20% over 1989 – not bad for a recession year.

Your analysis points to a longer term earnings growth rate of at least 15-17% annually for the next several years. If your projections prove correct, the company's per share earnings would be about $8.50 in 2000. Assuming a P/E of 20, the stock price would be close to $170. Not bad!

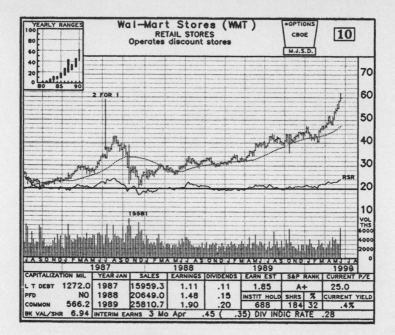

Wal-Mart Stores (WMT)
RETAIL STORES
Operates discount stores

OPTIONS CBOE · M.J.S.D. · 10

CAPITALIZATION MIL		YEAR JAN	SALES	EARNINGS	DIVIDENDS	EARN EST	S&P RANK	CURRENT P/E
L T DEBT	1272.0	1987	15959.3	1.11	.11	1.85	A+	25.0
PFD	NO	1988	20649.0	1.48	.15	INSTIT HOLD	SHRS %	CURRENT YIELD
COMMON	566.2	1989	25810.7	1.90	.20	688	184 32	.4%
BK VAL/SHR	6.94	INTERIM EARNS 3 Mo Apr	.45 (	.35)	DIV INDIC RATE	.28		

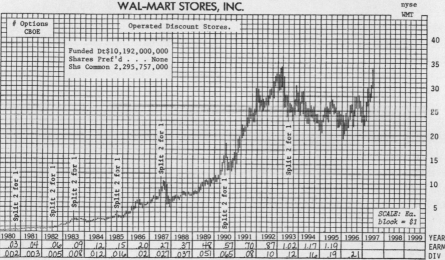

WAL-MART STORES, INC.

nyse WMT

Options CBOE

Operated Discount Stores.

Funded Dt$10,192,000,000
Shares Pref'd . . . None
Shs Common 2,295,757,000

SCALE: Ea. block = $1

YEAR	1980	1981	1982	1983	1984	1985	1986	1987	1988	1989	1990	1991	1992	1993	1994	1995	1996	1997	1998	1999
EARN	.03	.04	.06	.09	.12	.15	.20	.27	.37	.48	.51	.70	.87	1.02	1.17	1.19				
DIV	.002	.003	.005	.008	.012	.016	.02	.027	.037	.051	.065	.08	.10	.12	.16	.19	.21			

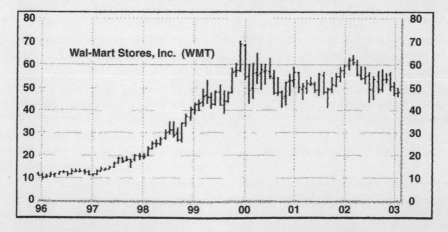

Wal-Mart Stores, Inc. (WMT)

Your purchase price was 25.4 times your 1990 earnings projection – a P/E 1.6 times your expected growth rate. However, you purchased only 100 shares, feeling uneasy about buying an equity that is up 100% in the past twenty-four months.

In the few months that followed the stock did nothing but go down, despite a 2-for-1 stock split shortly after your purchase.

However, you remain convinced about the company's prospects for annual growth of at least 15%. Wisely, you reject the advice of at the so-called experts who believe that "Investors should immediately cut their losses if the stock declines by 8%." This rule is okay for traders … but NOT growth stock investors. Nevertheless, ALWAYS review the fundamentals. It is far better to be averaging UP than to average DOWN.

Now it's December, 2002. Wal-Mart's stock was split 2 for 1 in 1993 and 2 for 1 again in 1999. Your original 100 shares is now 800. In 2000 the company reported earnings of $1.40 per share, well ahead of your original projection – 17.3% per year between 1990 and 2000. Today your original $5,800 investment in 1990 has:

• A market value of $40,408; plus,

• An annual dividend check of $224, equal to roughly 3.9% of the original investment.

Notice the timeframes on the Wal-Mart charts. As the years roll by, your analysis continues. One logical question to ask at Wal-Mart's next annual meeting: Could saturation become a problem? How much longer can the company grow at a rate exceeding 10% or 12%, given its size? The questions and analysis will never cease as long as the shares are owned.

At What Price? "What is a share of this company worth?" is the most difficult of all Wall Street questions. A precise answer cannot be found; it is simply a matter of careful analysis and judgment.

In the short term – in a period of days, weeks, or months – the price of a stock fluctuates around a consensus of value based on earnings and dividend expectations. This consensus usually changes gradually … but not always. Over the long term – a few years or more – the stock price will rise or fall in line with the company's actual earnings, dividends, and financial condition. This is especially true for growth stocks.

Valuing stocks is extremely complicated because investors always have alternative investment opportunities. Bonds, money market instruments, savings accounts, real estate, art, or personal business ventures are among many examples.

Alexander Graham Bell (1847–1922) shown with the new telephone device he invented. Bell Telephone Company was founded in 1877.

Therefore, an investor should make a value decision at three levels:

(1) The investment environment (i.e., the potential return that all stocks offer versus alternative investment opportunities).

(2) The value of the stock relative to other stocks.

(3) The value of the stock based on its individual merits and growth prospects.

Since the 1930s, there has been a steady decline in the purchasing power of the dollar. Most dramatic during this time were periods of accelerated inflation in 1946-47, in 1973-74, and in the early 1980s. Despite the gradual decline in the inflation rate since the 1980s, this long term trend in the loss of purchasing power is not likely to be reversed, unfortunately.

Interest rates, as measured by the prime rate charged by banks, remained at a low 23% level from 1935 until 1951, climbed gradually through the 1950s to about 5%, and maintained that level until about 1966. Since then, the prime rate has risen and fallen sharply, reaching peaks of 8-9% in 1969-1970, 12% in 1974, and over 20% in 1981. Of course, it has since returned to more reasonable levels in recent years.

Surprisingly, yields on both stocks and high-quality bonds in the fifty years,

1925-1975, averaged about the same – roughly 4.5%. Between 1925 and 1955 stock yields almost always exceeded bond yields, but in the years since 1955, the reverse has been true. Many observers attribute the shift since the 1940s to taxes and to a change in inflation expectations.

History also shows how a changing investment environment can affect P/E ratios. A typical stock P/E ratio in the late 1940s and early 1950s was 8 to 12 times earnings. Throughout most of the 1960s, a 15 to 19 range was considered normal. In the late 1970s, the DJIA P/E ratio dropped below 8 times earnings. Just before the stock market crashed in 1987 the ratio exceeded 20 and then returned closer to its 50-year average of about 14 over the following three years. At the peak of the market bubble in 2000 the Dow P/E went to levels above the high of 1987. The P/E ratio for "the market," as with individual issues, should be used with great care. A P/E of 20 has a totally different meaning when corporate earnings are projected to be rising in the years immediately ahead – as opposed to a time when earnings are expected to decline.

It stands to reason that growth equities typically command higher P/E ratios and lower yields than ordinary shares. Clearly, two stocks having the same P/E ratio or dividend yield are not equally attractive if one is a growing and the other is not.

Thomas A. Edison (1847–1931) said "Genius is two percent inspiration and ninety-eight percent perspiration." The Edison General Electric Company, founded in 1878, was a predecessor to the General Electric Company.

Assuming everything else is equal, the company that grows at a faster rate should command a higher P/E ratio. Throughout history securities analysts and market theoreticians have worked tirelessly to devise formulas to value growth stocks. The well-known financial textbook, *Security Analysis,* co-authored by David L. Dodd, Sidney Cottle, and the late Benjamin Graham, presents a valuation formula based on a seven-year time horizon. Their work concluded that a company with no growth deserved, at least, the nominal P/E multiple of 8.5 times earnings while, at the other extreme, a company growing at an annual rate of 20% could be assigned a P/E multiple of 41.5 times earnings. By 1974 it became obvious that interest rates have an influence (an inverse relationship) on P/E ratios. So the popular Graham & Dodd P/E formula was revised to read as follows:

$$P/E = \frac{37.5 + 8.8g}{i}$$

g – The expected earnings growth rate for the next 7-10 years.

i – The prevailing interest rate for Aaa bonds.

37.5 and **8.8** —Constant values based on experience

By using this formula and applying various growth rate and interest rate combinations to it, one can construct a P/E ratio table for easy reference, as shown on the next page.

To use the table, an investor must first estimate the company's annual earnings growth rate for the next seven to ten years. By crossing this growth rate with the prevailing interest rate on the table, the investor can obtain the same P/E multiple had the formula been used.

This formula has one serious shortcoming that should not be ignored, however. If the prevailing interest rate is 7% and there are two companies growing at the same rate of, say, 12%, both stocks deserve a 20.4 P/E ratio according to the formula and the table.

Suppose the first company has a higher return on equity and is, therefore, able to pay a higher dividend to its stockholders. Should both companies sell at the same 20.4 P/E multiple? Obviously, no. Another factor to consider is the reliability of the growth projection, which depends on the quality of management, the sophistication of products, the strength of competition, patent protection, the capital intensive nature of the business, and so on. Thus, investors using this table to compare stock values should be prepared to make a few adjustments.

Price/Earnings Ratios Assuming Different Growth Rates and Interest Rates

Prevailing Interest Rate

		3%	4%	5%	6%	7%	8%	9%	10%	11%	12%	13%	14%	15%
	20%	71.2	53.4	42.7	35.6	30.5	26.7	23.7	21.4	19.4	17.8	16.4	15.3	14.2
	19%	68.2	51.2	40.9	34.1	29.2	25.6	22.7	20.5	18.6	17.1	15.7	14.6	13.6
	18%	65.3	49.0	39.2	32.7	28.0	24.5	21.8	19.6	17.8	16.3	15.1	14.0	13.1
Expected	17%	62.4	46.8	37.4	31.2	26.7	23.4	20.8	18.7	17.0	15.6	14.4	13.4	12.5
Growth	16%	59.4	44.6	35.7	29.7	25.5	22.3	19.8	17.8	16.2	14.9	13.7	12.7	11.9
Rate	15%	56.5	42.4	33.9	28.3	24.2	21.2	18.8	17.0	15.4	14.0	13.0	12.1	11.3
	14%	53.6	40.2	32.1	26.8	23.0	20.1	17.9	16.1	14.6	13.4	12.4	11.5	10.7
	13%	50.6	38.0	30.4	25.3	21.7	19.0	16.9	15.2	13.8	12.7	11.7	10.9	10.1
	12%	47.7	35.8	28.6	23.9	20.4	17.9	15.9	14.3	13.0	11.9	11.0	10.2	9.5
	11%	44.8	33.6	26.9	22.4	19.2	16.8	14.9	13.4	12.2	11.2	10.3	9.6	9.0
	10%	41.8	31.4	25.1	20.9	17.9	15.7	13.9	12.6	11.4	10.5	9.7	9.0	8.4
	9%	38.9	29.2	23.3	19.5	16.7	14.6	13.0	11.7	10.6	9.7	9.0	8.3	7.8
	8%	36.0	27.0	21.6	18.0	15.4	13.5	12.0	10.8	9.8	9.0	8.3	7.7	7.2
	7%	33.0	24.8	19.8	16.5	14.2	12.4	11.0	9.9	9.0	8.3	7.6	7.1	6.6
	6%	30.1	22.6	18.1	15.1	12.9	11.3	10.0	9.0	8.2	7.5	6.9	6.5	6.0
	5%	27.2	20.4	16.3	13.6	11.6	10.2	9.1	8.2	7.4	6.8	6.3	5.8	5.4
	4%	24.2	18.2	14.5	12.1	10.4	9.1	8.1	7.3	6.6	6.1	5.6	5.2	4.8
	3%	21.3	16.0	12.8	10.7	9.1	8.0	7.1	6.4	5.8	5.3	4.9	4.6	4.3

Henry Ford (1863–1947), pictured in 1915 with his first automobile, formed the Ford Motor Company in 1903. His work signaled the beginning of an industry that enjoyed substantial growth in the early part of the 20th century.

Most analysts prefer to use three to five-year periods when studying the stock market or individual growth stocks. As mentioned earlier, Graham & Dodd used seven years. *Here, a 12-year investment time horizon is recommended.*

Any objective analysis of growth stocks requires a time period long enough to encompass at least one to three full economic business cycles, as well as enough time to allow a company to grow. However, the time horizon should also be short enough to allow an investor to estimate the future without too much "blue sky." Thus, ten to twelve years seems to be a good time frame.

Further, whether by accident, political contrivance, coincidence, or whatever, there has been a very distinct four-year buying cycle to the stock market as measured by the Dow Jones Industrial Average. While this pattern may never again repeat, history clearly shows that, with the exception of only one instance (1930), each fourth year since 1914 was an excellent time to buy stocks:

1914	1934	1954	1974	1994
1918	1938	1958	1978	1998
1922	1942	1962	1982	2002
1926	1946	1966	1986	
1930	1950	1970	1990	

A period of three full market cycles, or twelve years, seems appropriate since twelve-year periods play an interesting role in U.S. history. It was exactly twelve years between the U.S. entry into World War I (1917) and the beginning of the Great Depression (1929), and then the U.S. entry into World War II (1941). Twelve years after the end of World War II (1945-1946) was the first significant post-war economic recession (1957-1958). Twelve years later there was another recession (1970); and twelve years after that, the greatest of all bull markets began.

The "12-Year Present Value Method" is used to compare the relative values of stocks over a twelve-year period. This approach is based, as the name implies, on the present value of future earnings.

If "Company X" succeeds in growing at 14% annually over the next twelve years, each $1 of earnings today would become $4.82 in the twelfth year. If another firm, "Company Y," of similar quality, grows at 11% per year, each $1 of earnings would become $3.50 after twelve years. What is the value of the $4.82 and $3.50 today, not twelve years from now? Of course, the answer depends on the annual return the investor is seeking.

By using the 12-Year Present Value Table shown on the next page, it can be seen that the $4.82 (14% growth) has a present

U.S. Panel Seeks to Speed Approval of New Drugs For the Desperately Ill

12-Year Present Value Table
Desired Return

Expected Growth Rate	4%	5%	6%	7%	8%	9%	10%	11%	12%	13%	14%	15%	16%	17%	18%	19%	20%
4%	1.00	0.89	0.80	0.71	0.64	0.57	0.51	0.46	0.41	0.37	0.33	0.30	0.27	0.24	0.22	0.20	0.18
5%	1.13	1.00	0.89	0.80	0.71	0.64	0.57	0.52	0.46	0.42	0.38	0.34	0.30	0.27	0.25	0.22	0.20
6%	1.26	1.12	1.00	0.89	0.80	0.72	0.64	0.57	0.52	0.46	0.42	0.38	0.34	0.31	0.28	0.25	0.23
7%	1.41	1.25	1.12	1.00	0.89	0.80	0.72	0.64	0.58	0.52	0.47	0.42	0.38	0.34	0.31	0.28	0.25
8%	1.58	1.40	1.25	1.12	1.00	0.90	0.80	0.72	0.65	0.58	0.52	0.47	0.43	0.38	0.35	0.31	0.28
9%	1.76	1.57	1.40	1.25	1.12	1.00	0.90	0.80	0.72	0.65	0.58	0.53	0.48	0.43	0.38	0.35	0.31
10%	1.96	1.75	1.56	1.39	1.25	1.12	1.00	0.90	0.81	0.73	0.65	0.59	0.53	0.48	0.43	0.39	0.35
11%	2.10	1.96	1.74	1.55	1.39	1.25	1.12	1.00	0.90	0.81	0.73	0.65	0.59	0.53	0.48	0.43	0.39
12%	2.44	2.17	1.94	1.73	1.55	1.39	1.24	1.12	1.00	0.90	0.81	0.73	0.66	0.59	0.53	0.48	0.44
13%	2.71	2.41	2.15	1.92	1.72	1.54	1.38	1.24	1.12	1.00	0.90	0.81	0.73	0.66	0.59	0.54	0.48
14%	3.01	2.68	2.40	2.14	1.91	1.72	1.54	1.37	1.24	1.11	1.00	0.90	0.81	0.73	0.66	0.60	0.54
15%	3.34	2.98	2.66	2.38	2.12	1.90	1.71	1.53	1.37	1.24	1.11	1.00	0.90	0.81	0.73	0.66	0.60
16%	3.71	3.31	2.95	2.64	2.36	2.11	1.89	1.70	1.53	1.37	1.24	1.11	1.00	0.90	0.81	0.74	0.67
17%	4.11	3.67	3.27	2.92	2.61	2.34	2.10	1.88	1.69	1.52	1.37	1.23	1.11	1.00	0.90	0.82	0.74
18%	4.56	4.06	3.62	3.24	2.89	2.60	2.33	2.08	1.87	1.68	1.52	1.36	1.23	1.11	1.00	0.90	0.82
19%	5.04	4.49	4.01	3.58	3.20	2.87	2.57	2.31	2.07	1.86	1.68	1.51	1.36	1.23	1.10	1.00	0.90
20%	5.58	4.97	4.43	3.96	3.54	3.18	2.85	2.55	2.29	2.06	1.85	1.67	1.51	1.36	1.22	1.10	1.00
21%	6.16	5.49	4.90	4.37	3.91	3.51	3.14	2.82	2.53	2.28	2.05	1.84	1.66	1.50	1.35	1.22	1.10
22%	6.79	6.05	5.40	4.83	4.32	3.87	3.47	3.11	2.79	2.51	2.26	2.03	1.83	1.65	1.49	1.35	1.22
23%	7.49	6.68	5.96	5.32	4.76	4.27	3.82	3.43	3.08	2.77	2.49	2.24	2.02	1.82	1.64	1.49	1.34
24%	8.26	7.36	6.56	5.87	5.24	4.70	4.21	3.78	3.39	3.05	2.75	2.47	2.22	2.01	1.81	1.64	1.48
25%	9.09	8.10	7.23	6.46	5.78	5.18	4.64	4.16	3.74	3.36	3.02	2.72	2.44	2.21	1.99	1.80	1.63
26%	10.01	8.92	7.96	7.11	6.36	5.70	5.11	4.58	4.11	3.70	3.33	2.99	2.69	2.43	2.19	1.98	1.79
27%	11.01	9.81	8.75	7.82	6.99	6.27	5.62	5.04	4.53	4.07	3.66	3.29	2.96	2.68	2.41	2.18	1.97
28%	12.09	10.77	9.61	8.59	7.68	6.89	6.17	5.53	4.97	4.47	4.02	3.62	3.25	2.94	2.65	2.40	2.17
29%	13.28	11.83	10.56	9.43	8.43	7.56	6.78	6.07	5.46	4.91	4.42	3.97	3.57	3.23	2.91	2.63	2.38
30%	14.56	12.98	11.58	10.35	9.25	8.29	7.43	6.66	5.99	5.38	4.85	4.36	3.91	3.54	3.19	2.89	2.61

value of $1.54 and the $3.50 (11% growth) has a present value of $1.12 when the investor is seeking a 10% annual return. If the investor would prefer to have a 12% annual return, the present value of Company X's future earnings is $1.24 while Company Y's is $0.90.

To show how the 12-Year Present Value method works, consider the real-life experience of an investor comparing "Growth Stock A" with "Growth Stock B" and the Dow Jones Industrial Average during the 12-year period between one recession and the next (1990 to 2002):

Growth Stock A
Current Stock Price: $19
Current EPS: $1.14
Est. 12-year earnings growth rate: 12%
Current P/E ratio: 16.7 times earnings
Desired investment return: 10% per year

Growth Stock B
Current Stock Price: $26
Current EPS: $1.34
Est. 12-year earnings growth rate: 9.5%
Current P/E ratio: 19.4 times earnings
Desired investment return: 10% per year

Dow Jones Industrial Average
Current DJIA Level: 2,625
Current EPS: 172.05
Est. earnings growth rate: 7%
Current P/E ratio: 15.3 times earnings
Desired investment return: 10% per year

The present value of future earnings for each can be found by simply multiplying the current earnings per share by the appropriate figures found on the 12-Year Present Value Table (Growth Stock A $1.14 x 1.24; Growth Stock B $1.34 x 0.95 and DJIA 172.05 x .72). From these figures, an investor could have calculated P/E multiples based on the *present value* of future earnings rather than current earnings. The results proved interesting:

Growth Stock A
13.5 times PV earnings of $1.41

Growth Stock B
20.5 times PV earnings of $1.27

Dow Jones Industrials
21.1 times PV earnings of 123.88

Using this method of comparison today, Growth Stock A was much more attractive than the Dow Jones Industrials, not less attractive, as implied by the current P/E ratios. Moreover, Growth Stock A was also much more attractive than Growth Stock B as the stock market performance proved over the twelve years that followed:

Performance as of December 31, 2002

Growth Stock A	+458%
Growth Stock B	+223%
Dow Jones Industrials	+218%

Industrialist John D. Rockefeller, Sr., photographed in New York in 1894. Rockefeller (1839–1937) founded the Standard Oil Company.

When the 12-Year Present Value Method is being applied, one should also take into account any dividends received over the twelve-year period.

Investors can use the table to compare today's investment values by simply performing these same calculations with current earnings projections. However, the key to successful growth stock investing is good fundamental research and a correct analysis of the company's growth potential. Without the proper input, formulas such as these are practically useless.

Stock Market Manias

The next chapter explores the "Mania," a forever-recurring condition of excessive enthusiasm. It was apparent with Avon Products, Polaroid, and Xerox during the "Nifty-fifty years" of the early 1970's. And the internet and optical networking craze of 1995-2000, like the Tulip Mania in Holland, the dot-com bubble was no less absurd.

As experienced investors now realize, there can be a point when growth stocks become so overvalued that even capital gains taxes, as confiscatory as they are, should not be a deterrent to profit-taking.

In 1972, Avon Products touched $140 per share or 64.8 times current earnings. At its peak the total market value of Avon's stock was just over $8 billion, eight times its

sales, which had just surpassed the milestone $1 billion mark. If one assumed a 15% annual growth rate for earnings per share for the twelve years that followed (actually, 10% was attained until 1979, but problems were encountered in the years after), the stock had a multiple on present value earnings of 37.9 – that is, assuming a desired annual return of only 10%! (This was calculated as $2.16 per share x 1.71.) Avon did not return to its 1972 highs until 1997, twenty-five years later! What were rational investors thinking in 1972?

In 1999, Amazon.com reached $113 per share. The 370 million shares outstanding had a total market value of more than $40 billion at its peak. By 2002, revenues were almost $4 billion and the company attained modest profitability. Although Amazon's progress was notable, company profits were hardly enough to justify its peak price. By 2001, once the stock had lost 95% of its market value, investors had obviously become very discouraged.

The story of Corvis, an optical network company, during this same period is perhaps one of the most dramatic of all. Its stock price rose to $114.75 in 2000 giving the company a total market value of more than $40 billion! Yet the firm had minimal sales and no hope for profitability in the near future. Corvis' stock price has since dropped to pennies per share.

Thomas J. Watson, Sr. (1874–1956) became president of a small tabulating company in 1914 and built the business into a major corporation, now called IBM.

The price of JDS Uniphase hit $153 at its peak in 2000. With 1.4 billion shares outstanding, its market value eclipsed $200 billion while SALES had yet to reach $3 per share, let alone be profitable. At about the same time, the shares of Yahoo! touched $237 for a total market value of $135 billion. Sales at the time were about $1 billion. However, unlike JDS Uniphase, Yahoo! earned a profit. Within two years both stocks declined by more than 95%.

Even the professionals were caught up in the 2000 stock market bubble. When the stocks were near their peaks, both Yahoo! and JDS Uniphase were added to the S&P 500 Index. In fact, this was one reason why the S&P 500 Index underperformed the Dow Industrial Average once the bear market hit prices in the years to follow.

Other Methods When the late Benjamin Graham, known as the "Dean of Security Analysts," was asked for his approach to common stocks, he offered the following: He wanted a stock selling below its working capital (net current asset value), giving no weight the firm's plant and other fixed assets – although he realized this approach could be limited. He also favored other conservative methods: (1) paying no more than 7 times reported earnings of the past 12 months; (2) requiring a yield of at least 7%; and (3) companies with a book value greater than 120% of the stock price.

Unfortunately, growth stocks are rarely available at such attractive levels because investors also place a value on future earnings prospects, as they should.

Several top mutual fund managers in recent years have gained good reputations using an approach called "value investing," merely a contemporary term that describes a variation of Ben Graham's original work.

The basic idea is to buy shares of companies that have assets "undervalued" by the marketplace. It is important to realize, however, that unless these assets are used to produce higher earnings and dividends in future years, the idea of acquiring undervalued assets is nothing more than another application of the "Greater Fool Theory." Buying a stock with the hope that, someday, a greater fool will come along to pay a higher price is not the best way to invest!

This Decade and Beyond For the growth stock investor with a sense of history and some imagination and foresight, identifying growth areas should not be a difficult undertaking. It is a continuous process of inquiry, analysis, and review, never losing sight of the "big picture."

The population in the years ahead will be better educated, affluent, and will be a ready-market for products and services of

every type. Also, this population will be aging. People in the coming decade will be spending money on different products and services than when they were younger. In many markets, innovative entrepreneurs will create new businesses of all kinds.

Automation and the internet will continue to change the way people accomplish daily tasks. Health care, entertainment, and communications will remain good areas of growth to meet the needs of this group.

There are four broad concepts that hold some promise for possible investment opportunities in the coming decade:

Medical Devices – As the baby boomer generation ages the need for medical devices should grow significantly. And, unlike pharmaceuticals where generics are a factor, pricing pressures should be less.

Biotechnology – Amgen and others have already proven this research concept to be valid. The problem lies with the money and time required to develop new drugs. As a general rule, biotech stocks are best avoided until the drug has passed through the FDA process, or at least into Phase III testing, at the earliest.

Alternative Fuels (to oil) – There are three categories within this group: Fuel Cells, Wind Power, and Solar Power. The main challenge for fuel cells is one of physics.

That is, it takes power to make power. So fuel cells, while promising, will probably never be a cheap source of energy. Both Wind and Solar are proven technologies and should offer some profit opportunities even with their environmental limitations.

Wireless Communications – Wireless technology is already with us, of course. Some observers are talking "saturation," but the applications for wireless have just begun. New chips, devices, and services are all logical areas of opportunity.

A Growth Stock List

All the companies listed here could offer some opportunity as growth stocks for the years ahead. Many are already established in this regard, while others only hope to be. Note this is not a list of recommended issues, but merely a group of companies worthy of further analysis. In fact, a few possess extremely high market risk. This selection is just a starting point for growth stock investors seeking new ideas.

Technology

AT&T Wireless (AWE)
Automatic Data Processing (ADP)
Cisco Systems (CSCO)
Cree Inc. (CREE)
Dell Computer (DELL)
Intel Corp. (INTC)
Intergraph Corp. (INGR)

Barry Diller is the founder of InterActiveCorp, a leader in internet consumer services.

International Business Machines (IBM)
J2 Global Communications (JCOM)
Microsoft (MSFT)
Oracle Corp. (ORCL)
Qualcomm Inc. (QCOM)
Texas Instruments (TXN)
Xilinx Inc. (XLNX)

Health Care

Amgen Inc. (AMGN)
Anthem Inc. (ATH)
Baxter Laboratories (BAX)
Becton, Dickinson (BDX)
Biogen, Inc. (BGEN)
Boston Scientific (BSX)
Charles River Labs (CRL)
Johnson & Johnson (JNJ)
Medtronic, Inc. (MDT)
Merck & Company (MRK)
Mylan Laboratories (MYL)
Pfizer, Inc. (PFE)
St. Jude Medical (STJ)
SurModics, Inc. (SRDX)
Watson Pharmaceuticals (WPI)

Retail

Applebee's International (APPB)
Bed Bath & Beyond (BBBY)
Cracker Barrel Old Country (CBRL)
Home Depot (HD)
Krispy Kreme Doughnuts (KKD)
Lowe's Companies (LOW)
Outback Steakhouse (OSSI)
P.F. Chang's China Bistro (PFCB)

Miscellaneous

Coca-Cola Co. (KO)
Colgate Palmolive (CL)
eBay Inc. (EBAY)
Electronic Arts (ERTS)
InterActiveCorp (IACI)
Int'l Game Technology (IGT)
JetBlue Airways (JBLU)
Lilly, Eli (LLY)
3M Company (MMM)
Omnicom Group (OMC)
PepsiCo Inc. (PEP)
Procter & Gamble (PG)
Rent-A-Center Inc. (RCII)
Southwest Airlines (LUV)

As the next chapter explains, growth stock investors should be especially wary of "investment fads." An industry will sometimes flourish for only one or two years allowing its participants to resemble true growth companies. Examples, among many others, include boating in the late 1950s, bowling and certain electronics businesses in the early 1960s, conglomerates and computer leasing in the late 1960s, warehouse merchandising in the early 1970s, and airlines, spurred on by takeover rumors, in the late 1980s.

An investor can avoid being deceived by correctly identifying the strengths and weaknesses of the industry, understanding the economics of the business, and by maintaining a long term perspective.

Manias, fads, and panics

7

Introduction In the contemporary Foreword to Charles Mackay's 1841 classic, *Extraordinary Popular Delusions and the Madness of Crowds*, a reference was made to this colloquy:

"Have you ever seen, in some wood, on a sunny quiet day, a cloud of flying midges – thousands of them – hovering, apparently motionless, in a sunbeam? ... Yes? ... Well, did you ever see the whole flight – each mite preserving its distance from all others – suddenly move, say three feet, to one side or the other? Well, *what made them do that*? A breeze? I said a *quiet* day. But try to recall – did you ever see them move directly back again in the same unison? Well, what made them do *that*? Great human mass movements are slower but much more effective."

We may never know the answer to the question, *"What made them do that*?" but lessons can be learned from emotional market experiences such as those described here.

This chapter will show the psychology of investing from the Tulip Mania that began in the early 1600s to the dot-com bubble that ended in 2000. An investor who recognizes a mania or a fad when it occurs might profit by it, but is far less likely to lose money in the crash that inevitably follows.

Human Nature? "It's GREED and FEAR that move stocks," said the savvy Wall Street trader. "When prices are rising, enthusiasm and optimism rule. When the bids dry up, a fear of losing money takes over … and whatever promise the future holds is put aside!"

Almost since the beginning of time, the action and the excitement of the moment tend to stir these emotions, often to an extreme. People temporarily forget the fundamental reasoning behind the investment in the first place. When the long term outlook *does* change, one can expect prices to eventually reflect that change, gradually or suddenly.

History offers several glaring examples of greed and fear. As always, it is very easy to be critical of others with the benefit of 20/20 hindsight. But how is it possible for someone to pay a life's fortune for a few flower bulbs? Or invest in the cargo of a ship without knowing what the goods are or where they will be sold? Or buy shares in a company when its profit outlook is, by any reasonable analysis, questionable at best. When these tales are told, try to imagine how these "investors" became victims of their own greed and fear. Also, consider the similarities between each experience and the common lessons to be learned. In the end, investors who know and understand the fundamentals of the companies they own will be successful.

The Tulip Mania (1633-1637) The tulip, a bulb plant with long, broad, pointed leaves and a large, brightly-colored flower resembling a turban, was introduced into Europe from Turkey some time after 1550. These long-stemmed beauties rapidly gained popularity, especially by the wealthy in Holland and in Germany. By 1610, a single bulb of a new variety was said to be acceptable as dowry for a bride!

Since that time, about 100 species and at least 4,000 varieties have been identified. Indeed, these fragile flowers were a prize and they were displayed as such. That is, until it became too extravagant to do so.

In the early 1630's, Holland's general population became much more interested in the rising market value of the Tulipe Brasserie variety than in the beauty of the flower's continuous two-month spring time bloom. In 1635, a suit of clothes could be purchased for 100 florins – only a fraction of the going price for a single Semper Augustus at more than 5,000 florins.

From 1633 until the market peaked about four years later, it was not uncommon for homes and estates to be mortgaged merely to obtain contracts on bulbs that had never been out of the ground. And, based on experience, buyers KNEW that tulip bulbs could always be sold to other eager investors at much higher prices in the weeks or months ahead. As prices rose, almost

overnight, many citizens of modest means became rich. Farmers, shopkeepers, sailors, servants - everybody - enjoyed the prosperity of the tulip trade.

By this time, the wealthy no longer kept the flowers in their gardens. Instead, they sold them for an immediate cash profit. In 1636, tulips were actually traded on the stock exchange of Amsterdam; and also publicly traded, although to a lesser extent, in the Exchanges of London and Paris.

By 1637, the equivalent prices of hundreds of dollars – and in some cases, thousands of dollars – for a single bulb began to raise doubts. And then, when an investment of 3,000 florins would fetch only 300 florins six weeks later, or even less a few weeks after that, contract defaults became commonplace. It was becoming a major cause of social unrest. Unfortunately, the courts found it difficult to intervene and "come to the aid of the gamblers." Within just a matter of months, a great many hard-working Dutch citizens, who had been lured into trading much of their property for a handful of tulip bulbs, were left in ruin. Holland's Tulip Mania and the crash that followed serves as a classic lesson that may never be forgotten!

Mississippi Scheme (1718-1720)

John Law, the Scottish adventurer, gambler, economic theorist, and (at least by some accounts) financial wizard, was born in Edinburgh in 1671. At the age of only fourteen he worked in his father's bank, and set out for London three years later when his father died.

John Law's study of trade led to the publishing of his financial doctrines in his late 20's and early 30's. His work soon gained attention among politicians. He traveled on the Continent during the early 1700's and, while in Paris, established a friendship with the Duke d'Orleans, who later became an important figure in the French Government when King Louis XIV died in 1715.

In August, 1717, with the support of his friend, Law created the Compagnie d' Occident (Company of the West) and obtained exclusive privileges from the government to develop the French Mississippi Valley territories in North America. He was also granted the right to collect taxes and issue money. The initial capital consisted of 200,000 shares, each valued at 500 livres (the currency predecessor to the franc).

By mid-1719, his Compagnie des Indes (Company of the Indies), as it was renamed following several acquisitions, had exclusive

trading rights for other parts of the world as well … including the East Indies, China, and the South Seas. As the company's business opportunities opened up, demand for Compagnie shares increased.

Since new stock was being offered to the public in exchange for state-issued notes (billets d'etat), nearly everyone within the entire population saw the opportunity to share in the promise of the Compagnie and, at the same time, retire the national debt. The government obliged and approved additional shares which had attained a "good as money" stature. By this time, 625,000 shares had been issued and the market price of each had risen to about 18,000 livres. Most citizens could provide a current quote, although few could explain where the new territories were actually located.

The government continued to print more money which was readily accepted as before because it could be used to buy more shares in the Compagnie. However, the system's collapse began in early 1720 when share prices dropped sharply in the face of a developing scarcity of specie. Coins were being hoarded, which became evident to everyone by that time while all confidence in paper money was lost. It took years for the country to recover, and eventually the enormous debts were paid off with higher taxes.

South-Sea Bubble (1719-1720)

The South-Sea Company, incorporated by act of parliament, was organized by Harley Earl of Oxford in 1711. Its purpose was the assumption of government debts in exchange for exclusive trading rights to the South Seas.

Initially, the company would trade mainly in slaves with Spanish America. And even though the Treaty of Utrecht, made with Spain in 1713, proved less favorable than originally hoped, investors anticipated more positive developments. After all, the gold and silver deposits in South America were thought to be vast.

John Law's successes in France in the latter part of the decade did not go unnoticed by the public or the politicians, who began deliberations on the matter in January, 1720. Also, the fact that King George I was governor of the company inspired confidence in the venture.

Between the times the House of Commons opened discussions to authorize new stock in January, and the passage of the bill by the House of Lords in early April, amid rumors and speculation, the stock rose from 128.50 to over 300. The stock price was about 300 (quoted as a percent of capital) when the bill received final approval although, unknown to most investors, many influential people in government had a financial interest in its passage. By May, after two successful subscriptions and a price rising to about 400, most were convinced of the merits of the investment. The stock continued to climb, reaching 1,000 in early August.

The success of the South-Sea Company in 1719 and 1720 led to many "Bubbles," as they were aptly called, throughout Great Britain. And the speculative fever that swept the country encouraged ventures of all types. Among others, were bubbles seeking capital for: buying and selling goods, purchasing land, importing furs, and various insurance schemes.

The beginning of the end for the South-Sea Bubble came in August, 1720 once word spread that Sir John Blunt, Company Chairman, along with a few others, had sold their stock. This shook investor confidence and the decline that began quietly that month, accelerated. By the end of September the price had plunged to under 130. The ramifications of this crash were less severe than the debacle that occurred in France at the same time. However, this was not reassuring to those citizens who had used their South-Sea investment as collateral for other business dealings. In most cases, they, too, found themselves financially destroyed.

The South-Sea Company survived until 1853 even though most of its rights were sold to the Spanish government in 1750.

The 1929 Stock Market Crash The "Roaring 20's" came to a quiet halt on September 3, 1929. The steadily rising stock market with its well-publicized gains, especially late in the decade, seemed to confirm a popular notion that the United States had entered a "New Era" – a time of "permanent prosperity" – and one that might never end. The rapid rise of prices between late 1921 and September, 1929, and the violent crash and bear market that followed, are used today as a classic benchmark whenever market observers discuss the emotions of "greed" and "fear."

For some investors during the 1920's, a financial panic was not a totally new experience. The stock market had shut down for nearly two weeks in 1873; and many could recall when J. P. Morgan almost single handedly halted the panic of 1907. Also, the sharp 46% drop between 1919 and 1920 had not been forgotten.

But almost everyone agreed that the 1920's were very different. This was the new age of the consumer. Radios, air conditioners, washing machines, and automobiles were all being purchased with "buy-now-and-pay-later" plans. By 1929, consumer credit was helping the average family enjoy the prosperity of the day. Business was good, profits were up, and stocks, which were also being purchased on credit, were soaring.

October, 1928
Presidential candidate
Herbert Hoover

Even though stock prices were reflecting investor optimism, as they normally do, there were also several behind-the-scenes factors that contributed to the high equity valuations and to the vulnerability of the stock market in late 1929.

Margin on Equities

Stocks could be bought on 10% margin in 1929. Any investor could purchase shares having a market value of $10,000 with only $1,000 of capital. When stocks advanced, the profits generated were being used to purchase additional shares. This leverage, investors soon learned, worked very much to their favor when stocks were rising – and greatly to their detriment when prices were falling.

Perhaps most surprising was the magnitude of change in stock market credit. In January, 1928, total brokers' loans had reached $3.8 billion. A year later, the figure rose to $5.3 billion and continued soaring to a peak of $6.8 billion in early October, 1929. Of course, with the crash, equity credit also declined and was back to $3.4 billion by the end of the year.

Stock Manipulation

The late 1920's saw notorious stock price manipulation. Much activity considered legal then is no longer permitted today. In 1929, investor "pools" were formed to trade stocks. The pool would buy the shares, use media contacts to spread favorable news or rumors, and then "paint the tape" with large, meaningless trades between themselves. This would draw attention to the stock, thus allowing the pool to sell the shares, usually at much higher prices, to an unsuspecting public.

One of the most infamous manipulations of the time was the RCA pool headed by broker-specialist Michael J. Meehan. The pool managed to push up RCA's stock price by almost 50% between the 8th and 17th of March, 1929. Then, on the very next day, March 18th, the pool sold its entire holdings and divided the profits – about $100 million, by today's standards.

The trading activities, rumored or real, of William Durant, Jesse Livermore, and others, were popular topics of discussion in brokerage houses across the country.

Periodically, experienced market observers such as Roger Babson and Bernard Baruch would warn of the consequences of the speculative market environment. Unfortunately, few took these warnings seriously because both had been repeating similar messages for up to two years before the early September peak.

Allied Chemical	General Foods	Paramount Publix
American Can	General Motors	Radio Corporation
American Smelting	General Railway Signal	Sears Roebuck & Co
American Sugar	Goodrich	Standard Oil (N.J.)
American Tobacco	International Harvester	Texas Corporation
Atlantic Refining	International Nickel	Texas Gulf Sulphur
Bethlehem Steel	Mack Trucks	Union Carbide
Chrysler	Nash Motors	U.S. Steel
Curtiss-Wright	National Cash Register	Westinghouse Electric
General Electric	North American	Woolworth

The 1929 Fed

In the months between late-1927 and June, 1929, the nation's personal income and industrial production rose steadily. At the same time, Wholesale Prices (now called Producer Prices) remained flat, or were declining, as they had been doing for several years following the inflationary consequences of World War I. In addition, President Hoover, in keeping with the mood of the nation's working class, favored a continuation of high tariffs and protectionism. Meantime, the Federal Reserve Board encouraged easier credit.

On March 22, 1929, investors were relieved when the Federal Reserve failed to take action, thus encouraging further speculation. Yet observers seemed unaware of the consequences of the Fed's move in July when it raised the Discount Rate from 5% to 6%. And it was clear to some that personal income and industrial production were no longer rising. During the two months between the actual peak in the economy in August, 1929, and the October crash, personal income and wholesale prices were declining, and industrial production was actually plunging.

Following the crash the Discount Rate was quickly returned to 5% and many declines followed in 1930. By October of that year production had fallen 26%, personal income 16%, and product prices 14%. In terms of the creation of new money, it can be said that the Federal Reserve was very much "behind the curve" in the 1930 to 1933 period. The death of Benjamin Strong (the New York Bank governor and chairman of the newly-created Open Market Investment Committee) in 1928 led to a diffusion of leadership when the Fed needed it most.

Corporate Profits

From 1926 through 1929, earnings of the Dow Jones Industrial Average climbed 33% from about 15 to 19.94. Earnings remained strong year-to-year going into the last quarter of 1929. However, a slowdown was evident in some areas as early as the third (September) quarter of 1929; and the fourth quarter, normally higher than the third, was slipping. A substantial decline in profits occurred in 1930 and in the year following. The Dow Jones Industrial Average posted a *loss* for the entire year 1932. Not until the third quarter of 1948 did the Industrial Average post earnings greater than it did in 1929.

Corporate Dividends

More than 60% of DJIA company profits were paid out to shareholders in 1929. And in the four years that followed, 1930 to 1934, dividends paid, although lower in each successive year, exceeded the actual earnings of the companies.

New York Daily
Investment News
12,894,650 Day Smashes Old Peak by 4 Million
STOCK MARKET CRISIS OVER
Stock Houses Survive Worst Day in History

**Premature news on
"Black Thursday"
October 24, 1929**

Chronology: The 1929 Crash

The Dow Jones Industrial Average began 1927 at roughly 150 and climbed steadily throughout the year but stalled at 200 late in the last quarter. That mark was finally shattered on December 19, 1927. The Dow then advanced to 300 by November, 1928. In just five days in early December the Dow retreated 15%, but then rallied to close out 1928 at exactly 300. Volatility was becoming more prevalent – but more or less accepted by the public.

Volume on the New York Stock Exchange was picking up as well. During the sharp swing in December of 1928, daily volume reached approximately 5-6 million shares. In late 1928, and through most of 1929, a monthly total of 80 to 100 million shares was typical. Saturday trading, which was the practice during this period, saw volume at roughly half the activity of a weekday.

Between January 1 and June 1, 1929, the Dow Industrials fluctuated between 280 and 333. Exactly twenty-one weeks before the October crash the Dow began its final climb from 290 to its 386.10 peak on September 3. From that day on, a steady decline consumed the entire month of September. The Dow would not see 386 again until 1954, about 25 years later!

On January 24, the NYSE celebrated a membership increase from 275 to 1375.

October 24, 1929 (Black Thursday)

On Wednesday, October 23, the Dow closed at 305.85 in a busy session of 6,369,000 shares. Early Thursday, the market rallied 7 points and then a wave of selling hit the Exchange. To its lowest point, the Dow had reversed 40 points, or 13%, before closing at 299.47, down only 6.38 (2%) on the day. Volume totaled a record 12.9 million shares.

It can be said that "Black Thursday," as it soon became known, marked a "day of awareness" for 1929 Wall Street. The record trading activity that day was more than 50% greater than the March record and Wall Street's back offices struggled to keep up. The new high speed ticker tape ran hours behind and the paperwork was still being sorted and corrected on Friday.

On Saturday, activity returned to normal and the financial community seemed to believe the worst had past. The Dow closed Saturday's session at 298.97.

On Monday morning a story in the *New York Times* hit on many of the concerns of the day. The subtitle to the article was: **"Wall Street Hums on the Day of Rest to Catch Up on Work"**

"Wall Street, usually as deserted and quiet on Sunday as a country graveyard, hummed with activity yesterday as bankers and

A crowd gathered at the corner of Wall and Broad on "Black Thursday" October 24, 1929.

brokers strove to put their houses in order after the most strenuous week in history, in which all previous records for the exchange of securities on the New York Stock Exchange, the Curb Market, and over the counter were broken."

The article explained in a colorful way how weekend sightseers gazed curiously at the stock exchange building and, here and there, picked up from the street a vagrant slip of ticker tape, as visitors would seize upon spent bullets as souvenirs from a battlefield. A NYSE official was quoted saying that the members, many of whom were on the job Sunday morning, "have the physical work well in hand." And the article continued …

"There will, nevertheless, be great interest in today's stock fluctuations and those of subsequent days this week, or until the last vestige of the market upheaval has disappeared."

"Possibly, now that the nervousness has passed and holders of stocks or prospective holders of stocks have the opportunity to delve into the merits of their securities, especially in the points of earnings, dividends and outlook, the forecast may safely be made that it will be the best of stocks which will give the best accounts of themselves, no matter what the condition of the market."

U.S. Steel announced that its directors would be meeting on Thursday, leading many to believe that an important, positive announcement could be forthcoming.

"It would not surprise Wall Street in the least to see several leading corporations adopt a policy of greater liberality to their stockholders during the balance of the year, in view of the crisis which has developed and passed. Money is expected to continue cheap and plentiful."

"Business in most lines, according to all of the farometric indices, continues good and record Christmas trade is expected because of the high rate of employment. Ratios of operation in basic lines are not as high as in late summer and early fall, and the edge has been dulled measurably. On the other hand, the general state of trade compares favorably with this time last year, and corporate earnings as a whole, for the complete year, will show gains, it is expected, of between 20 and 25 per cent, over the full year 1928."

"Stocks of all sorts, those that have been selling at five times earnings, at ten times earnings, and those that have been selling at 75, 100, and even in extreme cases 150 times earnings, are now expected to engage in a quiet era of readjustment, in which the earnings will determine their worth, rather than the market value governed by the anxiety of speculators in all parts of the country to own them."

Monday, October 28, 1929

The Dow opened on a gap down at 295, three points lower. The popular blue chip U.S. Steel opened at 202¼, off 1¼. Upon reflection on Sunday, many were expecting some organized support at the open. They were disappointed. Prices plunged during the remainder of the session. Tuesday's *New York Times* described the action:

"There was but one brief respite during the day. At 1:10 P.M. news tickers reported that Charles E. Mitchell (broker, President, National City Bank) had just entered the Morgan offices. Wall Street jumped to the conclusion that another banking conference was on, and stocks steadied momentarily."

During the day most brokerage offices simply gave up posting prices on their chalk boards. The ticker was so late that prices put on the boards had no meaning by that time. In effect, FEAR ruled the day.

"Steel," as it was then called, closed down 17½ at $186, off almost 9% from Saturday and 29% below its $262 September high.

Monday's session closed down 38.33, almost 13%, on 9.2 million shares. On Monday, $14 billion of total market value had vanished. Lower prices, some observed, were fueled by the stop-loss orders placed weeks earlier and by margin calls that "went out by the thousands."

Tuesday, October 29, 1929

The opening bell on Tuesday saw a flood of sell orders – immediately prices were lower. By the end of the first half hour 3.3 million shares had traded hands. Soon stocks were being sold at whatever bid was available. Everyone wanted to sell.

From the opening bell, Steel plunged nearly $20 to $166½, down 11%, before closing at $174, down $12. Late in the day, the company's Board of Directors declared an extra $1 per share dividend.

The losses were wide-spread among all shares. Air Reduction closed at $120, off $25; General Electric at $222, down $28; International Telephone at $71, down $17; and Sears at $95, down $16¼. DuPont 's action was typical for those hectic days. The stock closed on Tuesday at $116, off $34 (50½ below Saturday's price) and 46% below its high set in September.

Union Carbide & Carbon (UK), listed in 1926, was a popular stock at the time. In mid-September, it reached $140. On Black Thursday, the stock's high was $106 and its low was $90. On Saturday, October 26, its price was near $102, the level it opened for trading on Monday. UK hit a low of $81 that day and $66 on Tuesday, a 35% drop in two days. By 1932, UK had fallen to $15½, exactly 89% below its 1929 high, a price not seen again until April, 1955.

At Tuesday's low, the DJIA hit 212.33, down 48.31 (18.5%) from Monday's close, 29% below Saturday, and 45% below its September 3 peak. Most issues enjoyed a recovery late in Tuesday's session. The Industrial Average ended its two-day panic closing Tuesday at 230.07. The day's volume totaled 16,410,030 shares, a record not eclipsed for nearly forty years.

On Wednesday, newspaper headlines were screaming ...*Variety*'s was a classic.

After the 1929 Crash

The emotional wave of selling finally ended on October 29th, although stock prices did move lower, hitting 195.35 on November 13th, before a healthy five-month rally began. By April, 1930, the Dow Jones Industrials had climbed back to 300, the precise point from which it crashed in late October. But by that time, the deteriorating fundamentals had become more obvious. It was then that the bear market took hold, and it extended until July 8, 1932, when the average hit its final low at 40.56.

The 1929 crash and the 1930-1932 bear market that followed had a devastating impact on individual stocks. U.S. Steel hit its final low in 1932 at $22, down 92%, and did not return to its 1929 peak until May, 1955. In the meantime, Chrysler declined from its 1928 high of $140 to $13 in 1930, a staggering 91% decline in just two years.

At the market peak on September 3, 1929, the P/E multiple of the Dow Industrials was 19.4 times estimated 1929 earnings and 35.0 times eventual earnings for 1930. The payout ratio was comparatively high in 1929 (64%) and the yield was 3.3%. At its low on October 29th, the P/E was 10.6 and the yield climbed to 6.0%.

Could the 1929-1932 debacle have been made less severe? Yes, most likely.

There were many major changes to the securities markets after the 1929 crash. Reforms included the establishment of the Securities and Exchange Commission (the SEC) in 1934 and the requirement of SEC filings by companies; the formation of the Federal Deposit Insurance Corporation (the FDIC); and the prohibitions of pools and manipulations of stock prices.

The huge profits that Jesse Livermore realized by selling short into an extremely weak market, for example, would have been more difficult given today's "up-tick" rules, option hedges, exchange "circuit breakers," and substantially higher margin requirements. By the same token, it can also be said that the emotions of "greed" and "fear" cannot be regulated from the marketplace, as we witnessed once again during the crash fifty-eight years later. However, the ability now to see prices without delays reduces the great fear and anxiety that accompanies the unknown.

The sinking of the battleship USS Arizona at Pearl Harbor on December 7, 1941

Wars and Shocks A study of the stock market's performances following shocking developments suggests that there is no precise pattern for a market reaction, but the market's ability to anticipate is clear.

Pearl Harbor and World War II

It can be said that World War II was a factor that helped end the Depression of the 1930s. It altered the unemployment picture dramatically and eventually added to the activity of the nation's economy.

The surprise attack on December 7, 1941 produced a sudden but relatively mild reaction. At the time, most issues had experienced a five-year bear trend up to that point ... and some experienced an immediate bottom. The majority, however, continued in a downtrend until May, 1942. In general, most stocks performed very well between 1942 and 1946. The Dow Industrial Average rose more than 70%.

One interesting observation regarding World War II: The stocks of military suppliers such as Grumman, for example, rose as one would expect. Between 1942 and 1945 the company's earnings climbed sharply from $2.16 to $11.28 per share and the stock advanced 500%. Yet, many consumer stocks such as PepsiCo, with relatively flat profits during the period, climbed even more dramatically. Airlines and utilities also did well.

One of the biggest winners during World War II was Chadbourn Gotham, Inc., the manufacturer of women's hosiery. When the Japanese bombed Pearl Harbor in December, the stock was priced below $2 with earnings per share of $1.43. In early 1946, the stock peaked at $43. By the time earnings finally peaked at $4.88 per share in 1948, the stock had already lost its luster and had returned to the teens.

The years 1937 to 1942 represented a no-growth period for most companies with little earnings progress while the battles were being fought. But the stocks rose anticipating a post-war profit boom. Deere & Co. was a good example: In 1942, the stock was $20 with $3.52 earnings per share. By 1946, Deere shares were $58 but earnings were only $2.48. By 1949, the stock had slipped to $40, yet profits rose to an astounding $12.40 per share.

The nation's war experiences since World War II have produced mixed investment results. The wars in Korea, Vietnam, and, more recently, in the Mid East did affect daily market fluctuations, each one more quickly than the one before it. In recent years minute-to-minute reports have been seen on television right from the battlefield.

The terrorist attack of September 11, 2001 resulted in a market shutdown for several days and it eventually caused dislocations within many segments of the economy.

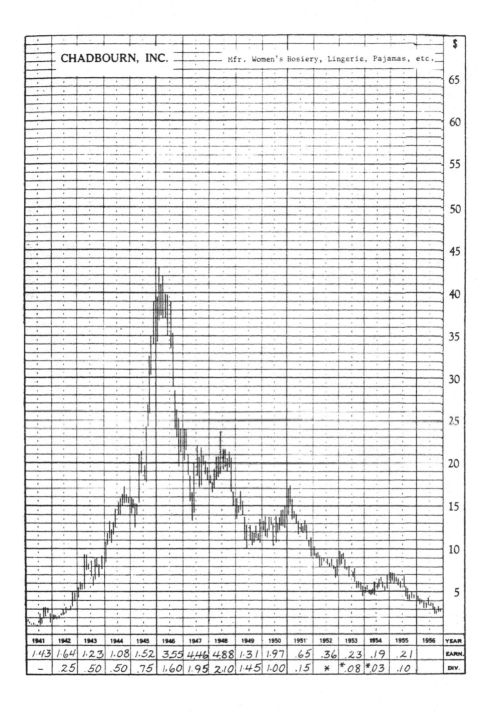

CHADBOURN, INC. — Mfr. Women's Hosiery, Lingerie, Pajamas, etc.

YEAR	1941	1942	1943	1944	1945	1946	1947	1948	1949	1950	1951	1952	1953	1954	1955	1956
EARN.	1.43	1.64	1.23	1.08	1.52	3.55	4.46	4.88	1.31	1.97	.65	.36	.23	.19	.21	
DIV.	–	.25	.50	.50	.75	1.60	1.95	2.10	1.45	1.00	.15	*	*.08	*.03	.10	

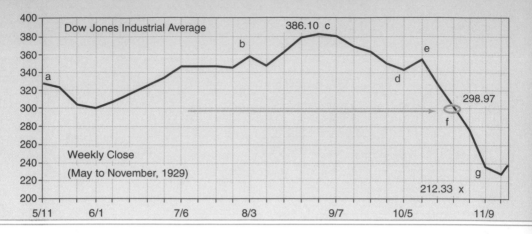

Dow Jones Industrial Average

386.10 c

b

e

a

d

298.97

f

Weekly Close
(May to November, 1929)

g

212.33 x

400
380
360
340
320
300
280
260
240
220
200

5/11   6/1   7/6   8/3   9/7   10/5   11/9

The 1987 Stock Market Crash

The economic circumstances and fundamental footing for businesses in 1987 were very different from 1929. But the technical similarities between the two periods were striking. First, the fundamentals:

1987 Background

The investment environment in the seven years immediately preceding the 1987 crash was as favorable, if not moreso, than the years prior to the 1929 crash. Inflation and interest rates, which peaked in 1980 and 1981, respectively, had been declining steadily. Even though wholesale prices had been climbing, they were not much higher than five years earlier.

In late 1986, industrial production began climbing at a pace much faster than in the prior two years. By the third (September) quarter of 1987, industrial production was growing at an annual rate of almost 6% and showed no signs of slowing.

Through the year 1986, the Fed reduced the Discount Rate from 7%, set in early March, to 6.5% in late April, to 6% in early July, and then to 5.5% in late August. This trend was reversed when the Fed *raised* the Discount Rate from 5.5% to 6% in early September, 1987 ... déjà vu?

From an investment standpoint, 1987 was very different from 1929 in two respects:

First, when the Dow Industrials peaked in 1929, stock yields were just over 3% and bond yields were about 4-5% (a spread of less than 2%). In contrast, the competition for investment funds was actually greater in 1987. Yields on equities were below 3%, while bond yields had advanced to over 10% by September, reflecting a fear that inflation might be rekindled. So, with the spread closer to 7%, stocks in 1987 were far less attractive relative to bonds.

Second, unlike 1929, there was little or no evidence in 1987 that corporate earnings and dividends would be declining anytime soon. In 1987, stock prices appeared high and, although a shift to bonds could take place at any time, there did not seem to be any fundamental reason to do so.

Still, by early October, 1987, the technical stage was set.

Technical Picture, 1987 vs. 1929

The charts above illustrate the weekly closing prices for each period. As a reminder, for most of the 1929 era, the markets were open for trading six days a week, Monday through Saturday. In 1987 trading was occurring five days a week, Monday through Friday, as it is today.

Most historic accounts refer to the "1929 Stock Market Crash" as the panic that hit the markets on Tuesday, October 29. As the earlier discussion shows, however, the

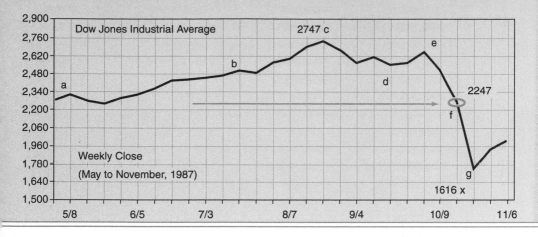

Dow Jones Industrial Average — 2747 c

Weekly Close
(May to November, 1987)

2247

1616 x

a, b, c, d, e, f, g

Y-axis values: 2,900 / 2,760 / 2,620 / 2,480 / 2,340 / 2,200 / 2,060 / 1,960 / 1,780 / 1,640 / 1,500

X-axis values: 5/8 / 6/5 / 7/3 / 8/7 / 9/4 / 10/9 / 11/6

actual crash was a two-day event that began Monday, October 28th, and merely continued into the following day, just as it did in 1987.

Compare the DJIA charts above. In both cases, the intraday market highs (386 in 1929, and 2747 in 1987) were just over 2.5 times the DJIA level of 36 months earlier. In 1929, the P/E ratio was 19.4, up from about 10 at the end of 1926; and, in 1987, the P/E was 20.7, up from almost 11 at the end of 1984. In other words, in both cases, earnings grew and P/E multiples expanded at very close to the same rate.

At the high in 1929, the DJIA yield was 3.3%. In 1987 it was 2.6%.

In 1929, and again in 1987, the top was formed with a distinct pattern, labeled "a" through "g." In both cases, the high ("c") was 18%+ above the peak of "a." In 1929 and in 1987, the actual high of "c" was hit on a Tuesday. Exactly six weeks later, the high of "e" was attained.

Again, in both cases, prices dropped sharply for two weeks. On Saturday, October 26, 1929, the DJIA ended its second week at 298.97 and opened down with a gap on Monday (at "f"). In 1987, the second week ended on Friday, October 16, at 2,247 and also opened Monday with a gap down. The intraday crash lows were 212.33 on Tuesday, October 29, 1929, and 1,616 on Tuesday, October 20, 1987.

In both cases, 1929 and 1987, the gaps that occurred on Monday marked exactly half way between "c" and "g" ... and both occurred 21 weeks after the trough of "a".

At the October 29, 1929 low (45% below "c"), the P/E ratio had dropped to 10.6, while the yield rose to 6.0%. In 1987 (at 41% below "c"), the P/E had dropped to 12.1 while the yield rose to 4.4%.

This is a significant technical pattern and it has been observed at other times, albeit less severely. Yet, although similar, the crash in 1987 was mostly *technical*. The event 58 years earlier was *fundamental*.

Fads Wall Street investors are a forward-thinking lot. And their ideas often lead to viable concepts ... but these concepts can be taken to an extreme. It seems that every decade the community will embrace a promising new investment theme and then look for its "pure plays."

Once this new concept is accepted by a larger audience the story has become well known and valuations become excessive. Unfortunately, in the years that follow, the initial earnings projections are rarely achieved; or if they are, not for many years. But the excitement and momentum can produce a thrilling ride.

Like manias, fads usually end the same way every time – with what called a "blow-off." When profit projections are revised or delayed, usually for valid reasons, investors begin to review and analyze the data and their assumptions much more carefully. Once this happens, earnings estimates are reduced and serious doubts begin to develop about the concept itself.

By the time it is obvious to the crowd that even the lowest, most conservative projections are not likely to be attained, the stocks have already begun their plunge. After the selling ends, the stocks are usually abandoned, sometimes for years. In most cases, a complete "cycle" will take years, depending on the madness and the degree of earnings disappointment.

Oftentimes, the leading companies within the group do produce impressive growth records for a time. And one or two viable long term investments may emerge. Most marginal firms are either acquired or fail.

Among the most notable fads over the past fifty years:

Leisure Time Stocks (1957-1961)

Brunswick Corp., AMF, Outboard Marine

The leisure-time stocks in the late 1950's enjoyed great popularity. Brunswick and AMF were the leaders in bowling. Also included were boating issues: Outboard Marine, Glasspar, NAFI (later Chris-Craft), and others.

Between 1957 and 1960, the shares of Brunswick Corp., adjusted for splits, rose from about $3 in early 1957 to almost $75 in March, 1961. BC's earnings progression after 1955 was also very impressive: $0.39; $0.69; $1.07; $1.71; and $2.28. Earnings peaked at $2.56 per share in 1961. By 1964, however, profits were back to breakeven levels and the stock price was well below $10 once again.

Conglomerates (1962-1967)

Litton Industries, Gulf & Western, IT&T

The art of merging lower-quality and/or lower-multiple companies into a larger entity to attain "synergy" and an apparent growth record has been an everlasting fad on Wall Street with mixed results.

Fertilizer Stocks (1964-1967)

Freeport Sulphur, Texas Gulf Sulphur

Sulphur (now usually spelled sulfur) and fertilizer stocks were a rage in the mid 1960s. As it often happens, when playing commodities, investors can forget that prices can be hurt by additional supply.

The "Nifty-Fifty" (1970-1974)

The excessive valuations attained by a relatively small group of growth stocks, dubbed the "nifty-fifty," contributed to the

Even Though Profits Exceeded 1972 Levels 12 Years Later, Winnebago's Stock Price Did Not Return to that Peak Until 2002!

devastating market debacle of 1972-74. They included Avon Products, Polaroid, Xerox, IBM, 3M, and others. Supposedly, these companies had reliable earnings streams that could be projected years into the future. Not so. At the same time, there were several individual groups that gained attention among growth stock investors. Among them were recreational vehicle stocks including Winnebago, Fleetwood, and Elixir Industries.

In fact, not many Wall Street fads turned from "Cinderella" Into a "Queen of the Ball" and back to a "Cinderella" as fast as this one did. Adjusted for splits, Winnebago's stock rose from $4 in 1970 to a high of $48 in 1972. By the end of the following year when gasoline prices and supplies became a factor, the stock had returned to $4.

Biotechnology (1989-1992)

Amgen, Chiron, Genentech, Biogen

Except for the astounding Internet Mania that occurred years later, no other industry with such modest immediate earnings prospects had ever raised as much new seed capital as did this one. Biotech IPO's were being spawned weekly in early 1991. The rapid rise and fall between 1989 and 1992 was noteworthy since the year-long shakeout effectively separated companies that had the most promising and lasting earnings prospects from those that didn't.

It was the Food & Drug Administration's "efficacy challenges" to Xoma, Centocor, and to others that changed the investor sentiment. Yet, some biotech companies have since had their drugs approved and developed into rapidly-growing drug companies in their own right.

Amgen, for example, rose from an adjusted $8 in early 1990 to almost $80 in 1992 as earnings soared from $0.04 per share, to $0.67, to $2.43 per share in the same timeframe. The stock's 50% decline in 1993 in sympathy with the industry's shakeout did nothing more than provide a buying opportunity for investors who had done their homework. But the same could not be said for many others in the group.

The Dot-com Bubble (1995-2000)

The Internet Mania that came to a sudden halt in 2000 is labeled the "granddaddy of all bubbles." The huge dollar losses in the millions of portfolios due to the dot-com bubble easily exceeded $1 trillion.

This book's later chapter, The Internet, explains the fascinating story behind this extraordinary method of communication. Why investors became so enamored is now very clear. In effect, imaginations ran amuck without any realistic understanding of potential profitability – or its lack thereof.

The bubble was fueled by enthusiasm for numerous products and services that could eventually be developed using the web: Software Sales, Internet Service Providers, Search Engines, Portals, Web Services, Website Auctions, Web Sales, and Business-to-Business Networks were among the many ideas to be developed. In addition, the internet system would require greater capacity and speed. Thus, billions – or maybe trillions – of dollars of network equipment would be needed. By 1995, the investment concept was born.

The big question was: "Who will profit?" Eventually, the answer became clear to most internet investors: "Not everybody!"

Netscape Communications was founded by young visionary Marc Andreesen and a savvy millionaire entrepreneur, James Clark. Netscape was an early leader in the field with an advanced browser software called "Navigator." Revenues increased rapidly and the company's initial public offering on August 8, 1995 was the most successful ever up to that time.

In only four months, the stock advanced from the IPO price of $28 to $171 per share. At its high, the company's shares attained a market value of more than $6.5 billion, or roughly 80 times 1995 revenues! Many seasoned observers held that Microsoft's momentum as a chief competitor was the turning point for Netscape, eventually acquired (after a plunge of 80%) by America Online.

Amazon.com's story is one of an evolving strategy by flamboyant founder Jeff Bezos. The venture began as an online bookstore and eventually expanded into many of the merchandise categories of big department stores including toys, clothing, electronics, and other products. The company has yet to post a significant profit but, so far, it has survived the burst of the bubble.

America Online emerged as one of the primary survivors largely due to its merger with asset-rich, media-giant Time Warner. However, to this day, many questions still plague the AOL franchise. At the high, its market value exceeded $350 billion.

Cisco Systems has been John Chambers' success story of sorts. The stock rose from under $1 to $82 (adjusted) before losing 80%+. Yet the company, with a wild acquisition spree, became a $20 billion enterprise ... and a profitable one at that.

Ebay Inc. has been one of the few dot-com companies to continue to grow and to earn a respectable profit. Like Amazon.com, Ebay has developed its forte (auctions) into a well-known internet franchise.

JDS Uniphase emerged as one of the leading suppliers of internet products. Like Yahoo, it became a mutual fund darling and was named to the S&P 500 once its market value ballooned above $150 billion.

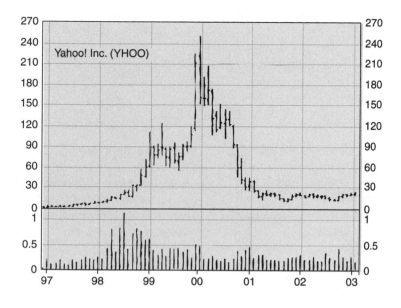

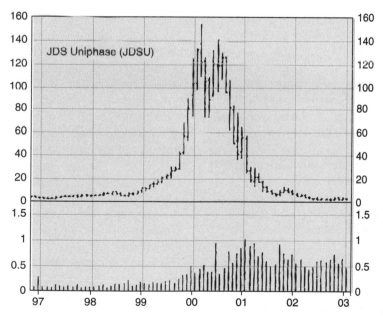

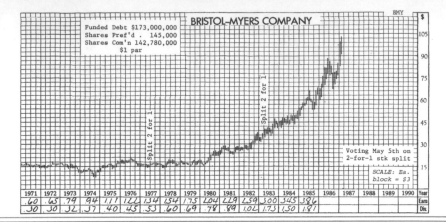

BRISTOL-MYERS COMPANY

Funded Debt $173,000,000
Shares Pref'd . 145,000
Shares Com'n 142,780,000
$1 par

Year	1971	1972	1973	1974	1975	1976	1977	1978	1979	1980	1981	1982	1983	1984	1985	1986	1987	1988	1989	1990
Earn	.60	.65	.79	.94	1.11	1.22	1.34	1.54	1.75	2.04	2.29	2.59	3.00	3.45	3.86					
Div.	.30	.30	.32	.37	.40	.45	.53	.60	.69	.78	.89	1.02	1.73	1.50	1.81					

Voting May 5th on
2-for-1 stk split

SCALE: Ea.
block = $3

Yahoo's rise from $1 to $250 (adjusted) and its slide to under $10, plus being added to the S&P 500 along the way, makes this stock a dot-com bubble "classic." To date, Yahoo's profits have been modest, but thus far the stock has survived.

One of the great ironies of the Internet Mania was the number of "conservative investors" unknowingly hurt by it. Once an internet stock was added to an index, such as the S&P 500, index holders who never owned it going UP rode it going DOWN.

Hundreds of other internet stocks were less fortunate. Some are still struggling to survive today. Here are just a few of the many past high-flyers that have since been reduced to penny-stock status or worse:

Avanex Corp. – Fiber optic-based products
High: $273 ($19.0 billion)

Corvis Corp. – Networking equipment
High: $115 ($41.3 billion)

Drugstore.com – Internet-based drug store
High: $70 ($4.7 billion)

Homestore.com – A service for real estate professionals. High: $138 ($16.2 billion)

Priceline.com – Internet buy-sell services
High: $165 ($37.1 billion)

Conclusion There is a certain degree of logic to the stock market and to the psychology that rules it when one examines and takes into account the imponderables of greed and fear. If they are understood, profits can result.

In late 1972, Bristol-Myers' shares were $70 with EPS of $2.60. Two years later, the stock was 50% lower and the earnings figure was $3.76. The P/E had dropped from 27 to 9 within twenty-four months. Twelve years later, BMY was earning four times as much and paying a cash dividend of $8.48 annually. Once the P/E multiple partially recovered those who panicked had good reason to be unhappy. The stock had tripled and was still rising! In effect, they let their emotions rule and temporarily disregarded the fundamentals.

The same emotions that drove the price of tulips down in 1638 … the fear of losing more money … led investors to sell BMY shares that offered a measurable value.

The lesson is simple. Over time, those investors who are better informed by having done their homework, and who recognize their emotions, should enjoy greater success in the stock market.

Bonds, preferred stocks and the money market

Introduction Sophisticated investors tailor their investment portfolios to meet their individual financial needs. They realize, too, that an individual's needs change with time; that an elderly widow has a different financial objective than a young business executive just starting a family.

Many investors find they require more current income and greater safety of principal than can be expected of a portfolio invested entirely in common stocks. This chapter will explain several alternatives including bonds, preferred stocks, and issues of the United States Government. It will also explain the Federal Reserve System and touch on the meaning and content of the "money market" where short-term credit instruments and negotiable paper are traded.

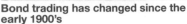
Bond trading has changed since the early 1900's

Bonds Explained News commentators frequently conclude their daily reports with a description of the day's stock market activity, but there is seldom, if ever, any mention of bonds. Widely regarded as the most conservative investment, bonds generally do not experience the dramatic day-to-day price changes that make for exciting reporting. Yet, the bond market is actually larger than the stock market. In recent years a majority of new corporate financing has been accomplished through bonds. Further, it has been estimated that nearly as many individuals own bonds as own common stocks.

Bonds are issued (sold) by corporations, state and local governments or their agencies, the United States Government, foreign governments, and Federal agencies. Professional bond traders use one-word designations for the bonds of each issue which are, respectively: corporates, municipals, governments, and agencies.

Although each type of bond has certain unique characteristics, bonds in general have one basic function: they are formal IOUs in which the issuer promises to repay the total amount borrowed on a predetermined date. In addition, for the use of the money, the issuer will also compensate the bondholder with, typically, semiannual interest payments at a fixed percentage rate during each year the bond

is owned. In the language of bonds, the total amount to be repaid is called variously its "principal amount" or "face value" or "par value." The repayment date is known as the "maturity date," the interest rate is the bond's "coupon," and the period of time the bond is outstanding is called its "term." All this information is printed on the face of the bond.

In the past, nearly all bond certificates came with coupons attached. The coupons were periodically clipped from the bond and presented for payment. This is, in fact, the derivation of the term "coupon," which became synonymous with fixed interest payment. Bonds can be issued in "registered" form (the owner's name is registered with the corporation and interest payments are mailed directly to the bondholder) and "bearer" form (the bond is presumed to belong to whomever possesses it). Most corporates are registered bonds while municipals, on the other hand, are still issued as bearer bonds.

A bond certificate, then, is a certificate of indebtedness spelling out terms of the issuer's promise to repay. Sometimes, this promise is reinforced by collateral such as equipment or property, but usually bonds offer only the "full faith and credit" of the borrower (bonds of this type are called debentures). Thus, obligations issued by the U.S. Government are regarded as the safest investments available. After all, as

Corporate Bonds

BONDS		CUR YLD	VOL	CLOSE	CHG
Dole	7 7/8 13	7.9	115	99.88	0.50
Duke En	6 7/8 23	6.8	38	101.50	0.75
Duke En	6 3/4 25	6.8	84	98.63	−1.00
FstData	6 5/8 03	6.6	23	101.00	unch
FstData	2s 08	cv	3	105.13	−1.25
FordCr	6 3/8 08	6.3	67	99.38	−0.63
GBCB	8 3/8 07	8.4	9	99.25	0.38

the saying goes, only the government has the ability to print money!

A corporate certificate of indebtedness contrasts sharply with a common stock certificate, which signifies ownership. If the company prospers, its common stockholders can expect to share in the expanding profits through a combination of dividend increases and a higher stock price. The bondholder cannot share in the company's growth and can only expect repayment of the principal amount and the fixed annual interest payments. If the company fails, however, the bondholders and owners of preferred stock, which resemble bonds in many ways, must be paid in full before the common shareholders get a cent. For this reason, bonds and preferred stock are known as "senior securities."

Bonds are issued with various face values or "denominations" . . . usually set at $1,000 a bond. When the bond trades in the open market, however, its price is quoted at 1/10 of its value. Thus, a bond selling at par, or $1,000, would be listed as 100; a bond selling above par or, in other words, at a "premium," say $1,100, would be shown as 110. A bond trading below par or at a "discount," say $880, would appear as 88. Bonds trade at fractional prices, but are noted in dollars and cents and rounded up when it is appropriate.

Thus, a bond priced at 88 1/8 corresponds to a dollar value of $881.25. A bond at 105 7/8 is the same as $1,058.75. If the change during the day happened to be 1/8, it would appear as $0.125 and rounded to $0.13 as it would appear in the bond table.

Government bonds are traded in a similar fashion but their fractions are expressed in thirty-seconds. A government bond selling for 90.12 means 90 12/32, which reduces to 90 3/8 or a dollar equivalent of $903.75.

Shown above is a typical excerpt from the New York Exchange corporate bond table that appears daily in The Wall Street Journal and other newspapers.

Consider the bond of Duke Energy, a well-known energy company, as an example. Reading from left to right, the investor learns that the bond was issued by Duke Energy, pays an annual interest rate of 6 3/4 percent, matures in 2025 and, on this particular day, carried a "current yield" of 6.8 percent, which will be explained shortly. The remaining figures describe that day's trading. They tell the reader that $84,000 of this specific issue traded that day. The final trade of the day was 98.63 (98.625), which was 1 point ($10.00) lower than the final price recorded in the preceding trading session.

The investor may wonder why bond prices fluctuate at all since the bondholder has

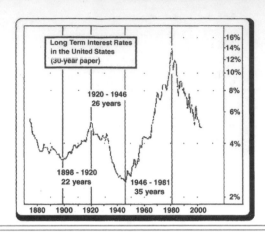

Long Term Interest Rates
in the United States
(30-year paper)

1920 - 1946
26 years

1898 - 1920
22 years

1946 - 1981
35 years

16%
14%
12%
10%
8%
6%
4%
2%

1880 1900 1920 1940 1960 1980 2000

An interest rate can be regarded as the purchase price of money.

been promised full repayment at maturity. This question can best be answered within the larger context of interest rates – the key to understanding bonds.

An interest rate can be regarded as the purchase price of money. Basically when there is high demand for money by business, consumers, and governments, and the supply is limited as it is during a period of economic expansion, the cost of money (expressed by the interest rate) rises. When demand is slack and money is freely available, as it is during an economic slowdown or recession, interest rates tend to fall.

There is no single interest rate, but several. These include the Prime rate, the interest rate that banks charge their most credit-worthy borrowers; the Federal Funds rate, the interest rate charged on loans made between banks that are members of the Federal Reserve System; the Federal Reserve Discount rate that member banks pay on funds borrowed from their Federal Reserve Bank; and Money Market rates (including issues of the United States Government such as Treasury Bills). Although there are frequently differences between the interest rate levels of various issues, all rates tend to move together (note the chart). At any given time, interest rates reflect not only current conditions, but also investor expectations of future trends.

Yields New bonds are issued at rates dictated by economic conditions and expectations. As rates change, the return investors expect from bonds already trading in the open market (called "yields") must be adjusted to remain competitive and attractive to investors. Since the annual interest payment is fixed throughout a bond's life, the adjustment must be made through the price of the bond itself.

Like common stocks, a bond's current yield is found by dividing its annual interest payment by its price (with stocks the expected annual dividend is divided by its price). When a bond is bought at par, or face value, its current yield is, obviously, identical to its coupon rate. However, if it is purchased at any other price, its current yield will be more or less than its coupon rate. As the example illustrates, the yield on a $1,000 par value bond paying $90 can decline or rise in response to a change in the price of the bond. A bond's price and its yield always move in opposite directions.

(1) When the bond price is at par: $\dfrac{\$90}{\$1,000} = 9.00\%$

(2) When the bond price rises, its yield declines: $\dfrac{\$90}{\$1,100} = 8.18\%$

(3) When the bond price declines, its yield rises: $\dfrac{\$90}{\$900} = 10.00\%$

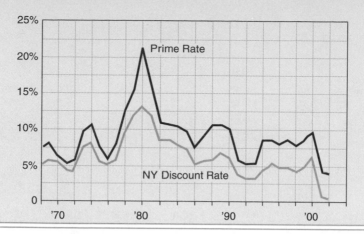

Price, then, is the basic adjustment mechanism that conforms yield to the general level of interest rates. To repeat, even though bondholders receive full face value at maturity, a bond's price will fluctuate during its life for a very simple reason: If all other factors are equal, an investor would never buy an existing bond from another bondholder when new comparable issues being offered elsewhere are providing higher returns.

While bond prices normally do not swing as widely or as rapidly as common stock prices, potential bond investors should realize that bond prices do fluctuate nevertheless. If a bond must be sold before its maturity date, it is possible that the bondholder will receive less than face value, and perhaps substantially less.

The term "current yield" was adequate to explain why and how bond prices change, but the most important measure of a bond's return to the long term bondholder is called the "yield to maturity."

At par, a bond's yield to maturity equals its current yield and its coupon rate, but if a bond is purchased at a premium or at a discount, its yield to maturity will be either less or more than its current yield. At any price other than par, the yield to maturity differs from and is more accurate than the current yield. It recognizes that, in addition to the annual interest payments received

during the life of the bond, the bondholder can also receive a capital gain or loss at maturity if there is a difference between the purchase price and the face value.

Yield to maturity computes the compound annual interest gained or lost on this difference, assigns (or more exactly "amortizes") a portion to each year of the bond's remaining life, and expresses the result as a single annual percentage rate. In effect, if a bond is purchased at a discount, the yield to maturity is greater than the current yield. If a bond is bought at a premium, the yield to maturity is less than current yield.

Although in practice, a bond's yield to maturity is usually calculated today by computer programs and calculators, it can also be approximated by using a bond value table. The bond value table gives the yield to maturity at various maturities, coupons, and prices. The yields are expressed in whole percentages and smaller measurements known as "basis points." A basis point is 1/100 of 1%. In other words, 100 basis points are equal to 1%. For example, a bond yield of 7.63% is 5 basis points less than a bond yield of 7.68%. The accompanying page shows a sample table from a bond value book.

As an example, if a 6 1/2% 2024 bond (currently selling at, say, 85 with a current yield of 7.6%) was being considered, the

6½%

YEARS and MONTHS

Yield	18-6	19-0	19-6	20-0	20-6	21-0	21-6	22-0
4.00	132.46	133.05	133.63	134.19	134.75	135.29	135.83	136.35
4.20	129.38	129.90	130.41	130.91	131.40	131.88	132.36	132.82
4.40	126.39	126.85	127.30	127.74	128.17	128.59	129.00	129.41
4.60	123.50	123.90	124.29	124.67	125.05	125.41	125.77	126.12
4.80	120.69	121.03	121.37	121.70	122.02	122.34	122.64	122.94
5.00	117.97	118.26	118.55	118.83	119.10	119.37	119.62	119.88
5.20	115.33	115.57	115.81	116.05	116.27	116.49	116.71	116.92
5.40	112.77	112.97	113.16	113.35	113.54	113.72	113.89	114.06
5.60	110.29	110.44	110.60	110.75	110.89	111.03	111.17	111.30
5.80	107.88	108.00	108.11	108.22	108.33	108.44	108.54	108.64
6.00	105.54	105.62	105.70	105.78	105.85	105.93	106.00	106.06
6.10	104.40	104.46	104.53	104.59	104.64	104.70	104.76	104.81
6.20	103.27	103.32	103.37	103.41	103.45	103.50	103.54	103.58
6.30	102.17	102.20	102.23	102.26	102.28	102.31	102.34	102.36
6.40	101.08	101.09	101.11	101.12	101.13	101.15	101.16	101.17
6.50	100.00	100.00	100.00	100.00	100.00	100.00	100.00	100.00
6.60	98.94	98.93	98.91	98.90	98.89	98.87	98.86	98.85
6.70	97.90	97.87	97.84	97.81	97.79	97.76	97.74	97.72
6.80	96.87	96.83	96.79	96.75	96.71	96.67	96.64	96.60
6.90	95.86	95.80	95.75	95.70	95.65	95.60	95.55	95.51
7.00	94.86	94.79	94.72	94.66	94.60	94.54	94.48	94.43
7.10	93.87	93.79	93.72	93.64	93.57	93.50	93.43	93.37
7.20	92.90	92.81	92.73	92.64	92.56	92.48	92.40	92.33
7.30	91.95	91.85	91.75	91.65	91.56	91.47	91.39	91.30
7.40	91.01	90.90	90.79	90.68	90.58	90.48	90.39	90.30
7.50	90.08	89.96	89.84	89.72	89.61	89.51	89.40	89.31
7.60	89.17	89.03	88.91	88.78	88.66	88.55	88.44	88.33
7.70	88.27	88.12	87.99	87.85	87.73	87.60	87.49	87.37
7.80	87.38	87.23	87.08	86.94	86.81	86.68	86.55	86.43
7.90	86.51	86.34	86.19	86.04	85.90	85.76	85.63	85.50
8.00	85.64	85.47	85.31	85.16	85.01	84.86	84.72	84.59
8.10	84.79	84.62	84.45	84.28	84.13	83.97	83.83	83.69
8.20	83.96	83.77	83.59	83.42	83.26	83.10	82.95	82.81
8.30	83.13	82.94	82.75	82.58	82.41	82.24	82.09	81.94
8.40	82.32	82.12	81.93	81.74	81.57	81.40	81.24	81.08
8.50	81.51	81.31	81.11	80.92	80.74	80.57	80.40	80.24
8.60	80.72	80.51	80.31	80.11	79.93	79.75	79.58	79.41
8.70	79.94	79.73	79.52	79.32	79.13	78.94	78.77	78.60
8.80	79.18	78.95	78.74	78.53	78.34	78.15	77.97	77.79
8.90	78.42	78.19	77.97	77.76	77.56	77.37	77.18	77.00
9.00	77.67	77.44	77.21	77.00	76.79	76.60	76.41	76.23
9.10	76.94	76.70	76.47	76.25	76.04	75.84	75.65	75.46
9.20	76.21	75.97	75.73	75.51	75.29	75.09	74.90	74.71
9.30	75.49	75.25	75.01	74.78	74.56	74.36	74.16	73.97
9.40	74.79	74.54	74.29	74.06	73.84	73.63	73.43	73.24
9.50	74.09	73.84	73.59	73.36	73.13	72.92	72.71	72.52
9.60	73.41	73.15	72.90	72.66	72.43	72.22	72.01	71.81
9.70	72.73	72.47	72.21	71.97	71.74	71.52	71.31	71.12
9.80	72.06	71.79	71.54	71.30	71.06	70.84	70.63	70.43
9.90	71.40	71.13	70.87	70.63	70.39	70.17	69.96	69.75
10.00	70.76	70.48	70.22	69.97	69.73	69.51	69.29	69.09
10.20	69.48	69.20	68.94	68.69	68.44	68.22	68.00	67.79
10.40	68.25	67.96	67.69	67.44	67.19	66.96	66.74	66.53
10.60	67.04	66.76	66.48	66.22	65.98	65.74	65.52	65.31
10.80	65.87	65.58	65.31	65.04	64.79	64.56	64.33	64.12
11.00	64.73	64.44	64.16	63.90	63.65	63.41	63.18	62.97
11.20	63.62	63.33	63.05	62.78	62.53	62.29	62.07	61.85
11.40	62.54	62.25	61.96	61.70	61.45	61.21	60.98	60.77
11.60	61.49	61.19	60.91	60.64	60.39	60.15	59.93	59.71
11.80	60.47	60.17	59.89	59.62	59.37	59.13	58.90	58.69
12.00	59.47	59.17	58.89	58.62	58.37	58.13	57.91	57.70

The "yield to maturity" can be found quickly in a bond values book.

buyer would first locate the 6 1/2% coupon rate shown in the upper left-hand corner of the page.

Next, the investor would locate the price closest to the expected purchase price in the column of prices appearing under the actual number of years to maturity; in this case, 2003 (today) to 2024, or 21 years. The price $85.00 falls between the prices 85.76 and 84.86, which, in the far left column, correspond to yields of 7.90% and 8.00%. A more exact yield can be found by interpolation. Therefore, because the bond price is now $85 (below par), the yield to maturity is greater than the 7.6% current yield.

Besides providing a more accurate picture of a buyer's potential return, yield to maturity also makes it possible to compare bonds of varying maturities and coupons. But even yield to maturity cannot be used blindly because a bond may be "called" before reaching the maturity date, which can change the yield significantly.

Calling "Calling" a bond means the issuer exercises a right stated on the face of the bond to retire the bond before its maturity date. Most bonds are now issued with call provisions. The right to call a bond gives the issuer greater flexibility to respond to changes in the general level of interest rates. For example, if a corporation had issued bonds with a 10% coupon during a period of high interest rates, and if interest rates subsequently declined to a level where the same bond could be issued with an 8% coupon, it would be to the corporation's advantage to retire the 10% bonds and reissue new bonds at 8%. In fact, the annual interest savings can be so significant, often measured in millions of dollars, that issuers usually redeem the bonds at a premium above face value. Typically, the premium amounts to one year's annual interest. Thus, a $1,000, 10% bond might be called at $1,100.

Most bonds are not subject to a call provision until a specified number of years have elapsed, say 5 or 10. After that period, the bonds can be called at any time at one specified price or the issuer can stipulate a declining scale of prices, one for each year remaining after the first call date.

In addition to the optional call method, many bonds and preferred stocks are also retired through the use of a "sinking fund."

Once established, the issuer must set aside a certain number of dollars each year for periodic retirements. This enhances the security of the remaining bonds. When new bonds are being issued, investment bankers often say they are "floating" a new issue; so it is understandable that a bond retirement

Ratings are important to both borrowers and lenders.

fund be called a "sinking" fund. The bonds or preferred stock to be retired each year can either be called at a specific price or they can be purchased in the open market. Occasionally, the sinking fund payments are allowed to accumulate while earning interest, so the entire issue can eventually be retired at one time.

Any investor who ignores a call feature could be subject to an expensive surprise. If bonds are called unexpectedly, a bondholder might get the principal amount back sooner, but lose what may have been an attractive yield. In some cases, the bondholder may even lose part of the principal. This would occur if a bond had been purchased at a substantial premium but called at a price close to par. For these reasons, the potential bond buyer should carefully examine call and sinking fund provisions with a broker or bond dealer to better understand the risks involved.

So far, it has been shown that bond selection must include a consideration of the type of issuer, maturity, coupon, yield, and call features. There is yet another important factor that must be included – a bond's "rating."

Ratings Ratings measure the probability of a bond issuer repaying the principal amount at maturity and meeting the scheduled interest payments. Viewed another way, ratings rank issues according to their perceived risk of default. They are computed and published by objective, independent organizations. The two best known rating agencies are Standard & Poor's Corporation and Moody's Investor Service Incorporated. Their ratings are available on a subscription basis and in a variety of publications that can usually be found at a local library or brokerage office.

Together, the two agencies rate most of the publicly held corporate and municipal bonds. In addition, Moody's rates many Treasury and government agency issues. However, they do not rate privately placed bonds, unless they are asked to on a fee basis. In recent years, nearly fifty percent of all bond issues have been placed privately, which simply means that investors, usually institutions, have purchased the bonds directly from the issuer without any public distribution. Although preferred stocks have ratings which appear identical to bond ratings, they are not directly comparable because bonds represent debt and preferred stocks are equity (ownership).

The rating agencies use a simple system of letters to indicate their judgment of an issue's safety of principal and interest payment stability. Standard & Poor's ranks bonds from highest quality to lowest by using the first four letters of the alphabet in groups of three, as follows: AAA, AA, A, BBB, BB, B, and so on through D. Bonds

S&P Lowers Debt Ratings

carrying a D rating are in default. Investors commonly refer to the highest rating as "Triple-A." Moody's uses a similar system, stopping at C, as follows: Aaa, Aa, A, Baa, Ba, B, Caa, Ca, C. Some of the bonds in Moody's C categories could be in default.

When appropriate, both agencies use other symbols to further refine a given rating. Thus, Standard & Poor's might add a plus or a minus sign to a rating. For example, an A+ rating is a shade higher than an A rating. In its municipal bond ratings, Moody's uses A1 and Baa1 to indicate the highest quality bonds falling within those two specific categories.

In both systems, rating groups from Triple-A through B carry the same meaning. Thus, Moody's opinion of an Aa bond is basically identical to Standard & Poor's opinion of its AA bond. Further, both systems clearly have a boundary line established with the BBB and Baa ratings, which are the first categories indicating some speculative investment characteristics. Bonds above BBB are believed safe investment candidates for both individuals and institutions. Bonds below BBB should receive careful analysis because they are inherently more speculative.

But ratings are more than interesting academic notations. They are gauges of risk and, in the marketplace, investors demand greater returns as risk increases. Thus, the lower an issuer's rating, the greater the annual interest payments demanded.

Since ratings can translate into millions of dollars of interest savings, the rating agencies are understandably thorough in researching their opinions. Each agency employs a staff of security analysts who examine the financial condition, operations, and management of a given issuer. They also study specific documents such as the bond's "indenture," which describes certain legal and technical details of the issue. Perhaps the most important factor is an evaluation of the company's future earnings potential, which calls for analytical techniques like those used in appraising common stocks. In general, bond analysts test an issuer's strength under adverse business conditions with an objective to determine the safety of principal and interest payments. After a rating is given, it is reviewed periodically and sometimes changed to reflect any improvement or deterioration in an issuer's overall condition.

Convertible Bonds Convertible bonds, as these debentures are commonly called, are usually subordinate to other debt. However, they have all the features discussed thus far – a par value, coupon rate, maturity date, yield and often a rating

**In the New York Exchange bond room
before the move to new quarters in
1977**

159

and a call date. But they differ from other bonds in one important respect: They can be converted into a specific number of shares of the issuer's common stock.

Convertibility closely links the price performance of the bond with that of the underlying common stock. Thus, although a convertible bond offers some of the relative safety of principal and interest characteristic of so-called "straight" or nonconvertible bonds, they usually fluctuate in price more widely and more rapidly due to the convertible feature. In this sense, convertible bondholders participate directly in the changing business fortunes of an issuer whereas other bondholders cannot.

If the common stock is selling above the conversion price, the convertible bond will tend to move more closely with the common. When the stock is below the conversion price, the bond's market price will tend to more closely reflect prevailing interest rates and the company's ability to maintain the bond's interest payments. In short, convertible buyers usually give up some safety and interest in exchange for potential capital gains.

Corporations select convertibles to raise additional capital for several reasons. Convertibles, as opposed to a new common stock issue, limit the dilution of existing stockholders' equity. Convertibles also offer tax savings to the issuer because interest payments on convertibles, and on other bonds, are deductions before Federal income taxes, while cash dividends are paid from after-tax earnings. Finally, the interest rates on convertibles usually yield more than equivalent common stock dividends but less than comparable straight bonds. If interest rates in the conventional bond market are high, an issuer can frequently obtain a lower rate by offering the convertibility feature as a sweetener.

Convertibles may offer an attractive opportunity for capital gains as well as income, but they also place greater demands on the investor's analytical resources. Several new terms and calculations, which will be presented in the hypothetical example to follow, must be understood before convertibles can be used effectively.

Consider a 7% convertible subordinated debenture with 10 years remaining to maturity convertible into common stock at $40. The bond is currently selling at 90 ($900). The underlying common stock is selling for $32 a share.

The investor first must determine the maximum exposure to loss by calculating the bond's price as if it were selling as a "straight" bond. This price, often called the "investment value," is usually computed by the same organizations that publish bond ratings. The investment value is that price which causes the bond's yield to maturity to equal the yields offered by straight bonds of similar quality and maturity. Suppose our bond carries a Baa rating (convertibles rarely receive higher) and that straight bonds in this category are currently yielding 9%. The appropriate calculations indicate that our bond must sell for approximately $835 to yield 9%.

The investment value represents the theoretical downside risk, the floor beyond which the bond's price should not fall in the current market environment. Again, it is theoretical and based on comparative values that are subject to change. In this case, however, it does tell the investor that, without its convertible feature, the bond could decline roughly 7% from the purchase price to its value as a straight bond.

Next, the convertible buyer will want to compare this risk with the possible reward.

Since the $1,000 bond is convertible into common stock at $40, the investor knows that each bond has a "conversion ratio" of 25. In other words, at the $40 "conversion price" each bond can be exchanged for 25 shares of common stock ($1,000 divided by $40 = 25). Although the bond is convertible at $40, the stock is actually being bought at $36 because the same conversion privilege

is being obtained at a discount. This price is called the stock's "conversion parity price." It is obtained by dividing the bond's actual purchase price by the number of shares that will be received upon conversion ($900 divided by 25 = $36). Viewed another way, the investor is at the break-even point at the conversion parity price. As the stock price advances beyond conversion parity, the bond's value should follow in step with at least an equal percentage move. In this case, the conversion parity price of $36 is roughly 12% higher than the stock's current price of $32.

From the break-even point, the buyer now explores the potential gain that might ultimately be realized. The investor should have some reasonable profit target in mind. Assume, after a thorough study of the issuer's business and prospects, the bond investor concludes that the common stock will rise to $50. At $50 per share, the bond would be worth $1,250 (25 shares $50 per share = $1,250), representing a profit of nearly 40% on the $900 investment. In addition, the investor receives a steady stream of interest payments.

The sophisticated convertible buyer attempts to limit risk by selecting a bond where:

Disney Plans Zero-Coupon

• The current price is close to the investment value.

• The conversion parity price is close to the common stock's current price.

• The common stock is expected to appreciate considerably.

Rarely, however, are actual situations as clearly defined as this example. A convertible bond can be a complicated security.

Zero-Coupon Convertible Bonds

This unique variation of a subordinated convertible bond emerged as a popular instrument in many years ago. The "zero" convertible, also referred to as a Liquid Yield Option Note (or "LYON") by Merrill Lynch, is a convertible bond priced at a deep discount. The bondholder receives no ("zero") annual interest payments, but is promised a face-value payment at maturity.

Zero convertibles are attractive to the issuer because the implied interest payments may be deducted from taxes. Although bondholders are required to pay taxes on the implied interest they receive, they benefit by the convertible feature. To date, these bonds, usually convertible into the issuer's common stock at any time, have been used most successfully by growth companies to raise funds for expansion.

If an investor believes that long-term interest rates will be trending lower in the year(s) ahead, buying zeros might be a leveraged way to participate. Zeros tend to be more sensitive to interest rate swings because the bond's interest payments are reflected in the discount. Some speculators use 20-year or 30-year "stripped" Treasury bonds (called Treasury Strips) to play interest rate moves. While these zeros are not convertibles, of course, they can produce considerable profits or losses if interest rates fall or rise by just a small amount.

Investing in zero convertibles requires special care for two reasons:

(1) Zeros often have a call feature at the discretion of the issuer. An investor should never purchase a zero without first calculating how much might be lost if the bond is callable and redeemed unexpectedly.

(2) A zero will be sensitive to the price movement of the equity into which it is convertible. If the price potential of the stock appears limited, the zero will probably be less attractive in the marketplace relative to other bond opportunities.

Municipal Bonds Municipal bonds are issued by states, cities, towns, political subdivisions, or authorities, such as housing authorities and bridge and tunnel authorities. They are usually issued to finance new construction for such diverse purposes as hospitals, bridges, tunnels, and sports stadiums.

Municipal bonds differ from straight corporate bonds in three ways. First, and most important, the interest on municipals is exempt from Federal income taxes. Further, if the investor lives in the state of issue, they are usually exempt from state and local taxes as well. This tax exempt feature sets municipal bonds apart from all other bonds and explains why municipals are frequently called "tax exempts." Note the useful calculation above.

Secondly, municipals are usually issued with "serial" maturities as opposed to the "term" maturities characteristic of corporate bonds. Serial maturity means that a portion of the total issue matures annually until the entire issue is retired. Unlike sinking fund retirements, each year of a serial issue has its own interest rate or is priced to provide a specific yield.

Many years ago, for example, the State of Maryland issued $145 million of 15-year Triple-A general obligation bonds at a net interest cost of 4.86%. The bonds were reoffered to investors on the following

partial "scale," as the series of yields is known: 1977 priced to yield 3.70%, 1980 to yield 3.90%, 1981 to yield 4.10%, and continuing with a 5.20% yield in 1991. The higher rates in later years reflect inflation expectations, of course.

Thirdly, most municipals are issued in $5,000 principal amounts, whereas corporate bonds usually have a $1,000 principal amount. Further, municipal bonds are traded entirely in the over-the-counter market unlike corporate bonds which are also listed on some of the national exchanges. An investor interested in a specific issue must consult a bond dealer for a price. Municipal prices are usually not quoted in daily newspapers. The dealers themselves frequently consult The Blue List of Current Municipal Offerings, a daily publication, which gives pertinent data such as price and yield on available offerings. Although municipals usually have a $5,000 principal amount, their prices are nonetheless quoted as if the principal amount was $1,000 (i.e., at 100 or some premium or discount to 100).

There are several types of municipal bonds. Most common is the General Obligation Bond where the issuer promises full faith, credit, and taxing power to ensure that principal and interest payments are made on time. These general obligation bonds are considered to provide the greatest security

Here is a simple formula to calculate whether a tax-free investment is more advantageous than a taxable one:

Subtract your tax bracket from 1.0 (for example, if you are in the 28% tax bracket, 1.0 − .28 = .72). If you have a tax-free yield of 5%, you can find its taxable equivalent by dividing it by .72. In this case, the answer is 6.9% (that is, .05 divided by .72 = 6.9%).

and, as a result, usually have the lowest yields. Revenue bonds are backed only by the earning power of the facility constructed with the proceeds of the bond issue. Other types include general obligation bonds with a provision limiting the amount of taxation that can be applied, as well as special tax bonds, and industrial revenue bonds.

In general, because of the tax exempt feature, municipal bonds have interest rates several percentage points below the going rate on corporate bonds of comparable quality. In other words, a municipal bond will often provide the same after-tax yield to an investor as a corporate bond priced to yield several points more. The benefit of this tax-exempt feature improves as an investor's annual taxable income and tax bracket increases. For example, the tax rate for a husband and wife filing a joint return with a $65,000 taxable income is about 21%. To equal a 7% municipal bond yield, they would have to find a corporate bond yielding about 8.8%. A family earning $100,000 would be paying taxes at a higher rate, close to 24%, and must find a corporate bond yielding at least 9.2% to get the same after-tax return that a 7% municipal offers.

Preferred Stocks At first glance, many preferred stocks might appear to be bonds without a maturity date. They offer relatively attractive yields, they can be called, some can be converted into common stock, some

are rated, most are issued at a stated par value (usually $100), and all are commonly listed as "senior securities." Indeed, some preferred stocks are thought to be of such high quality that their prices tend to parallel the price trends of high-quality, long-term bonds.

There are, however, two important distinctions investors should appreciate before buying preferreds:

(1) Dividends – Although the dividend is set at a fixed annual rate, it can be changed by the issuer at any time. It can, in fact, be omitted entirely. For this reason, most investors seek a "cumulative preferred stock," which means that if dividends are "passed" by the board of directors, they are allowed to accumulate and must eventually be paid when money becomes available.

(2) Claims – As its name implies, a preferred stock has preference over the common stock in the receipt of dividends and in any residual assets after payments to creditors if the company is dissolved. But a creditor, such as a bondholder, has a legally enforceable claim against an issuer who defaults on an interest payment. A preferred stockholder has no such claim should a dividend be omitted.

"Participating" preferred stocks enable the owner to share in any extra dividend

U.S. Government Securities—
A treasury bond, a treasury note,
and a treasury bill. Certificates
are no longer in use.

165

payments, although most preferreds are "nonparticipating," which limits the annual return to the fixed annual dividend payment.

Corporations have favored bonds over preferred stocks as a method of raising new capital. Preferred dividends are paid from after-tax earnings whereas bond interest is paid from earnings before taxes. Thus, preferred stocks can be more expensive to the corporation.

A preferred stock is a blend of the characteristics of a bond and a common stock. It can offer the higher yield of a bond; it has priority over the common in equity ownership, but it does not have the safety of a bond and its participation in the company's growth is limited.

Preferred stocks are usually bought for income. The investor should strive for high income with greater safety (a preferred with little debt ahead of it) or high income with growth (a preferred convertible into common stock). Otherwise, it is probably better to own the bond or the common stock.

U. S. Government Securities The
Federal government, much like state and local governments, also uses debt obligations to finance various projects and programs. Three types, generally differentiated according to maturity range, are used most frequently. They are: Treasury BILLS, with maturities up to and including one year; Treasury NOTES, with maturities between one year and seven years; and U.S. government BONDS, with maturities between seven years and thirty years. There can be exceptions to this general classification, however. For example, there are 10-year notes.

Government securities offer the investor:

• Maximum safety of principal since they are backed by the word of the government itself;

• Competitive yields, although seldom equal to yields on less-secure corporate bonds;

• A high degree of liquidity through active trading in secondary markets both listed and over-the-counter;

• Limited taxation because they are free of state and local taxes, although not from federally imposed taxes.

Today, treasury securities are no longer issued in paper form as depicted in the photograph. All treasury securities are now in electronic book-entry form.

Treasury bills, commonly called "T-bills," account for the bulk of government financing. They are sold by the Treasury at a discount through competitive bidding. A weekly auction is held for bills with three-month and six-month maturities. Monthly auctions are held for the remaining two maturities – nine-month and one-year bills. Treasury bills are issued in five denominations from $1,000 to $1,000,000. The return to the investor is the difference between the purchase price and the bill's face value received at maturity.

Most treasury securities can be purchased through a program called TreasuryDirect. Bills can be sold in the secondary market before maturity. Individuals can purchase bills directly at no charge either from a Federal Reserve Bank or the Bureau of the Public Debt by sending a certified personal check or cashier's check for the bill's face value to:

Bureau of the Public Debt,
Securities Transactions Branch,
Washington, D.C. 20226.

Better yet, investors can now transact business using this internet website:

www.publicdebt.treas.gov

Bills can also be purchased for a fee from certain commercial banks, government securities dealers, and brokerage firms. As discussed shortly, T-bills are the major vehicle used by the Federal Reserve

System in the money market to implement national monetary policy.

Treasury notes have become increasingly popular with individual investors for three reasons. First, they are usually issued in $1,000 denominations, the same as a minimum T-bill investment. Second, their longer maturities usually offer higher yields than T-bills. And, finally, notes are now being issued more frequently. The treasury sells various securities, including notes, at more than 150 auctions held throughout the year.

Notes have a fixed rate of interest payable semiannually, and they can be purchased without charge at issuance from Federal Reserve Banks or their branches, or directly from the Treasury. Investors can also buy them for a fee from some commercial banks, brokerage houses, and other government securities dealers.

Government bonds can also be purchased without charge at issuance directly from the Treasury and Federal Reserve Banks and in low denominations. In many ways, they resemble straight corporate bonds. They have fixed rates of interest, fixed maturity dates and, before 1985, were callable.

No 30-year bonds have been issued since October, 2001.

The government likes to say that if U.S. Treasury bills, notes, and bonds are the world's safest investments, then the Treasury Inflation-Protected Securities are the safest of the safest because their ultimate value cannot be diminished by inflation. These "TIPS," as they are called, are like other notes and bonds. Interest payments are received every six months and a payment of principal when the security matures. The principal value is adjusted by inflation (using CPI) and at maturity it is redeemed at its adjusted principal amount or original par value, whichever is greater. The fixed rate of interest is applied not to the par amount of the security, but to the inflation-adjusted principal. TIPS can be purchased three times each year. A 10-year note is auctioned in July and then reopened in October and January.

Many investors were first exposed to government bonds through the famous Series E Savings Bond used during World War II. Savings bonds, unlike Treasury Bonds, are not "marketable securities" (that is, they do not have a secondary market). Today, the "Series I Savings Bond," the second of two types of inflation- indexed government securities, is available with face value denominations of 50, 75, 100, 200, 500, 1000, 5000, and 10,000 dollars. The I-Bond has an interest return that is a combination of a fixed rate, which applies for the life of the bond, and the inflation rate.

For example, the November 2002 I-Bond offers 1.60%, plus 2.46% as an inflation hedge (CPI-Urban adjusted; see the Appendix), for a total return of 4.08%. Cashing in a Series I-Bond before five years has a 3-month earnings penalty and I-Bonds are state and local tax exempt (federal income tax is deferred until the bond is cashed).

Nearly twenty other government agencies issue short-term notes, debentures, and participation certificates to finance their specialized operations. Most "agencies" have maturity dates, fixed interest rates, and face values, but are rarely callable. Unlike the direct obligations of the U.S. Treasury, however, only a few agencies are backed by the Federal government. As a result, they usually offer higher yields than Treasury issues.

The best-known agency issues are sold by the Federal National Mortgage Association and the Government National Mortgage Association, commonly called "Fannie Mae" and "Ginnie Mae." These are corporations created by Congress to support the secondary mortgage market. In general, these two agencies strengthen the market for certain types of mortgages. Their mortgage-backed securities are sponsored, but not guaranteed, by the government.

The Money Market Securities comprising the capital market primarily serve investors and borrowers who have a time horizon extending beyond one year. But many investors have surplus cash they want to employ for shorter time periods, even as short as overnight. Similarly, many borrowers need to raise money quickly for only short-term use. In both cases, the money market provides the ideal solution.

The money market is actually composed of several individual markets, one for each of its short-term credit instruments. Thus, there are markets for Treasury bills, commercial paper, negotiable certificates of deposit (CDs), and bankers' acceptances (drafts drawn on banks to finance international trade on a short-term basis). In addition, commercial bank borrowings from each other at the "Federal Funds Rate" and commercial bank borrowings from the Federal Reserve Banks at the "Discount Rate" are also considered important parts of the money market. Unlike the other transactions, however, neither method of bank borrowing creates "negotiable paper" (marketable promissory notes pledging the return of principal at maturity and fixed interest payments in the meantime).

In any case, all transactions have maturities within one year and most are 90 days or less. Although each credit instrument is different, the rates tend to move closely together.

Investors, including commercial banks, state and local governments, some individuals, large non-financial businesses, foreign banks, and non-bank financial institutions, are drawn to the money market for three basic reasons in addition to attractive yields:

(1) It is a liquid market capable of handling billions of dollars with slight effects on yields.

(2) It offers a high degree of safety of principal because issuers, in general, have the highest credit ratings. Investors should realize, however, that certain credit instruments can never be considered completely risk-free. When the Penn Central went bankrupt in 1970, for example, it had $82 million in commercial paper outstanding.

(3) Money market maturities are short and thus there is little risk of loss due to interest rate changes.

Borrowers, in turn, including the U.S. Treasury, commercial banks, and non-financial corporations, seek the market's attractive rates, which are generally below bank loan rates even to prime borrowers.

By far, the most important participant in the money market is the Federal Reserve.

Trading Room of the Federal Reserve Bank of New York where specialists buy and sell government and federal agency securities.

169

The Federal Reserve System

On December 23, 1913, President Woodrow Wilson signed the Federal Reserve Act establishing the Federal Reserve System (also referred to as the "Fed"). Its original purpose was to improve the nation's financial system with a stable monetary framework. Thus, the country would have a more elastic currency, facilities would be available for discounting commercial paper, and there would be an improved supervision of banking. The primary concern of the Federal Reserve System was, and is today, the flow of credit and money – although, since its formation, its responsibilities have been broadened considerably.

Generally speaking, the Federal Reserve System consists of: (1) its Board of Governors, (2) the Federal Open Market Committee, (3) the twelve Regional Federal Reserve Banks and their branches, (4) the Federal Advisory Council, and (5) the 5,500+ commercial banks that are members of the system and all other institutions subject to its rules. The Fed is, in effect, a bank for individual banks and their lender of last resort.

The Fed's Board of Governors is located in Washington, D.C. and is the System's top administrative body. There are seven Board members, each appointed by the President and subject to confirmation by the Senate.

The members are appointed for 14-year terms with one term expiring every two years. The President also appoints the Chairman and Vice-Chairman of the Board from among the members for four-year terms that may be renewed.

The Federal Reserve's principal function is monetary policy which it controls with three tools:

(1) Open market operations.

(2) The discount mechanism.

(3) Changes in reserve requirements.

Since the 1930s, open market operations has clearly become the Fed's major instrument. However, raising or lowering the discount rate (i.e., the cost of borrowing from the Fed) and changing the reserve requirements (i.e., shifting the allocations of required and non-required reserves of depository institutions) are also useful tools.

Through its Open Market Trading Desk at the New York Federal Reserve Bank, one of the twelve regional banks, the Fed implements the decisions of the Federal Open Market Committee (a 12-member body that meets about every three weeks).

The Board of Governors Chairman is also the chairman of the FOMC. The six other

CD Yields Are Steady At Major U.S. Banks

Board members, along with the president of the Federal Reserve Bank of New York, and four rotating Federal Reserve bank presidents comprise the Open Market Committee. The primary function of the FOMC is to determine the amount of securities to be purchased or sold by the Federal Reserve System. These securities are primarily Treasury bills, notes, and bonds. Also bought and sold are federal agency obligations and bankers' acceptances.

By selling and buying these various money market instruments, the Federal Reserve contracts or expands the reserve positions of the commercial banks that are members of the system. The resulting changes in member banks' reserve balances affect the ability of member banks to make loans and acquire investments. If the Fed wants a tighter monetary policy, which can produce higher interest rates, securities are sold to reduce member bank reserves.

Securities are bought by the Fed, which will increase member bank reserves, when it wants an easier monetary policy. In this way, the Federal Reserve influences monetary and credit conditions of the entire country – and it affects the international community as well.

When the Fed makes an open market operations decision, it must take conflicting factors into consideration. Assume, for example, it wants to pursue an easier monetary policy because the nation's unemployment rate is rising and lower interest rates are needed to stimulate the economy. The Fed simply bids up the price of securities high enough to purchase them from banks, bond dealers, or individuals. Will its move to ease stimulate inflation? How will the nation's exports and imports be affected? Will it become more difficult for the Treasury to sell its securities to refund its debt when the lower yields are compared with the returns available in other parts of the world? It is easy to see why the Federal Reserve, with each policy move, has its supporters and its critics.

Rates on money market instruments are generally scaled upward from the Treasury bill rate on comparable maturities. Otherwise, they could not compete with the nearly risk-less and highly flexible government security.

Yields on negotiable certificates of deposit (CDs), for example, are usually several basis points higher. CDs are issued by banks. They are receipts for funds deposited with them for a predetermined period of time on which the bank agrees to pay a specific rate of interest. A CD returns principal and interest to the owner at maturity, but it can also be sold in the secondary market should the owner need the money before maturity.

CDs are particularly popular with large corporations that use them in cash management as a backup to Treasury bills.

Maturity dates are usually selected to suit the needs of the purchaser. They range between one and eighteen months, but most CDs mature in four months and are issued in denominations from $25,000 to $10 million. In the secondary market, dealers usually trade in $1 million denominations.

Commercial paper is another money market instrument, although there is no secondary market. This instrument, sold in denominations from $5,000 to $5 million or more, is simply a short-term promissory note that credit-worthy businesses use in place of bank borrowing because, traditionally, it has been less expensive.

Tax anticipation bills, bankers' acceptances, and loans to and repurchase agreements with government securities dealers are also considered money market instruments. However, Treasury bills, CDs, and commercial paper comprise the bulk of money market transactions.

Money market instruments, along with bonds and preferred stocks, play an important role in the world of investments. They can be, for many investors, either an effective complement or a valuable alternative to common stocks.

The Internet

9

Introduction Since the early 1980's the computer has come into the lives of most American families in one way or another. And since 1991, no technological development has been more significant to this new computer-savvy community than the internet.

The personal and business applications of the internet are far more extensive than even the greatest visionary could have imagined at the time the World Wide Web first opened up to the general public.

Today, we take most of the internet's capabilities for granted as just part of our daily lives. E-mail, on-line shopping, telephony, music, video, and other applications are continuing to expand the popularity of this new medium. And no business will benefit more by the internet than Wall Street. One can almost say that the internet has developed into Wall Street's modern-day Curbstone Marketplace.

This chapter will offer some background and explain why this new medium became the subject of the dot-com bubble. It will address the application of the internet from the investor's standpoint and it will show how the internet can be used in both fundamental and technical analysis as well as being a direct link to Wall Street.

Tim Berners-Lee opened the internet to the public on August 6, 1991.

History of the Internet Tim Berners-Lee is credited with creating the world wide web while working at the European Particle Physics Laboratory at CERN in Geneva, Switzerland. The Oxford graduate was seeking a means of collaboration between physicists and other researchers in the high-energy physics community. His proposal, entitled *HyperText and CERN*, was written in 1989.

Three new technologies were soon incorporated into his proposal: HyperText Markup Language (HTML) used to write web documents; HyperText Transfer Protocol (HTTP) to transmit the pages; and a web browser client-server program to receive, interpret, and display the results at each website address.

One important concept of his proposal involved a client software allowing users to access information from many types of computers. The line mode user interface, called the World Wide Web, was completed in 1989 and his files were made available to the public for the first time on August 6, 1991. At that time all documents were stored on one main computer (called a "web server") at CERN.

By year end 1992, there were over 50 web servers, located mostly at universities and research centers. In mid-1999 the number of servers had grown to nearly 800,000 and by 2001 there were over 20 million.

It was 1990 when Tim Berners-Lee, using a NeXT computer, wrote the first web browser-editor, later called "Nexus." Three years later, another pioneer of the internet, Marc Andreesen, as an undergraduate at the University of Illinois, developed the graphic interface browser named "Mosaic." This software was the forerunner to the popular Netscape browser called "Navigator." (Netscape was eventually acquired by America Online as Microsoft's "Explorer" captured more of that business.)

By the end of 1993 various browsers could access about 600 websites. There were close to 10,000 sites by 1995; 100,000 by 1996; and about 650,000 going into 1997. There are more than 30 million sites today.

The internet has forced companies to adjust. The web has added yet another leg to the marketing stool making the business environment more competitive. And every day access is becoming faster and easier.

Over the years, internet access has been accomplished with a dial-up system using a modem. In 2003, roughly 65% of the 72 million U.S. internet households were dial-up and 35% used the faster "broadband" access. Experts expect that by 2007 the reverse will be true – 65% of the expected 88 million internet households will be broadband and 35% dial-up. This trend should accelerate acceptances of new products and services via the internet.

Michael Dell formed a computer company from a venture he started in his college dormitory. Dell's success today is due, in part, to the internet.

Dell Computer is a perfect example of how companies today are using the internet to further their business. Dell's sales are made to other businesses (80%) and directly to consumers (20%). Dell applies what is called a "Direct Business Model." Customized products are sold by using a combination of a direct sales force, an 800 number, a catalog, and the internet.

With progress come problems, and as the internet grows there will be challenges. The three most prevalent threats to the productivity gains of the internet are:

- Spam – unwanted advertising that clogs e-mails, wastes time and destroys user productivity.

  In 2002, 3.9 trillion internet e-mails were sent in North America and it is estimated about 60% was "junk mail."

- Virus attacks – criminal programs that spread unintentionally and disrupt normal internet activity.

- Terrorism – acts that purposely shut down systems for a time.

Most experts agree that the internet will overcome these problems in time. But more effective measures will have to be developed in the years ahead, especially as wireless modes become more popular.

Investing and the Internet The World Wide Web has become Wall Street's newest curbstone meeting place. Here, individual investors can find an untold wealth of information and services, oftentimes free. Yesterday's dirt path leading to the buttonwood tree is today's computer software program referred to as the "browser."

Now, with just a few keystrokes or a click or two of the mouse, an investor can find a website that offers information, products, or services to meet almost any need.

With the help of so-called "search engine" directories, such as "Yahoo!" or "Google" and others, a website address, called the Universal Resource Locator (URL), can be found quickly and with little effort. Want to purchase another copy of this book for a friend? Use a search engine to find an internet bookstore ("Amazon.com" is among the largest currently). Go to the internet bookstore's website and enter the book's title. After that, purchase is easy.

One of the most interesting and practical websites developed for active investors in recent years is the U.S. Government's URL address "www.publicdebt.treas.gov". At this internet location visitors can enter the "Virtual Lobby" to buy or sell T-bills, Notes, and Bonds online, 8 a.m. to 8 p.m.

An aseptic room at Johnson & Johnson Laboratories during the early days of a great company, circa 1910

The Company's Website

To illustrate the simplicity and utility of this worldwide communication network for investors, here is how a visitor might search for fundamental information on, say, Johnson & Johnson. The traditional analytical approach outlined earlier can be used, of course. But the worldwide web can greatly speed the research process.

First, the investor needs the company's URL address. A quick visit to Yahoo.com or Google.com, for example, will provide a URL address search by entering the company's name, "Johnson & Johnson." Immediately, the investor learns that the company's URL is "JNJ.com". The company decided to use its stock symbol as its URL. General Motors did the same. General Motors website is "GM.com." Frequently, the investor can learn the company's URL without searching. For example, by typing the company's name "JohnsonAndJohnson" immediately after the internet designation http://, the browser will automatically connect the investor to the company's website, JNJ.com.

Once Johnson & Johnson's website appears on the screen, a series of tabs or buttons can be clicked for directions to any one of several of the website's locations. They might include "Company Products," or "Careers," or "Investor Relations." From this location, the investor can then go to:

- Company background, historical data;
- Annual reports and Proxies;
- Dividend history and its reinvestment plan, if any;
- Financial reports;
- SEC filings;
- Recent news releases;
- JNJ's pharmaceutical "pipeline";
- Past corporate presentations;
- Webcast archives;
- The latest stock quote or chart;
- Request for other information.

Most company websites today, including Johnson & Johnson, provide far more data and information than could have been obtained from many different sources years ago. For example, recently, one of the major brokerage firms featured Johnson & Johnson at its "Pharmaceutical and Medical Devices Conference" where the company made a presentation. From JNJ's website, the investor can listen to this webcast and view the slides that were used during the presentation. In effect, the extraordinary power of the internet now allows every investor to participate directly in the complete investment process.

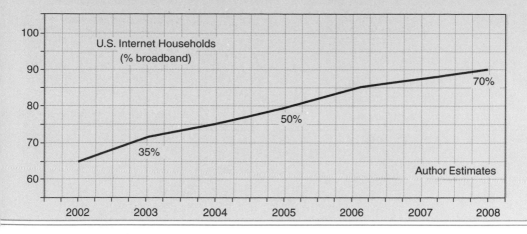

U.S. Internet Households
(% broadband)

35%

50%

70%

Author Estimates

The SEC and Other Sources

Besides the company's website, there are many other internet locations where an investor can collect information on nearly every public company. Other than research reports from brokerage firms, the investor can access SEC documents through a company called Edgar Online. Edgar is not affiliated with or approved by the SEC but the most important forms filed with the Commission can usually be obtained through the EDGAR service. The most important submissions to the Securities and Exchange Commission Include:

- **10-K** – The complete Annual Report

- **8-Q** – The complete Quarterly Report

- **8-K** – Unscheduled material events such as an arbitration judgment, etc.

- **4** – Changes in beneficial ownership

- **13-D** – A Statement of Ownership, or merger terms, etc.

Nearly all company investment information, apart from security analyst reports, can be obtained FREE from the corporation using the internet. In most cases, it should not be necessary for the investor to pay for, or subscribe to, the same information which is often found elsewhere on the web. The company's website is THE place to start.

Online Services

Current stock prices can be found on the Internet or through some "internet service providers" such as America Online, Microsoft's network (MSN), and others. Accessing the web using these services typically requires a low monthly fee. Thus, users can experience Wall Street through attractive and well-constructed sites that present current prices, charts, and ample abbreviated fundamental data. But this is not always an inexpensive approach.

Once on line, individual investors can conduct their own research and then monitor their stock portfolios on a regular basis, either independently, or through these services. Most of the time, the subscriptions provide a 15-minute lag from real-time prices, which is satisfactory for most investors doing preliminary research.

Perhaps one of the best free charting and corporate news site found on the internet is "BigCharts.com" a service from the CBS enterprise, MarketWatch.com (well known on the web for its financial news).

Investors who need real-time data for trading purposes, or for up-to-the-minute quotes, will discover that additional fees are usually required. If an online brokerage account is opened, all stock prices are, of course, real-time.

Lycos Finance (lycos.com) offers an online charting service called "LiveCharts." Like so many interactive services of this type, its operation seems to slow as it becomes more popular. Nevertheless, this website (noted here because it works satisfactorily, it's reasonably priced, and they have been in business for several years) is worth a visit. Lycos' LiveCharts offers a good comparison benchmark for other services.

Beyond the simple task of providing stock prices and charts, some websites can be a link to library-quality information, especially on products and product markets. More times than not these sites are associated with industry magazines and newsletters.

In addition, "bulletin boards" and "chat rooms" are available for open forums and discussions with other investors having similar interests. Once in a while other investors, perhaps knowledgeable about certain products, companies, and their markets, can stimulate and challenge. Of course, they can also very be misleading. Information from unofficial internet sources should always be used with caution.

In the late 1990s a great many internet "scams" were uncovered and prosecuted. Among them was a young man who used the internet as a platform to promote certain stocks for his personal benefit. Another notable case involved false press releases. Punishment was sure and swift.

Technical Analysis Almost every financial newspaper and magazine has advertisements for charts and charting services, oftentimes with free demos. Among the more popular is the TC2000 Service from Worden Brothers, Inc. at TC2000.com. Also, *Investor's Business Daily* offers daily graphs and other analysis data at Investors.com. Reuters has a charting service called "MetaStock." Most are, of course, directed to traders rather than investors. There are many good (and bad) and reasonably priced (or expensive) services available either from independent sources or brokers.

There have been many software packages developed in recent years to exploit the readily-available data from the internet. In 1996, this author introduced a program called *The Wall Street Trader* designed to produce short term technical indicators using, mainly, intraday and daily data from the Chicago Board Options Exchange. (*The Wall Street Trader* software helps identify the market's short term swings and is featured at the BullsOrBears.com site.) Its key indicators are described later in the "Principles of Technical Analysis" chapter.

For software programs like this, investors are less concerned with the application of real-time data. Most users, who are called "swing traders," have investment horizons of only days or weeks and they are interested in daily data primarily.

Brokerage Firms Years ago the net was the domain of, mostly, the online and discount brokers. This is no longer true. Almost all brokerage firms today have a presence on the internet and they are now similar in many ways. Investors have the ability to obtain real-time quotes, have access to research reports, and, of course, can buy and sell securities on line with a response time of under a minute.

Trading commission schedules vary but, normally, active online customers will pay less than with a full service broker. An independent investor can expect to pay $10 to $15, or less, for a single round lot (100 shares) transaction or perhaps up to thousands of shares. And, as one would expect, the fees and commissions tend to become lower as activity increases.

The so-called "full service" brokerage firms (as well as some of the discount brokers) can offer a broad range of capabilities on their internet sites. A typical website might include some or all of the following:

Services

- Account executive referrals
- Online record-keeping
- Money transfer
- Account protection
- Extended hours trading
- Wireless and touch tone services

Also, some site sections could be devoted to various calculations for time & risk, living yield curves, finding net worth, as well as bond calculations.

Types of Accounts

- Individual trading
- Margin
- Bank
- Corporate
- Custodial
- Estate
- Joint
- Retirement
- Trust

Products

- Stocks
- Bonds
- Annuities
- CD's
- IPO's
- Mutual funds
- Money markets
- Unit investment trust

Most major brokerage firms today are targeting the "wealth-management" market. This also means, of course, that investors should expect to pay fees for whatever products and services they order. Fee and commission schedules are frequently posted on the website. If not, a simple inquiry will answer the question.

Conclusion In the near future about 700 million wireless handsets will be sold annually, and probably 25-30% will include a pocket PC capability. Coupled with the millions of servers, desktops, and laptops already in use, little imagination is required to immediately visualize the possibilities the internet holds for all of us in the future.

Like home addresses, internet website addresses can change. So, listing any URL always presents a risk. In fact, many of the website addresses listed below may not exist a year from today. Recognizing this as an uncertainty, here is an alphabetical list of worthwhile sites to visit. Among the features are quotes, news, market activity, investor tools, and more.

http://
- BigCharts.com
- BullsOrBears.com
- cbs.marketwatch.com
- conference-board.org
- federalreserve.gov
- finance.lycos.com
- finance.yahoo.com
- kitco.com
- money.cnn.com
- moneycentral.msn.com
- nasdaq.com
- nyse.com
- wsrn.com
- www.cboe.com

Worldwide
investing

Introduction Enormous changes have occurred worldwide over the past thirty years, and none more startling than those in the areas of international politics and finance.

The implosion of the former Soviet Union and the unification of Germany, along with the fall of the Berlin Wall, marked the end of the so-called "Cold War." Today, the United States is the unchallenged military leader and has been given a greater responsibility in "the new world order."

In only a few decades, Japan, with a population less than half that of the U.S., became the second largest economy in the world. Then, the Japanese, operating many of the world's largest banks and industrial companies, and active in U.S. Treasury financing, fell into a depression unlike any since the 1930's.

As we now move further into the 21st century, it appears that future events will be no less dramatic. The dastardly 9/11 World Trade Center attack and other Islamic and rogue terrorist threats have served notice that the benefits of this new world order will not come easily or without major challenges. Nevertheless, the worldwide opportunities for businesses and investors are substantial. With the right leadership, there are many reasons to be optimistic for the years ahead.

Instantaneous communications and global, 24-hour trading capabilities are no longer science fiction. The ongoing integration of global financial markets will be taking Wall Street investors far beyond the canyons that meet at Broad and Wall.

This chapter will explore the subject of Worldwide Investing and discuss the promises and risks of this new arena.

Perspective Since the 1940s, most other economies of the world have greatly prospered by United States Government decisions and by the policies of the Federal Reserve System. Japan rose from the ashes of World War II without the considerable burden of a military complex buildup or Cold War competition from the Soviet Union. And in the years immediately after the war, West Germany, aided by the Marshall Plan and limited military obligations, saw a substantial recovery. West Germany enjoyed solid and healthy growth since its independence in 1955.

In addition, U.S. financial institutions and businesses invested huge sums of money in the economic development of other countries, not always with satisfactory returns. The recent conflicts with Iraq are still more examples of U.S. altruism as other nations, even more dependent than the U.S. on oil from the Mid East, have benefited by America's leadership role, initiatives, and spending.

This is not to minimize the economic achievements of the Japanese, the Germans, and others. Their educational efforts, investments, competitive products, and hard work have produced meaningful results, even considering their more recent problems. On balance, their economies have flourished with modest inflation, and they have created attractive environments for their businesses and investors.

The United States dollar (the world's principal monetary unit to date), the Canadian dollar, the Euro, the British pound sterling, the Japanese yen, the German deutschemark, and the others are convertible into one another at exchange rates determined by free market forces. Domestic inflation rates and productivities, balances in trade accounts, relative interest rates, political events, and many other factors all contribute to the supply and demand forces between currencies on the world markets.

Therefore, when a foreign investor buys a share of IBM, the value of that stock in an overseas portfolio can fluctuate in two ways. First, the price can rise or fall according to its supply and demand on the New York Stock Exchange. Second, its value to the foreign stockholder can move up or down, depending upon the exchange rate of the investor's currency versus the dollar. Thus, a Japanese investor in U.S. equities would watch the yen-to-dollar relationship, a German would monitor the mark-to-dollar rate, and so on.

The same holds true for a U.S. investor who buys shares in a non-U.S. enterprise. That company's sales and profits, balance sheet values, and stock price would all be denominated in the local currency. Of course, the U.S. holder would calculate the stock's portfolio value in U.S. dollars.

Thus, a decline of the U.S. dollar versus other currencies will increase the value of an investment in a foreign company since more dollars will be required in exchange when the foreign investment is later converted back into dollars. Conversely, if the dollar rises relative to other currencies, the dollar-denominated value of the foreign investment would decline.

But investors in foreign stocks should not overlook the other side of the equation either. If the dollar is rising in value, a foreign company will benefit if a large portion of its product line is exported to the U.S. That is to say, their products become more attractively priced in U.S. markets. Obviously, currency fluctuations are important in worldwide investing, but it is never simply black or white. An analysis of the company is still necessary.

Besides currencies, there are other external items to consider in worldwide investing: global politics, economic trends, unpredictable taxes, and the possibility of expropriation, to name a few. In analysis, it should be noted that accounting, auditing, and reporting standards have been less stringent than in the U.S. markets, adding further to the risks of foreign investing. And finally, the stocks in foreign companies can be less liquid, making the share prices more volatile. In short, to be successful in this arena, one must maintain a somewhat broader perspective than otherwise.

The Global Marketplace The marketplace for stocks and bonds is becoming more global every day. Millions of shares of many major U.S. companies are now traded daily on foreign exchanges. Similarly, U.S. investors, including mutual funds and other institutions, are finding it progressively easier to invest in companies abroad.

By the end of this decade, the New York Stock Exchange, as well as the American Stock Exchange, the Chicago Board Options Exchange, NASDAQ, and others, will be operating in various capacities 24-hours a day. It is almost possible now for any U.S. or foreign investor to buy or sell any popular stock, day or night, depending only on where the shares are being traded at that moment – Tokyo, London, New York, or elsewhere.

However, it is unlikely that today's dominant markets will become so integrated that they lose their identity. London and Tokyo prices for General Motors will still be largely determined by New York trading. Similarly, prices for Hitachi in London and New York will continue to be dictated by expected supply and demand in Tokyo.

Stocks Advance in Tokyo

The Japanese Stock Market The Tokyo Stock Exchange (TSE) was first opened in 1878, mainly for trading government bonds and gold and silver currencies. Stocks, which gained their popularity in the 1920s and 1930s, now represent more than 90% of all TSE transactions.

Since its postwar reopening in May 1949, the Tokyo Stock Exchange in Tokyo's Kabutocho financial district has experienced substantial growth. By year-end 1989, just before it began its steep decline, the total value of the Japanese market reached more than $4 trillion. In terms of the Nikkei Stock Average (an average of 225 of the nearly 2,200 TSE-listed stocks), equity values rose six-fold in the 1980s alone. During the decade, the Nikkei average, as it is called, climbed from 6,536 in 1980 to its peak of 38,916 in December 1989, and it was only twelve years earlier, in 1968, when Japan first required its brokers to be licensed by its Ministry of Finance. That year, the Nikkei was approaching 1,700!

In the 1990s and in the early years of this decade, the Japanese stock market has suffered greatly. The Nikkei dropped to under 10,000 once again and the steep decline of the Tokyo Stock Price Index, called the "TOPIX," has been no less dramatic, as the next chart illustrates. About 70% of the approximately 2,200 companies listed on the TSE are included in the exchange's first of its two sections, or groups. Companies with larger capitalizations dominate the first section, whereas the more thinly traded stocks are commonly found in the second group. In effect, the first tier accounts for about 90% of all TSE shares traded. A third group, called "Mothers" (Market Of The High growth and EmeRging Stocks), accounts for another 45 issues, and foreign stocks, fewer than 100 constitute the balance.

The TOPIX, a composite index of all common stocks listed in the first section, measures the change in market value with its base January 4, 1968. The TOPIX is also divided into thirty-three sub-indices allowing investors to examine the market by industry groups as well.

The Tokyo Stock Exchange enjoys a modern facility they call the "TSE Arrows" which includes an exhibition plaza, a museum, an information terrace, a media center, as well as the market center.

The operations of the TSE differ from those of the NYSE in many respects. There are two distinct 2-hour trading sessions in Tokyo each day, Monday through Friday. The morning session, called *zenba*, extends from 9 A.M. until 11 A.M. (7 P.M. to 9 P.M. Eastern Daylight Time), and the afternoon trading session, called *goba*, operates from 1 P.M. until 3 P.M. (11 P.M. to 1 A.M. Eastern Daylight Time).

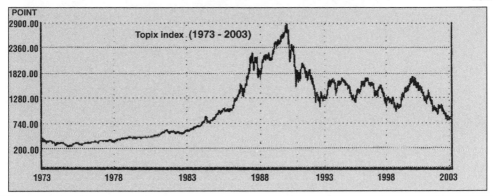

POINT

All but about 150 of the most active stocks on the TSE are traded electronically rather than through specialists. Moreover, a majority of all Japanese stock trading is accomplished through only a small group of brokerage firms and their affiliates — Nomura, Daiwa, and Nikko Securities. It was not until 1985 that U.S. and other overseas brokerage firms were permitted to participate in Japanese financial markets. It should also be noted that a small group of insurance firms and banks account for a large percent of the daily volume on the TSE.

In recent years, the volatility of the stock market in the United States prompted the NYSE to impose trading limits (popularly called "circuit breakers"). Actually, TSE rules have limited daily stock volatility (10%-20%) for decades. Some market observers credit the circuit breaker as one of the reasons why stock declines in Japan were more modest during the crash of the global markets in 1987. In fact, many TSE stocks never traded during those hectic October days.

As in the U.S., companies must meet certain size, profitability, and shareholder requirements to be listed on the Tokyo Stock Exchange. The companies on the TSE can be categorized into numerous business segments – fishing, mining, paper,

chemicals, rubber, textiles, and so on. In general, the list can be described as industrially-oriented and most of these businesses are well diversified. In the U.S., however, service companies are much more prevalent. To an analyst, the contrast is striking.

Four other exchanges in Japan make up the balance of Japan's stock market activity: the Osaka Securities Exchange, with more than 1,000 companies listed; the Japanese over-the-counter market, which is relatively small with 200 issues; and other small regional exchanges.

A Few Special Risks in Japan

Throughout the 1987-1990 period in particular, market analysts were especially critical of Japanese investing. The comments were many, but consistent: "A stock crash waiting to happen"; "a house of cards"; and "vastly overpriced." None of these critics were surprised by the Japanese stock market crash that began in early 1990.

Throughout the 1980s, the Japanese were apparently listening to Will Rogers' advice: "Buy land, 'cause He ain't making any more of it." Real estate in Tokyo is not usually quoted by the acre, but rather, by the square foot. Japan measures 146,000 square miles, just under the size of California. This

Nikkei Index Declines

is equivalent to about 1.2 square miles for every 1,000 people. Crowded? Yes. But this hardly explains Tokyo commercial real estate that was being quoted at an average of $6,000 per square foot, with many reports of substantially higher prices. As some analysts saw it Japan's vastly overpriced real estate represented a major risk to its banking industry and to its stock market:

• Japanese banks were known to lend money aggressively with land values placed as security. Critics contended that much of this money had been invested in the stock market.

• A large portion of commercial loans by Japanese banks were used to finance real estate purchases.

• Bank assets, even to this day, include substantial stock holdings.

• Frequently, a company's "hidden assets" (the value of its real estate holdings) were used to justify the price of its shares on the stock market.

Of course, investors are now more aware of this leverage. Thus, the continued decline in real estate and stock prices has made subsequent recovery in Japan that much more difficult. However, time has a way of healing. The outlook today is much brighter than it was in 1990.

For years, analysts called Japanese stocks overpriced based on the traditional measures of price/earnings ratios (over 60 were not unusual), yields (well under 1% typical), and profit margins that were well below the standards in the United States.

Defenders of these seemingly high prices explained that the accounting rules are different in Japan – depreciation is more liberal and not all profits are consolidated. The defenders also pointed to the faster growth rate of earnings, and, again, the "hidden assets" of real estate. Also, it was not unusual for companies to include non-operating trading profits from the stock market (Japanese businesses frequently invest in their suppliers or in other companies). However, lower stock prices have cured much of this problem.

Finally, it should be noted that in the United States, full disclosure of financial details is considered desirable. In Japan, management makes an effort to conceal noteworthy items whenever possible. In the U.S., the shareholder, the owner of the business, is held in high esteem; not so in Japan. Many Wall Street observers were surprised when, several years ago, astute investor T. Boone Pickens, bought a major interest in Japan's leading automotive component producer, Koito Manufacturing. Pickens' frustrated attempts to change Japanese tradition should be a lesson to anyone interested in this market.

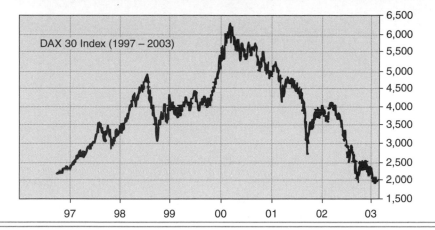

DAX 30 Index (1997 – 2003)

Even in the face of the declining market, Japan's GNP continued to grow through the early 1990's and peaked in 1995 at roughly $5.3 trillion dollars. From there, GNP either dropped or was stagnant throughout the remainder of the decade. Today, the Japanese economy seems to be on the road to a gradual recovery.

The following are typical leading Japanese companies that have grown and prospered globally: Honda Motor, Toyota Motor, and Hitachi Ltd. Tracking the progress of just these companies is easily accomplished and could help investors recognize the trends in Japan at any given point in time.

The New Germany The reunification of the Federal Republic of Germany (West Germany) and the German Democratic Republic (East Germany) reunited a country of more than 80 million people in an area roughly the size of Nevada. The new Germany is the third largest economy in the world with a Gross National Product about 20-25% of the U.S., larger than that of the U.K., but almost half that of Japan. In terms of exports, it is smaller than the United States in volume, but it is no less active than Japan.

After the fall of the Berlin Wall in 1989 and the reunification that was declared official on October 3, 1990, Germany encountered a period of digestion. Economists fully

expected to see years of problems and hardship as East Germany, which had been struggling for decades, was merged into the far more prosperous and well-managed West German economy. East Germany with its 14 million citizens (or 17% of the total) was contributing only 8% of overall economic activity. East Germany had close to one-half million young, lower-paid workers that needed work. Also, as East German productivity gained it faced competition of cheap labor from Poland and the Czech Republic. Germany's jobless rate is still high today.

German domestic sales remained flat through most of the '90's, the transition has been slow, and the country's growth has been mainly export-driven. Germany's principal exports have been aircraft, autos, chemicals, and electronics. Throughout the past decade Germany's overall growth rate has been less than half of the U.S., a big disappointment, but still above Japan.

There are eight stock exchanges that constitute the German bourse. The largest is the Frankfurt Stock Exchange, with well over half of all trading activity. The Frankfurt exchange has roughly 1,000 issues and many are listed internationally. Second in size is the Rhineland Westphalia Stock Exchange in Dusseldorf.

Another exchange, the West Berlin Stock Exchange, is small now, with only half as many companies as Frankfurt. The other exchanges are located in Munich, Hamburg, Stuttgart, Hanover, and Bremen.

Trading in Frankfurt occurs in a short, two-hour session from 11:30 A.M. until 1:30 P.M. (5:30 A.M. to 7:30 A.M. Eastern Daylight Time).

Traditionally, German public participation in the stock market has been relatively modest and, as indicated, the capital markets of Germany are still fragmented despite constructive efforts in recent years by the Bundesbank. It will be many years before the German markets emerge from the shadow of London.

The most widely followed indicator of stock market activity is the weighted German stock index, the Deutscher Aktienindex DAX, simply referred to as the "DAX." Like the Dow Industrials in the U.S., the DAX entered a bull market in 1982. The index rose from 670 to 2038 (year-end) five years later. The DAX declined more than 30% in the 1987 stock crash to a level below 1400 and then recovered. As the chart on the previous page illustrates, the DAX has also suffered in recent years.

Among of the more popular investment names in Germany over the past few years: Siemens, Volkswagen, Henkel, Schering, and Heidelberger Zement.

The London Stock Market In October 1986, London's International Stock Exchange experienced a changeover to its present methods of operation and the media euphuistically termed the event "Big Bang." However, for Great Britain, a country of tradition, this was, indeed, a major undertaking: foreign firms were admitted to trading, fixed brokerage commissions were eliminated, and a new technology was introduced.

Since Big Bang, trading on the International Stock Exchange has been virtually all-electronic in upstairs rooms rather than on the floor, as it had been done for centuries. Together with the Unlisted Securities Market, formed in 1980, and the Third Market, the London exchange stands ready to lead Europe and the new European Common Market into the 21st century.

A few years ago the exchanges in Paris, Amsterdam and Brussels formed an alliance called Euronext. The idea of a merger between the London and Frankfurt exchanges in May 2000, which has since been dropped, is, nevertheless, an indication of the ongoing trend in global finance.

London's seven-hour trading day begins at 9 A.M. (4 A.M. Eastern Daylight Time) and ends at 3 P.M., two hours after trading has begun in New York.

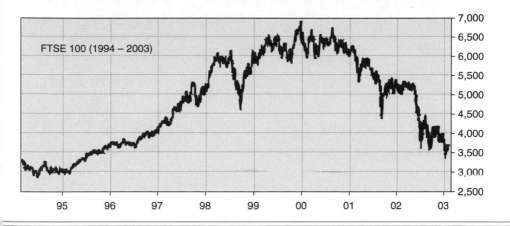

FTSE 100 (1994 – 2003)

Among the important companies in Great Britain are: Glaxo SmithKline, Unilever, Reuters Group, and Enterprise Oil.

China Not long ago *Understanding Wall Street* was translated and published in the Chinese language (there is also a Spanish edition of this book). These facts alone tell of the ever-expanding global interest in the stock market.

As an enormous country with 1.3 billion inhabitants, China also represents a huge new market for goods and services. During the 1990's the growth rate of the Chinese economy was roughly 10% per year. The expectation for China's growth rate for the next few years appears to be in the 6-8% range.

As one example of future growth in China, economists are predicting that automobile sales in that country could reach 5 million cars annually by 2007; still modest by Western standards, especially considering the size of the market, but to reach such figures, the world will see annual growth rates of more than 30%. In China, the automobile is a growth industry as it was in the U.S. in the 1920's.

China's GNP per capita is now a meager $790, versus more than $36,000 in the U.S. Yet, China's GNP is already ranked #5 in the world, just ahead of Russia, and not far behind the U.K. and France.

The risks of investing in China will remain extremely high as long as the government is Communist. However, investors willing to assume these extraordinary risks might find the rewards there, too.

For those who are interested in overseas markets, the opportunities to invest in all but the most remote parts of the world are there – limited only by the risks, of course.

Other Stock Markets There are many other international stock markets, including several that are never mentioned in the news. Most U.S. investors are familiar with the exchanges in Canada (Toronto and Montreal), where mining and industrial shares are actively traded every day; and some may know of the exchanges in Mexico, France, Australia, and Israel. But how many follow the activity in Iran, Thailand, Nigeria, Peru, or Nepal? Many years ago a stock exchange in Russia would have been the punch line to a joke. Today, the Russian stock market is anything but a joke.

ADRs American Depositary Receipts (ADRs) offer a way for U.S. investors to buy or sell shares in overseas companies without trading in markets outside the U.S. An ADR is a negotiable receipt for stock in a foreign company. Typically, the shares are held in a bank in the issuer's country, and a correspondent bank in the U.S.

creates ADRs, which are then traded in the open market in lieu of the stock. About two-thirds of the 150 or so ADRs available are listed on NASDAQ. Most of the others are on the NYSE. Investors should be familiar with the terms of the ADR at the outset.

Normally, one ADR is created for each share held, but not always. In addition, ADRs issued prior to 1983 were not required to be registered with the SEC and, therefore, some companies might not be obligated to disclose certain financial information. Finally, the shares might or might not be "sponsored" by the issuing company. If so, the ADRs would have voting rights and the holders would receive financial reports; otherwise, they would not.

Among the more active ADRs in recent years that trade in the over-the-counter market have been Reuters Holdings (Great Britain) and De Beers Consolidated Mines (South Africa). Glaxo SmithKline (Great Britain) and Sony Corp (Japan) have been two popular ADRs on the New York Stock Exchange.

Multinational Companies One of the best methods of worldwide investing is buying shares in U.S. multinational companies. Many major companies listed on the New York Stock Exchange derive significant portions of their annual earnings from overseas markets. Procter & Gamble,

Johnson & Johnson, Exxon, 3M, and many other U.S. companies have meaningful earnings contributions from overseas. Close analysis will reveal which companies participate with what products and where.

Profits from foreign operations can be both good and bad. In the 1970's, Xerox's worldwide profits grew at a very rapid pace largely due to the profit contributions from its overseas businesses, especially Rank Xerox in Europe and in Japan. Also, not too many years ago Disney investors were expecting a considerable boost in profits from its new theme park in France. Overseas profits can sometimes benefit results greatly. Conversely, years ago, Black & Decker's Great Britain facility was a constant drain on its consolidated profits. Foreign results should not be overlooked.

Closed-End Funds A number of closed-end "country funds," as they are often called, have been formed to offer direct participation in certain countries. Like other closed-end funds, they are traded on exchanges and will advance or decline according to their portfolio values, as well as supply and demand of their shares in the open market.

There are two country funds listed on the New York Stock Exchange that exemplify the emotion and volatility that seem to be normal for investments of this type.

Slump Predicted For Germany In Short Term

The **Mexico Fund** made its debut on the NYSE in June 1981 and promptly declined from $12 to about $2 as the fortunes of Mexico faded nearly as rapidly. The fund's price recovered nicely, then repeated the cycles several times since. Aside from its fluctuating portfolio value, moves in this fund could be due to political events, oil prices, concerns about loans to Mexico, currency rates, Mexican inflation, or any number of other items. Today the fund is selling below $12 and a 16% discount to current net asset value.

The **Germany Fund** was listed on the NYSE in July 1986 at about $10 and performed poorly for the next three years. When the reunification of Germany first caught Wall Street's attention and imagination in September 1989, the fund's price rose from below $9 to $25 in less than six months. The excitement of this dramatic event prompted the formation of other (unrelated) closed-end investment companies including the New Germany Fund, among others.

They, too, are listed and have nearly the same investment objectives but with different portfolios. These funds tend to move in a similar manner, although their premiums or discounts can differ markedly from time to time. For example, both of these Germany funds are selling at the low end of their ranges of recent years and roughly 16% discount to their asset values.

As with all closed-end funds, investors should monitor both the fundamentals and the degree of premium or discount the funds sell to their asset values. Clearly, market timing and patience are especially important ingredients in country fund investing.

International Mutual Funds For those who would like to invest only in a certain group of countries or in particular regions, an International or Global mutual fund could be an ideal vehicle. The advantages of professional management and diversification are even more compelling in this area than with domestic mutual funds. Among the benefits:

• Contact with an overseas management is nearly impossible for individuals, but easier for fund managers.

• The mutual fund analysts are likely to be more aware of the accounting anomalies.

• The risk of missing negative, local news items can be minimized through diversification.

The funds' descriptions found in their prospectuses are usually stated in general terms, although some can be very specific. "International" refers to non-domestic investments; whereas "global" means investments anywhere in the world – but including domestic stocks. Unlike closed-end funds, the prices of these investment companies directly reflect the net asset values of their portfolios at any given moment. In addition, similar to domestic mutual funds, International and Global funds can be load (with a sales charge) or no-load.

As discussed earlier, investors who want some degree of flexibility will find it beneficial to own funds that are part of a "family." In this way, money can be moved easily from one type of fund to another if international events, exchange rates, or price levels dictate a change. As with any investment program involving a mutual fund, it is necessary to read the fund's prospectus, review the portfolio, analyze the fund's record, and become familiar with (and be ready to judge) the people who make the investment decisions.

In the late 1990's and early part of the new decade, the managers of international and global funds have found it very difficult to produce positive results. In fact, some portfolio results have been awful. Even quality no-load managers such as **T. Rowe Price** (the T. Rowe Price International Stock Fund) and **Vanguard** (the Vanguard World International Growth Fund) found it difficult to produce positive results in recent years.

The following mutual funds have compiled respectable records of performance over the past few years in the face of a difficult environment. This not a recommendation list, but an example of the fund types available along with their strategies and objectives, in alphabetical order. Each is a member of a mutual fund family, and all have the same stated objective: growth, within the confines of each fund's charter.

The details are as of their latest 2002 reports. These comments and portfolio percentages are only for illustrative purposes since the data and information can change markedly from one year to the next – or even sooner.

Fidelity Overseas ($2.7 billion)
(No load)
(800) 544-6666

The Fidelity Overseas Fund began in late 1984 to invest in growth companies in Western Europe, the Far East, the Pacific Basin, and in the Americas outside the United States

The fund would like to keep its portfolio at least 80% in non-U.S. common stocks, with the stated objective: "Long term growth of capital." Today the principle geographic territories are represented approximately as follows: Japan 24%; the United Kingdom 13%; U.S.A. 11%; France 9%, and Switzerland 8%, with the balance in other countries.

The fund's larger holdings include: Nomura Holdings Inc. (Japan), Total Fina (France), Nikko Cordial (Japan), Unilever, Credit Suisse Group, and Nokia AB.

Today, the Fidelity Overseas Fund is 6% below its net asset value of six years ago.

There are also other overseas funds in the Fidelity Investments family.

Oakmark International ($1.7billon)
(No load)
(800) OAKMARK

The Oakmark International fund is a value-oriented fund with about 60% in Europe. Approximately 25% is in emerging Latin American and Pacific Rim economies.

The fund is managed by Harris Associates of Chicago and its two managers, David Herro and Michael Welsh, have been with Harris since 1992.

Examples of the fund's larger holdings are: Ericsson (Sweden), Vivendi (France), GlaxoSmithKline (U.K.), Daiwa Securities (Japan), and Aventis SA (France).

About 27% of total assets are in consumer cyclical stocks; 17% in financials; and 17% in capital goods.

The fund's net asset value is roughly 24% greater than it was six years ago.

Oppenheimer Global ($4.7 billion)
(5.75% load)
(800) 525-7048

Foreign securities represent more than 60% of this fund's net assets, although management indicates this ratio can change at any time. The fund maintains a broad agenda and a high-risk profile with its ability, under certain conditions, to buy or sell call options as well as put options for hedging. The fund can also invest in companies of all sizes, as well as stock index futures and other instruments.

This global fund is managed by Oppenheimer Management Corporation, which is controlled by a publicly held English company, British & Commonwealth Holdings PLC.

The fund is currently 21% in Information Technology stocks; 16% in Health Care; 16% in Financial stocks; and almost 16% in Consumer Discretionary stocks. The fund's largest holdings include Cadence Design, Qualcomm, Reckitt Benckiser PLC, and Sanofi-Synthelabo SA.

William L. Wilby has been the manager since 1995. The fund's net asset value has increased about 24% over the past six years.

Templeton Foreign Fund ($9.6 billion)
(5.75% load)
(800) 632-2301

The Templeton Foreign Fund has a very
widely diversified portfolio, well over its
stated goal of 80% in non-U.S. securities.
The portfolio is 8.9% in oil and gas stocks,
5.7% in bank stocks, 5.2% insurance
stocks, 4.6% chemicals, and almost 4% in
paper and forest stocks.

The geographic breakdown of the portfolio is
roughly 48% in Europe, 27% in Asia, almost
6% in North America, and 4% in Latin
America. Among its largest holdings are
Cheung Kong Holdings (real estate in Hong
Kong), Volkswagen AG, DSM NV (a
chemical company in the Netherlands) and
Aventis SA (a French pharmaceutical
company).

The fund is now headed by a young and
relatively-new manager, Jeffrey A. Everett.
The net asset value of the Templeton
Foreign Fund is approximately 8% above its
NAV of six years ago.

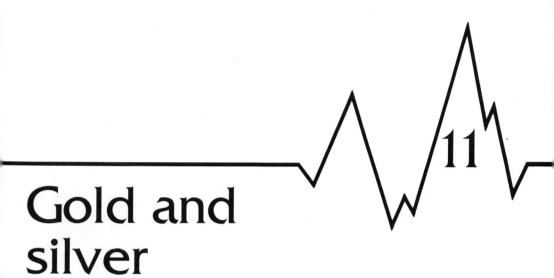

Gold and silver

Introduction "A barbaric relic," a learned economist once called it. This pragmatic fellow could not understand why gold rose from $35 an ounce in 1968 to more than $800 twelve years later. "After all, it has limited utility, it's expensive to store, and it doesn't offer any interest income. Who would want to own it?" he asked. He was serious, but it was clear – his college major was not History.

The answer was simple: Gold is the most ideal medium of exchange and "store of value" known to man. It is malleable, ductile, and easily divided into accurately measured quantities. Its quality is consistent; it does not rust, tarnish, or corrode; it's practically indestructible. Also, gold is attractive and relatively scarce. And, finally, it is recognized and accepted by almost everybody. It's "as good as gold," as they say.

This chapter examines gold, and also silver, from an investor's point of view.

Gold Soars

Background Gold is first known to be used in Central and Eastern Europe as far back as 4,000 B.C., as well as in Egypt in 3,000 B.C. Gold does not react to oxygen and remains free of tarnish and rust. The gold death mask of King Tutankhamen, entombed in 1352 B.C., was found to be in perfect condition when the tomb was unearthed in 1922.

Although no one knows for certain, it has been estimated that about 90% of all gold mined in the history of man is still in existence and that just over 125,000 tons (4 billion troy ounces) of gold are above ground and available to be traded in the marketplace. If this is so, all the gold in the world would fit into one large, four-story house.

For about one hundred years, from the early 1500s until the early 1600s, consumer prices in England increased relentlessly. Throughout this period, the prices of food, fuel and clothing advanced five-fold. And, during this same period, the price of an ounce of gold also increased steadily. By 1620, the year "Mayflower" landed at Plymouth, Massachusetts, one ounce of gold had appreciated to the equivalent value of about $17.56, with a purchasing power considerably more than today, of course.

In 1792, the U.S. currency was established as a viable form of legal tender, backed by gold and silver ("bimetallism"), and for many years, traded at a ratio of 16 to 1. In 1835, a little more than two hundred years after the Pilgrims landed, gold was discovered on Cherokee land in Georgia. That year, gold's value was approximately $20.67 per ounce.

President Andrew Jackson ordered government funds to be withdrawn from the United States Bank and placed into state banks in 1836. Many of these banks, particularly in the West, engaged in speculation, made unwise loans, and issued bank notes without sufficient specie (metal) backing. Concerned, the President then issued his Specie Circular of 1836, which instructed Federal land agents to accept only gold and silver in payment for public lands. Many banks were unable to meet the demand for specie, closed their doors, and a financial panic followed in 1837. Yet, the state-controlled banking system continued for another 76 years until the Federal Reserve System, headed by the Federal Reserve Board, was established on December 23, 1913.

Regarding the development of the gold market, a major turning point occurred with the discovery of gold at Sutter's Mill on the American River in January, 1848. It has been said that 92% of all gold produced has occurred since that California event. In

1851, gold was found in Australia, and South Africa had its first year of gold production in 1884. By the end of that century, South Africa had suddenly passed the U.S. to become the world's leading gold producing country.

The Civil War produced a substantial disruption to the country's monetary order. In 1862, "Greenbacks," which had no specie backing, were issued. Like the worthless "Continentals" issued by the Continental Congress in 1775, this new fiat money inflated the prices of almost all commodities – including gold, which nearly doubled in value at that time. Later, the attempted withdrawal of the notes led to a substantial decline in economic activity and commodity prices – and was, along with the overexpansion of the railroads, a major cause of the depression of 1873.

By 1880, gold had returned to its stated value of $20.67. Shortly thereafter, new gold discoveries in South Africa, Australia, and Alaska, along with improved methods of mining, made it possible to increase the nation's money supply. Also, the period from 1873 to 1896 marked the beginning of the demonetization of silver, a program that was officially completed in 1964 when the Treasury minted its last silver coins. The United States was officially returned to the gold standard when Congress passed the Gold Standard Act in 1900.

The 1896-1920 period saw inflation, attributed largely to the demands of World War I. During this timeframe, commodity prices quadrupled while gold remained at its fixed price of $20.67. In 1920, and into 1921, commodity prices declined sharply, business activity slowed, and the stock of money contracted. By 1922, the economy was improving. Money stock resumed its growth, commodity prices stabilized, and businesses were again profiting and growing. The price of gold was the same.

Following a sharp decline in land values in 1926 and the stock market crash of 1929, commodity prices resumed the decline that began in 1920. Money stock contracted and business activity and profits began to drop. The first banking crisis (of three) occurred in late 1930 when public confidence in the banking system waned. Bank failures, initially in the Midwest, led to widespread withdrawals of public deposits.

A second banking crisis occurred in mid-1931, and later that year, Great Britain abandoned the gold standard. Following numerous statewide "bank holidays," President Roosevelt declared a nationwide banking holiday in March 1933, which continued for a week. Gold redemptions and gold shipments to abroad were also suspended. The Gold Reserve Act of 1934 took the U.S. off the gold standard and the stated value of one ounce of gold was then raised from $20.67 to $35.00.

Budget Deficit Grew Sharply During July

The system of having money supply based on gold reserves ended officially with the Bretton Woods Agreement in 1947. Not surprisingly, United States gold reserves soon began to decline as central banks turned their dollars in for the precious metal. The nation's gold stockpile of 700 million ounces after World War II declined to less than half that amount by the time sales were suspended in 1968. After the window closed, gold was then allowed to seek its own price level in the marketplace, like silver, or any other commodity.

History tells us that gold does not create, nor does it prevent, business cycles or the excesses that occur in speculation or mismanagement of the economy. From the day the first grain of gold was discovered, it has been a universally accepted treasure and a viable medium of exchange. People turn to it during periods of uncertainty and concern, or when they see a currency not backed by specie rapidly losing its value.

The arguments in favor of a "gold standard" are compelling since gold is a valid check against currency debauchment. Actually, the world will always be on a "gold standard." Only governments and their policies change.

Today, the U.S. and other nations are using an international system of fiat money. Such systems usually fail because the monetary quantities (the amount printed) can never be held in check. Now, the major question is: "How long will the present system last?" The answer is not clear – perhaps many more years with proper management. A fiat money system will last only until its failings can no longer be tolerated. Then, as always, people will return to gold as the starting point for yet another new and better system.

A Store of Value Ardent supporters of gold, affectionately called "gold-bugs," are typically colorful personalities. They often maintain that gold is undervalued. Perhaps it is. But compared to what?

The man who used his ounce of gold to purchase a good-quality suit to wear in 1790 thought he knew what his gold was worth that day. The man who sold his ounce of gold more than two hundred years later, in 2003, to buy a good-quality suit knew what his gold was worth that day, too. And the person who bought the gold from him earlier that morning undoubtedly thought that the metal was undervalued at $340 per ounce.

A common mistake many gold investors make is to expect the world to stand still from one moment to the next. One cannot assume that if runaway inflation occurs and the price of gold increases to, say, $450,000 per ounce, then, finally, that "dream house" becomes affordable. Unfortunately, the home will probably be listed for sale at $562

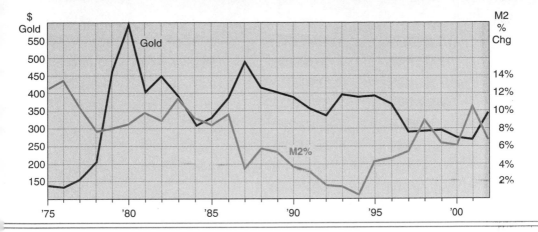

million. But, one day in the future, that same ounce of gold will most likely buy a good-quality suit to wear.

Today, it cannot be said that our dollar is "as good as gold." Nor can it be said for the euro, the pound sterling, the yen, the mark, or most other forms of exchange. Why? Because, unlike gold, these currencies do not offer "a store of value."

"Gresham's Law" Investors interested in the subject of gold and silver should become familiar with the monetary observations of Sir Thomas Gresham during the mid-1500s.

"Gresham's Law" is an economic theory that states, in effect, that bad money tends to drive good money out of circulation:

"When coins of equal value but different intrinsic value are put into circulation, side by side, the coin with the higher intrinsic value will be hoarded and only the coin of lower intrinsic value will be permitted to remain in circulation."

One example of Gresham's Law was the era of bimetallism during the nineteenth century when both gold and silver were in circulation at the same time. From time to time, one would drive the other out of circulation (i.e., one would be spent and the other would be hoarded), whenever their relatively-free market values would differ from the values

being dictated by the government. This monetary concept could apply once again if gold and/or silver are ever reintroduced as specie backing for United States currency. However, specie backing will also place a physical limit on the excessive printing of money.

Supply and Demand The supply of gold is fairly constant and predictable even though precise annual production figures are difficult. A significant portion of all gold mining is done in remote, politically sensitive areas of the world. But the increment from annual production is small relative to the total above-ground stock. In other words, the above-ground stock is not likely to change substantially in the near future since the addition to world supplies is only about 2% each year. Thus, the scarcity of the metal is well-assured.

For perspective, the world's entire above-ground stock of 4 billion ounces has a total market value of only $1.4 trillion at $350 per ounce, which is not more than 10% of the total market value of all U.S. equities.

Production and Supply

In the year 2000, U.S. gold production was almost 11 million ounces having a market value of approximately $3 billion that year. Nevada was, by far, the largest producing state – about 77% of all ounces mined in the U.S. North American production that year totaled close to 16 million ounces, accounting for roughly 20% of the world total of nearly 83 million ounces. Below are the author's estimates for 2000:

	Troy Oz.	%
South Africa	13.8 mm	17%
United States	10.6	13
Australia	9.5	12
China	4.8	6
Canada	4.8	6
Russia, et al	11.0	13
Other	28.0	34
Total	82-83 mm	100%

Ten years earlier, annual world production was estimated to be 73 million ounces with North America accounting for 15 million ounces or 21%. South Africa's production was more than 25% of world output that year and the Soviet Union, just before its implosion, was ranked second at just over 10 million ounces.

The cost to mine gold varies from $150 to $400 per ounce, with many of the deep South African mines (10,000 feet or more) at the upper end of the range, and the Canadian producers (1,000 feet or so) at the lower end. The largest mine in the world, the Muruntau facility in central Uzbekistan, is said to have a production cost of approximately $250 per ounce.

Historically, gold mining production has increased about 2% annually, in line with the growth of worldwide population. Even assuming a substantial increase in the price of the metal, it is unlikely that annual production will increase any more than 2% due to the complexities and high costs of the mining effort, especially in South Africa. However, there are numerous higher-cost facilities that could be made operational if the price remained above $500 or so for any extended period. Similarly, production would be reduced if gold's price remained below $300 per ounce. This is a very capital-intensive business, requiring hundreds of millions of dollars and 3-5 years to start a new mine.

Gold is a commodity and, when it is permitted to do so, will trade according to the basic laws of supply and demand.

Between 1933 and 1975 U.S. citizens could not, legally, own the metal without a special license, except in coin collecting. This suppressed the open market demand for gold during these years. During the 1970s the price rocketed, due largely to inflation, hitting an intraday peak of $870 on January 21, 1980. Tons of gold that had been hoarded for years, or perhaps even centuries, by governments and individuals were sold to the speculators. The price of gold encountered a bear market for the next 20 years taking it under $300 to a low of $250 largely due to hedging schemes created by greedy bankers and producers.

Modern equipment operated by remote control (photo courtesy of Barrick Gold Corp.)

Demand

Recent estimated gold reserves of the key member governments of the International Monetary Fund (IMF) can be seen on the following table. Central banks have been selling gold and ECB holdings have become more important due to the creation of the European Union.

Troy Oz (Millions)

United States	262
Germany	111
IMF	103
France	97
Italy	79
Switzerland	63
Netherlands	28
European Central Bank	25
Japan	25
China	16
Russia	12
United Kingdom	10

Gold stockpiles in other parts of the world are substantial. The greatest unknown continues to be the Middle East where reserves can accumulate whenever a conversion takes place from oil to gold as it did in the 1970s. Gold prices are influenced from time to time by Central Bank selling, hedging activities largely by producers, and jewelry demand, especially from India and the Middle East countries. For this reason, gold investors should also monitor the price of oil and try to anticipate investor demand trends from this region.

In recent years, the total world demand for gold used in jewelry, industry, and dental applications has been roughly 120 to 130 million troy ounces annually, with jewelry accounting for 95 to 105 million, or about 80% of this amount.

However, overall market demand for gold in the short term cannot be predicted with any confidence because the speculative and investment interest in the metal can change so dramatically from one day to the next depending on monetary news (especially dollar-related) and world events.

The Money Supply The dollar is the principal currency through which domestic and international trade is conducted. Therefore, the single most important fundamental factor to the gold investor is the U.S. currency ... its quantity, relative value, and its viability worldwide. It is fiat money, dependent solely on the competence of the people printing it and the confidence of the people using it.

The next chart shows the money supply of the United States, as measured by M-2 and, more importantly, its percent change from one year to the next. Today, total U.S. money supply, measured by M-3, is now over $8 trillion, up sharply from $4.2

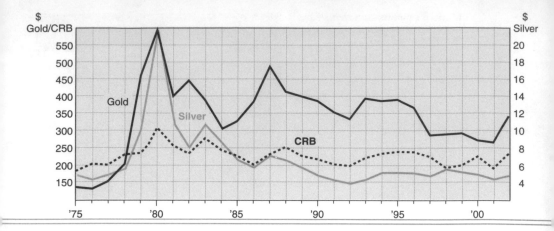

trillion in 1990 and $2 trillion in 1980. The annual increase in the money supply in recent years has far exceeded the rate of growth in the nation's economy. Gold enthusiasts are quick to remind us that this money supply is equal to roughly $30,000 per ounce of gold held at the depositories at Fort Knox and West Point.

Other key relationships or comparisons with gold can be seen in the chart that follows. It shows the Commodity Research Bureau Futures Index (CRB), and Silver prices. Over the past 20 years CPI inflation has averaged 3.2% per year.

Gold investors are constantly aware of the U.S. budget deficit and the nation's debt. They also note that the "legal debt ceiling" is being raised regularly. National debt now stands at over $6 trillion, nearly double the $3.4 trillion of 1990. In the U.S., as a percent of GNP, debt has been climbing gradually. In 1980, it was close to 40%. In 2000, it was 54%. And the percent figure is higher and still rising today.

A high debt level should be of concern because the cost of servicing that debt (i.e., the annual interest that must be paid) is added to federal outlays. The trend of lower interest rates in recent years has kept debt service from becoming an immediate problem. However, higher interest rates, for whatever reason, could very easily lead to a budget crisis.

To finance the excess of expenditures over tax revenues (the budget deficit), the Federal Government must borrow by selling Treasury securities, further increasing the nation's debt – a vicious cycle, to be sure. The Fed must either refrain from supplying the funds, thus allowing interest rates to climb, or supply the funds, thereby monetizing the debt. If interest rates climb, debt service rises, further aggravating the problem. Inflation tends to follow the year-to-year change in money supply by one or two years, especially when it is sharp and prolonged.

Silver Like gold, silver offers a "store of value" and a viable medium of exchange. Similarly, it has a monetary history and is recognized as such worldwide.

As a commodity, silver is much more abundant than gold, since its exploration and production is not dictated by its market price. Silver is mined primarily as a (lead) by-product to other metal mining activities. Since 1800, an estimated 56 billion ounces of silver have been mined and 36 billion since 1900. Today's annual production rate of silver is probably near 600 million ounces, not including silver recovery – almost 200 million ounces. Moreover, untold quantities of silver have been hoarded for centuries in India and other remote parts of the world, and large government stockpiles of the metal stand ready to be sold at higher prices.

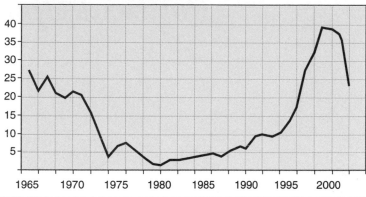

But, unlike gold, silver has enjoyed a stable demand from industry each year (photography, silverware, jewelry, and electronics). Despite the notable inroads of digital photography, which is silver-free imaging, and new recovery methods, a fairly constant industrial demand for the metal should continue for years to come.

The daily price quotations for gold and silver tend to move in tandem, as they should. The same monetary influences and concerns drive the prices of both metals, although gold may lead the way.

What Are the Risks? Gold and silver advocates have been among the most vocal critics regarding management of the U.S. economy. They maintain that the politicians are not capable of fiscal responsibility and that the Federal Reserve cannot contain the problem of excessive spending. The Fed, they say, will avoid high unemployment at all cost and will never be able to resist the temptation to print money in excess. They maintain that hyperinflation is a foregone conclusion. Could these critics be wrong?

The risks of holding gold and silver would be substantial if the U.S. economy were to enter a period of severe recession or depression. In such an environment, producer and consumer prices would, most likely, be declining; money supply would be contracting; interest income on savings and investments would be in demand; defaults would be commonplace; unemployment would be rampant; and gold and silver would be regarded more as commodities than as havens from inflation. In this case, gold and silver prices would probably be going down, not up.

Also, any legislation introduced to control government spending represents another risk for precious metals investors. The U.S. dollar will continue to lose value if government spending remains unchecked. A constitutional amendment to balance the budget or any legislation that might in some way limit pork barrel spending would clearly be a negative for gold and silver investors.

Investing in Gold and Silver For those who regard inflation as the major problem, and who want to buy gold, and perhaps silver, participation is possible in several ways. There are advantages and disadvantages to each approach, such as:

• Buying the metal directly as bullion, coins, medallions, or in other forms.

• Purchasing shares in mining companies.

• Investing in precious metal mutual funds.

In a hyperinflation environment, direct investments in gold bullion wafers (small bars) and gold and silver coins would probably outperform mining shares. At such a point of extreme circumstances, mining stocks could be subject to special government taxes and restrictions, similar to the "excess-profits taxes" oil companies faced in the 1970s. And, of course, the ownership of gold could once again be outlawed by the government, giving investors few places to hide.

Rare coins, which often gain attention when gold and silver markets are active, are frequently, and properly, cited as having performed well as long-term investments. But rare coins should not be regarded in the same context as bullion coins such as American Eagles, Canadian Maple Leafs, and Krugerrands, priced for their melt-down bullion values. Rare coins are collectibles, almost in the same vein as stamps, ceramics, or art. Coin grading, dealer credibility and competence, and comparison shopping are key elements to success in that market.

In a moderate-to-high inflationary period, mining stocks and mutual funds that invest specifically in companies of this type would probably be the best vehicles. The high commissions, handling costs, and storage fees associated with buying the metal outright can be largely avoided by purchasing equities. The dividends from gold mining shares could soar. These are the only companies in the world that produce REAL MONEY as its principal

product. South African gold-mining companies, available for investment through ADRs and mutual funds, typically sell at lower P/E ratios and offer higher dividend returns than do mining stocks in the U.S. and Canada. There are a several well-established South African mining companies such as AngloGold Ltd. and Gold Fields Ltd. However, many investors prefer not to buy the stocks of South African companies regardless of their prices, due to current trends in South African mining and the political risks.

The possibility of political unrest, strikes, or other problems in South Africa should not be ignored. As indicated earlier, RSA gold mining represents a large portion of worldwide production, employs more than 400,000 (mostly black miners), and contributes substantially to that country's economy and to its exports. Any significant disruption in supplies from South Africa could inflate gold prices and depress South African share prices, at least on a temporary basis.

For those who want a diversified participation in South African gold mining shares, there is ASA Ltd., a closed-end investment company, listed on the New York Stock Exchange. ASA has paid cash dividends every year since 1959.

Gold & Silver Mining Stocks

The following is an alphabetical list of the leading North American mining companies with activities located principally in the U.S. and Canada. This is not a list of recommended stocks, but a description of several well-established, NYSE-listed mining companies and their properties:

Barrick Gold Corp. (ABX)

This Toronto-based company has many producing gold mines in the U.S., Canada, Chile, and Peru. Its major operations include the Goldstrike Property in Nevada, an open pit mine in Utah, and properties in Ontario and Quebec, Canada.

With its acquisition of Homestake Mining a few years ago, Barrick gold production expanded to about 6 million ounces. HM's properties are located in South Dakota, northern California, and Nevada as well as in other parts of the U.S. and Australia.

Barrick, also a producer of silver (about 15 million ounces annually), has developed a good growth record overall. Unfortunately, Barrick's policy of forward-selling its gold production tends to make its stock an under-performer among the group due to that exposure.

Glamis Gold Ltd. (GLG)

Glamis, a small, non-hedged gold producer headquartered in Reno, Nevada, is engaged in the mining and extraction of precious metals by open-pit mining and the heap leaching method.

Goldcorp (GG)

Toronto-based Goldcorp is medium-sized, non-hedged gold producer that operates two gold mines, one underground mine and an open-pit mine. The company also operates two mineral divisions that produce sodium sulfate, limestone and processed lime. The company's annual gold production is below 1 million ounces.

Hecla Mining (HL)

Hecla Mining, headquartered in Idaho, is one of the few "pure plays" in silver mining. Domestic properties are located mainly in Idaho (the Lucky Friday silver mine and the Yellow Pine gold mine) and in Utah (the Escalante silver mine), as well as in Washington and Alaska.

Hecla is not close to the largest silver producers with just under 8 million ounces, but it represents one of the more attractive direct vehicles for those who want to buy into the silver market. HL is also a gold producer to a lesser extent.

Meridian Gold (MDG)

Meridian is a Reno-based company with three major properties in Idaho, Nevada, and Chile.

Newmont Mining (NEM)

This Denver-based company is now the world's largest gold company producing nearly 8 million ounces annually. The company's major properties include projects along the Carlin Trend in northern Nevada, as well as major projects in Peru, Australia, Russia, Indonesia, and in other parts of the world. The company's proven and probable gold reserves total close to 100 million ounces.

Newmont Mining is also a silver producer with an annual production level of more than 8 million ounces.

Pan American Silver (PAAS)

Pan American Silver is a well-managed, growing silver producer with a current annual output of about 7 million ounces.

Placer Dome Inc. (PDG)

This Vancouver-based precious metals company is one of Canada's largest producers of gold with well over 3 million ounces annually.

Placer Dome's properties include the Campbell, Dome, and Detour Lake mines in Ontario, as well as additional facilities in Quebec. The company also has operations in Nevada (Bald Mountain and Cortez), in Montana, and in Australia.

Like Barrick, Placer Dome has an active hedge book and forward-selling is not an investment positive when gold prices are rising.

Conclusion Investing in gold and gold stocks should be a decision based on long term considerations. Now that the 20-year bear market of gold prices may have finally come to an end, companies in this arena could be worth investigating.

There are numerous books on precious metals that discuss gold investing and its many options in great detail – and caution is strongly advised. Investors should be especially careful of mail-order schemes and unscrupulous dealers who promote gold and silver as a sure way to riches or safety. This could be an important area for investment. However, those who fail to do their homework or enter into transactions unknowingly can be easy targets for abuse.

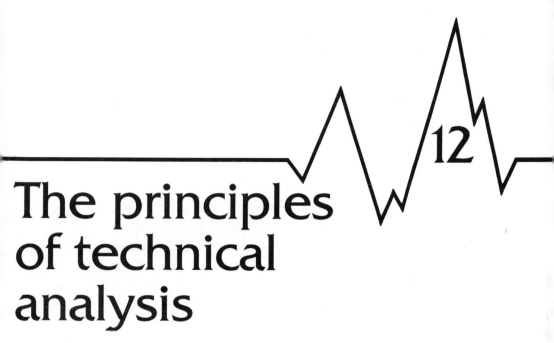

The principles
of technical
analysis

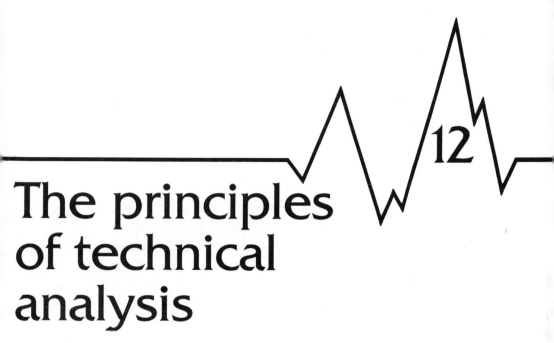12

Introduction On Wall Street there are two distinct approaches to the stock market. "Fundamental Analysis" is the study of all relevant factors that influence the future course of corporate earnings and dividends and, hence, stock prices. This approach involves the analysis of economic data, industry conditions, company fundamentals, and corporate financial statements. In contrast, "Technical Analysis" refers to the study of all factors related to the actual supply and demand of stocks. Using stock charts and various indicators, the "technicians," as they are called, attempt to measure "the pulse of the market" in their effort to forecast future stock price movements.

The substantial number of investors successfully using fundamental analysis attests to the merits of that approach. However, technical analysis also has considerable value because, ironically, not all investors believe in it. A wise Wall Street analyst once said "if everybody bought at the bottom and sold at the top, the bottom would be the top and the top would be the bottom."

The individual who understands both the fundamental and technical approaches knows the strengths and weaknesses of each and should, therefore, have an advantage on Wall Street.

Here is a key point from an earlier section that is worth repeating … "As a general rule, *investment selection* and *investment timing* are inversely important. When the investment horizon is longer, selection becomes more important than timing. But timing is far more critical when the horizon is shorter." And THIS is where technical analysis is most valuable.

Investors oftentimes find it frustrating to watch a stock decline immediately after it was purchased – or advance right after it was sold. Hopefully, this section will prove useful in this regard.

The chapter describes several popular technical methods and explains a few key principles that have been successful over the years.

Bar Charts A stock chart is a picture of price history. With just a glance, an investor can quickly see the stock's past action and gain valuable perspective.

There are several types of stock charts. The most popular, called a bar chart, shows the price of a stock and its volume (number of shares traded) over a period of time, usually measured in days, weeks, or months. A daily bar chart, for example, would show the highest, lowest, and closing prices each day, as well as the number of shares traded daily. Similarly, a weekly bar chart would show the highest and lowest prices for the entire week as well as Friday's closing price and the total volume Monday through Friday.

Online computer programs today are a great deal more sophisticated than they were even ten or fifteen years ago. Users can now construct real-time charts of all types with one, two, five, ten, fifteen, thirty, or sixty minute price ranges.

Investors who want to pinpoint the best price to buy or sell a stock will find the monthly price chart a good place to begin. Then, by gradually move down the time scale, the analysis can be "fine tuned." A thirty-minute scale with a moving average setting of "40," as explained shortly, can provide a good picture of a stock's daily action – especially when it is viewed in conjunction with a weekly chart.

To demonstrate exactly how bar charts are constructed, assume that a stock traded at the following prices over a period of four weeks (twenty trading days):

Date	High	Low	Close	Volume
First Week				
Mon. 2nd	29.75	28.50	29.00	13,400
Tues. 3rd	29.50	28.63	29.13	15,200
Wed. 4th	29.50	28.25	28.75	15,800
Thurs. 5th	29.00	27.88	28.50	17,500
Fri. 6th	28.63	27.00	27.50	14,300
Second Week				
Mon. 9th	29.00	26.75	29.00	40,200
Tues. 10th	29.50	28.75	29.00	16,100
Weds. 11th	30.25	29.00	30.00	29,400
Thurs. 12th	31.00	29.63	30.50	15,600
Fri. 13th	30.75	30.00	30.25	12,100
Third Week				
Mon. 16th	31.00	30.13	30.75	17,800
Tues. 17th	31.50	30.38	30.38	10,200
Weds. 18th	30.75	29.50	29.75	18,100
Thurs. 19th	30.00	29.13	29.75	15,000
Fri. 20th	29.75	29.13	29.63	13,100
Fourth Week				
Mon. 23rd	32.00	29.63	31.25	18,000
Tues. 24th	32.25	31.00	31.38	14,500
Weds. 25th	32.00	31.13	31.88	14,900
Thurs. 26th	32.50	30.75	30.75	17,300
Fri. 27th	31.63	30.38	31.50	11,700

A daily bar chart of these prices would appear as follows:

A weekly bar chart of the same prices would be simply a condensed version of the daily chart:

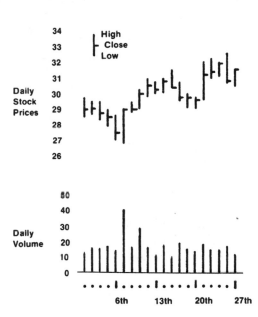

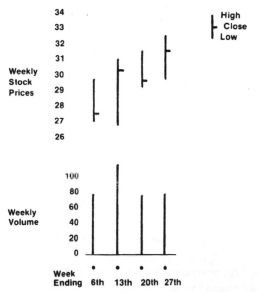

Typically, a complete daily chart displays several months (and sometimes more than a year) of data.

A complete weekly chart would normally show at least three to five years of weekly data.

One challenge all investors need to overcome with charts is PERSPECTIVE which will become more evident later when growth stocks are discussed. As a longer term investor with an investment horizon of many years, charts with "intraday" settings, or even "daily" or "weekly" settings, have less value as one looks further into the future. Charts are mainly *short term* tools.

Chart Patterns Once a bar chart has been constructed and maintained, over time various patterns appear. Each tells a different story and some are more valuable than others. "Support and resistance" patterns, for example, work well because investors have a tendency to remember past stock prices. Here are two typical support and resistance patterns and the psychological reasoning behind each:

Price Support

For several weeks or months this stock traded in a price range between $15 and $20, providing ample time for many investors to buy, sell, or just observe. When the stock suddenly rose above $20, an action that is called a "breakout," each person who bought the stock was saying "Wow, am I smart! This is a good one! If it returns to the $15 to $20 range, I'll buy more." The same can be said for the investor who sold it or watched it rise without owning it. "What a mistake! If the stock returns to that price range again, I'll buy it!" This is called a "Price Support" pattern.

The story would be completely different, of course, if the breakout happened to be down forming a "Price Resistance" pattern.

Price Resistance

In this case, the stockholders might be thinking "I knew that stock should have been sold! If it rallies back to $15 to $20, I'm going to sell it and use the money to buy a better stock!"

Price support and price resistance patterns have even greater meaning when the trading range is accompanied by large volume. This usually indicates that investment interest is high.

Normally, the moment the stock breaks out of its trading range – either up or down – volume increases. If it does, and the stock continues in the same direction, the pattern can be considered quite reliable.

When the stock breaks out of a price support or price resistance pattern the precise spot of the breakout is often called "the pivot point." Frequently, but not always, the pivot point represents half of the move before the stock returns to "test" the breakout. This pullback can be "one final chance" for investors to buy or sell.

There are two other types of support and resistance chart patterns:

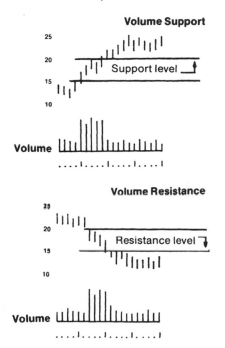

The increased volume, as illustrated above, highlights the accelerated trading activity at those particular price levels. For essentially the same psychological reasons mentioned earlier, support and resistance levels created by volume can also influence future buy and sell orders.

Note, too, that after an extended move, up or down, the volume support or volume resistance pattern can mark the beginning of the end of the stock's prior trend.

Ascending and descending triangles are interesting and useful variations of the price support and price resistance patterns discussed earlier. They are so named because the direction of the breakout is frequently indicated in advance by the shape of the triangle.

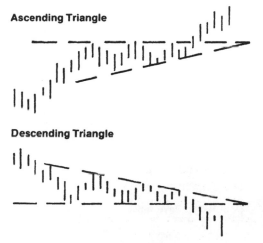

When the direction of a stock changes, specific chart patterns frequently develop as the turn occurs. Several of these so-called "reversal patterns" are shown on the next two pages. In some cases they develop gradually; at other times, the reversal occurs more suddenly.

The type of reversal pattern that appears is frequently determined by the nature of the advance or decline. Usually, the faster the move, the more rapid is the reversal.

Panic Reversal

Head & Shoulders Reversal

Neckline

Rounding Top Reversal

Descending Triangle Reversal

Double Top Reversal

Broadening Top Reversal

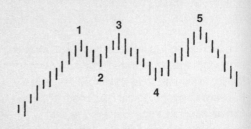

Selling Climax Reversal

Test

Climax

Inverse Head & Shoulders Reversal

Neckline

S   S

H

Rounding Bottom Reversal

Ascending Triangle Reversal

Double Bottom Reversal

1   2

Triple Bottom Reversal

1   2   3

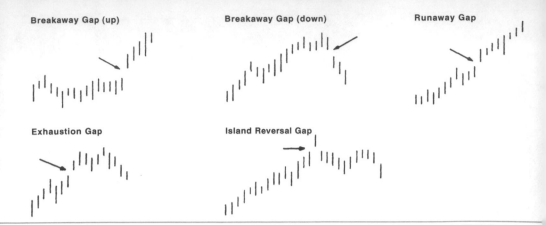

Breakaway Gap (up)

Breakaway Gap (down)

Runaway Gap

Exhaustion Gap

Island Reversal Gap

A "gap" occurs when the trading range on a given day is above or below the trading range of the previous day. Often the result of an emotional response to an overnight news item, a gap can be the first indication of a new price trend. However, if the stock's unusual volatility is partly due to a small float (i.e., a relatively small number of shares available for trading) the gap can be less reliable as a chart pattern.

Bar charts are amazingly geometric. As a result, technicians frequently draw trend lines and channels to identify future support and resistance points. In so doing, an experienced chartist will not ignore the "secondary points," which are the high and low points immediately before and after each peak or trough. Here are three trend line illustrations:

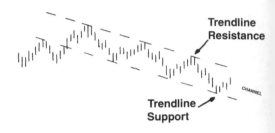

Trendline Resistance

Trendline Support

CHANNEL

Stock charts are like snowflakes – they are similar but never exactly the same. With the benefit of 20/20 hindsight and hours of experimenting, an investor can apply many of the same lessons learned time after time. Still, stock patterns present two major problems:

• If the pattern has developed completely, some of the move has already occurred.

• Chart patterns are never 100% reliable.

Most technical analysts who use bar charts prefer the regular scale graph paper, which is probably best for most investors. However, technicians interested in stock price movements on a percentage basis can obtain a somewhat different perspective by constructing the same charts on semi-logarithmic scale paper.

Of the few chart subscriptions available showing hundreds of companies in various formats, S&P has been the most reliable. These older charts show various formats. Today most technicians use the internet.

Trendline Support

Trendline Resistance

INTERNATIONAL BUSINESS MACHINES

nyse
IBM

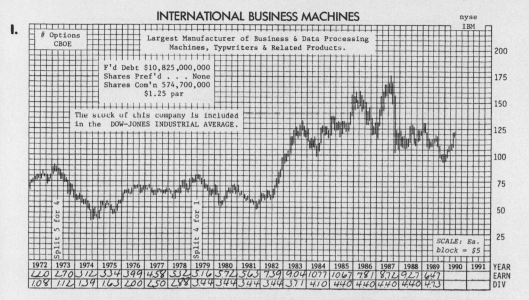

I.

Options CBOE

Largest Manufacturer of Business & Data Processing Machines, Typwriters & Related Products.

F'd Debt $10,825,000,000
Shares Pref'd . . . None
Shares Com'n 574,700,000
$1.25 par

The stock of this company is included in the DOW-JONES INDUSTRIAL AVERAGE.

Split 5 for 4

Split 4 for 1

SCALE: Ea. block = $5

	1972	1973	1974	1975	1976	1977	1978	1979	1980	1981	1982	1983	1984	1985	1986	1987	1988	1989	1990	1991	YEAR
EARN	2.20	2.70	3.12	3.34	3.99	4.58	5.32	5.16	5.72	5.63	7.39	9.04	10.77	10.67	7.81	8.72	9.27	6.47			
DIV	1.08	1.12	1.39	1.63	2.00	2.50	2.88	3.44	3.44	3.44	3.71	4.10	4.40	4.40	4.40	4.40	4.73				

★INTERNATIONAL BUSINESS MACHINES CORP. (IBM)

II. $

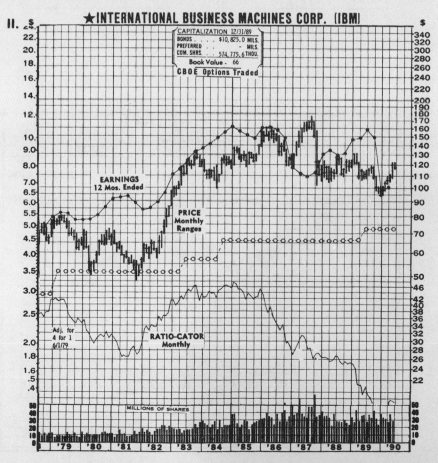

CAPITALIZATION 12/31/89
BONDS . . . . $10,825.0 MILS.
PREFERRED . . - MILS.
COM. SHRS. . 574,775.6 THOU.
Book Value - 66
CBOE Options Traded

EARNINGS
12 Mos. Ended

PRICE
Monthly
Ranges

Adj. for
4 for 1
6/1/79

RATIO-CATOR
Monthly

MILLIONS OF SHARES

'79 '80 '81 '82 '83 '84 '85 '86 '87 '88 '89 '90

III.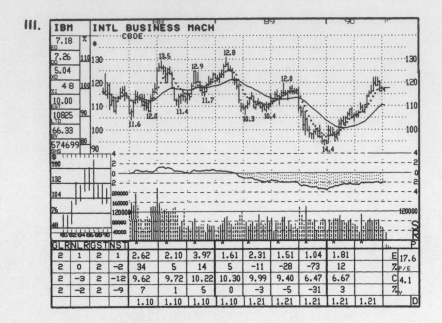

IV.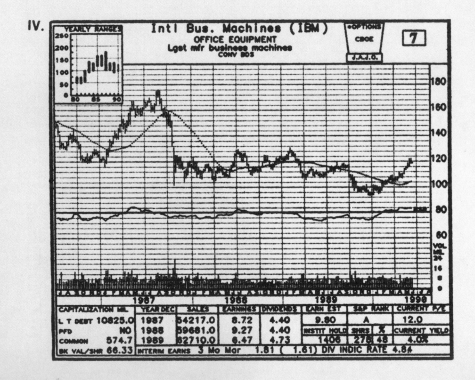

V.

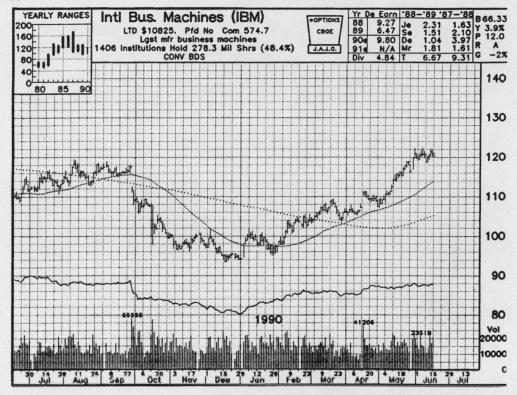

I. The Stock Picture
   M. C. Horsey & Company, Inc.
   120 South Blvd.
   Salisbury, MD 21801

II. 3-Trend Cycli-Graphs
    Securities Research Company
    101 Prescott Street
    Wellesley Hills, MA 02116

III. Mansfield Stock Chart Service
     R. W. Mansfield Company
     2973 Kennedy Boulevard
     Jersey City, NJ 07306

IV. Trendline's Current Market
    Perspectives
    Standard & Poor's Corporation
    55 Water Street
    New York, NY 10041

V. Daily Basis Stock Charts
   Standard & Poor's Corporation
   55 Water Street
   New York, NY 10041

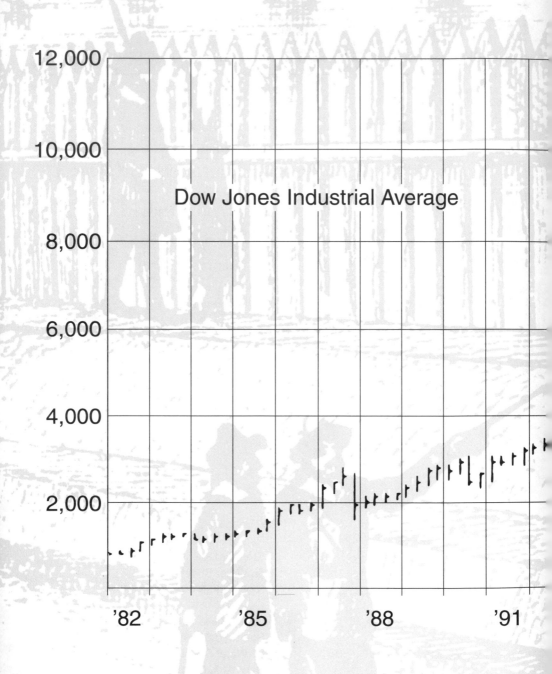

Dow Jones Industrial Average

The Dow Theory The Dow Theory is one of the oldest and most famous technical tools of the stock market. Its primary purpose is to forecast the future direction of the overall stock market by using, as a guide, the past actions of both the Dow Jones Industrial Average and the Dow Jones Transportation Average.

The Dow Theory is based mainly on the observation that market movements are analogous to movements of the sea. In other words, there are three movements in the market, all occurring simultaneously: Hourly or daily fluctuations (ripples); secondary or intermediate movements of two or three weeks to a month or more (waves); and the primary trend extending several months to a year or more (the tide). It is this primary trend that is generally referred to as either a bull or bear market.

According to early proponents of the theory, daily fluctuations are of little value. Secondary movements, however, are closely watched. They can retrace between one-third and two-thirds of the prior primary price change. The Dow Theory becomes useful when the secondary movements of the Dow Jones Industrial Average and the Dow Jones Transportation Average both signal a new primary trend by penetrating their previous secondary peak points. A new primary trend is not "confirmed" until both averages have produced the necessary signal.

Although most technicians believe the Dow Theory has been successful, they do not agree to what extent. The distinction between a primary and a secondary movement is not always clear. Still, many analysts find the tenets of the theory useful in their work.

The Elliott Wave Theory Like the Dow Theory, the Elliott Wave Theory uses past chart movements to forecast future price action.

The Elliott Wave Theory contends that movements in the stock market can be identified in five steps (forming three distinct waves). Once these five steps are complete, and the top or bottom has finally been reached, investors should anticipate a new trend.

But, also like the Dow Theory, not all of its proponents agree on its interpretation at any given time. What might appear to be a third step to one student could be the fifth step to another.

Despite its obvious shortcomings and, in some cases, misleading conclusions, the Elliott Wave Theory should not be totally dismissed. There are many bright and talented technicians who are using this theory successfully in one form or another.

The Moving Average Deviation

Technicians frequently watch a stock's progress by relating the stock price to its "moving average." A 40-week average, for example, is calculated by adding a stock's closing price of the current week to the closing prices of the previous thirty-nine weeks and dividing by forty. As time passes, this weekly average becomes a "moving average," which displays a smoothed trend of the stock's past prices.

Among the most popular moving averages is the 50-day moving average and the 200-day moving average (or 40 weeks).

A stock's momentum, or rate of change, is shown by its "Moving Average Deviation." Using a weekly chart and a 10-week moving average of the stock price, an investor can, each week, calculate the deviation by simply dividing the last stock price in the series by the 10-week moving average calculated for that week. This approach can be especially helpful in the technical analysis of highly volatile stocks (e.g., many growth and cyclical stocks). A new price trend is often indicated by the moving average deviation well before it actually takes place. It is also a good measure of an "overbought" and "oversold" condition that can result when a stock moves too far too quickly.

A weekly Moving Average Deviation chart would look like this:

Moving Average Deviation

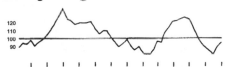

Sometimes calculating a 10-week moving average of the deviation figure and plotting it on the same (lower) scale will help the investor gain a longer term perspective and avoid being "whipsawed" by excessive short term activity.

Technician Gerald Appel is credited with what is called the "MACD" (the Moving Average Convergence/Divergence). This calculation consists of three exponential moving averages, instead of one or two. MACD is displayed as two separate lines that fluctuate above and below a base line. The second line is set at a longer time frame than the first (usually twice as long).

"Stochastics" is a popular technical tool that measures price velocity of a particular stock or market index. The investor sets a range and stochastics measures where the price is relative to that range (i.e., a stochastic of 100% means the price is currently trading at the extreme high of the range; at 0% the price is trading at the extreme low of the range). A moving average of the indicator is also used to smooth this otherwise volatile indicator.

Relative Strength The two most popular forms of relative strength are: The calculations used by *Investor's Business Daily*, a relative price strength rating for individual stocks they call the "RS Rating;" and the "Relative Strength Index" (the RSI) developed by J. Welles Wilder, Jr.

The *Investor's Business Daily* RS Rating measures a stock's relative price change in the previous twelve months versus all other stocks, and *IBD* is impressed when their RS Rating is above 80.

Based on the way Worden calculates their RS Index, a stock is declared "overbought" when it has an RSI of 70 or more and is considered "oversold" when their RS Index falls below 30.

Beta Many professional portfolio managers use a form of technical analysis in their attempt to measure a stock's market risk or sensitivity by calculating its "beta coefficient." Beta is a measure of the percentage change in the price of a stock relative to the percentage change of a market index.

Usually beta refers to the stock's relationship to the S&P 500 Index (i.e., the S&P Index = 1.00). A typical electronics stock, for example, might have a beta of 1.60, which means that the stock can be expected to move up or down by as much as 60% more than the general market. Conversely, an electric utility might have a beta of only .80 or less, which suggests the stock is expected to be 20% less volatile than the general market.

Portfolio managers often try to outperform the market by placing high-beta stocks into the portfolio when the market is expected to advance and by using low-beta stocks when they think the market outlook is less promising.

The major drawback to beta analysis is that beta never remains constant and predicting its future direction can be hazardous. For example, bank stocks were once thought to be low-beta issues, which has not been the case in more recent years. Thus, the beta formula must be monitored and not be taken too literally.

Point & Figure Charts

Quite different from bar charting is another method called "point & figure" analysis. Although a point & figure chart cannot measure time precisely and does not show volume, two important features of bar charts, P&F does have its advantages. Construction is simple and, once understood, a point & figure chart is easy to maintain and read. As with bar charts, an investor should spend at least several hours experimenting with old charts before any theories are put into practice.

Prior to starting a point & figure chart, examine the past price range and volatility of the stock. It is necessary to determine the appropriate denomination or "reversal" to be used on the chart. A high-priced stock (e.g., $50 or above) usually requires a 2-point, 3-point, or perhaps a 5-point reversal. A medium-priced stock (say, in the $20 to $50 range) is probably best represented by a 1-point, a 1.50-point, or 2-point reversal chart. A 0.50-point or a 1-point reversal is frequently used to chart low-priced stocks. Any one of these reversals will work on the same stock, but the chartist must decide which is most effective. With point & figure charts, the stock moves in only one direction at a time—either up or down. It does not change direction until a "reversal" of the desired amount occurs.

Once the scale has been drawn, mark the beginning price on the chart. If the price advances thereafter, place X's on top of one another. If the price declines, use O's placing them below one another. These symbols are used merely to identify the price direction. When the stock's direction changes by the required amount (the reversal), move to the next column. Do not place a new "X" or "O" on the chart until the exact price has been hit. As time passes, the result will be alternating columns of X's and O's.

For example, shown below is a 2-point reversal chart built from this string of prices: 29 (start), 32.75, 29.63, 33.25, 30.13, and 34.88.

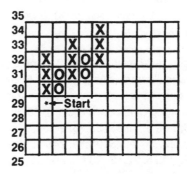

Point & figure charts, similar to bar charts, can show price support levels and price resistance levels.

Chart #1   1 Point Reversal

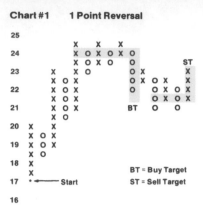

Chart #2   3 Point Reversal

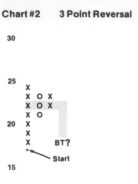

In addition, "breakouts" are easy to detect using the point & figure method:

Bullish

```
            X ←— Breakout
X     X     X
X  O  X  O  X
X  O     O
X
```

Bearish

```
X     X     X
X  O  X  O  X  O
X  O     O     O
X              O ←—Breakout
```

Many technicians use point & figure charts to predict how far a stock can advance or decline. There are several techniques, although none has been found to work every time.

The charts labeled #1 and #2 at the top of the page illustrate one approach. Both charts above are constructed from this same string of prices: 17 (start), 20.38, 18.13, 20.75, 19.63, 23.25, 21.50, 20.25, 24.63, 22.75, 24.75, 23.13, 24.75, 22.00, 23.13, 20.75, 22.50, 20.63, and 23.25.

According to point & figure practitioners, the greater the frequency of reversals at a certain level, the greater will be the stock's potential rise or fall from that level. As the 1-point reversal chart demonstrates, the base indicating the 21 Buy Target has a

count of six (shaded) across the 24 line. Six blocks below is the 21 price objective. Similarly, the Sell Target of 23.50 is the result of a base count of four (shaded) across the 21.50 line. The base to be used in the measurement can be found at the foot of the breakout regardless of whether the chartist is looking for a buy target or a sell target.

Point & figure charts can do many things. They can help an investor spot breakouts and new price trends. They can help identify support and resistance areas. And sometimes they can provide price objectives. But, for most investors, because it doesn't include volume, this charting method is best used as an adjunct investment tool to confirm or challenge other technical and fundamental work.

Japanese Candlestick Charts

One interesting variation of modern-day bar charts is the ancient Japanese Candlestick method of technical analysis. Actually, it is similar to bar charts, as explained earlier, except that opening prices are also included. In other words, the opening, high, low, and closing prices all appear on the chart rather than just the high, low, and close. The result is a chart notation that looks much like a candlestick.

Here is an example of how a candlestick chart illustrates a day when the closing price is lower than the opening price – and how it would be shown on the standard bar chart:

This is how they would appear when the closing price is higher than the opening quotation:

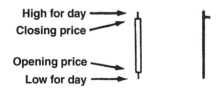

There is much more to this approach, of course, but the chart patterns are basically the same. The Japanese descriptive terms can be both interesting and exotic: Gaps are referred to as "windows," an intraday reversal can be called a "shooting star" or a "hanging man" or a "hammer." (The Japanese often name each symbol for its graphic appearance).

Japanese Candlestick Charts represent a colorful way to view the stock market. However, most experienced technicians dismiss candlesticks as a complex tool for an art that is best kept simple. And, in technical analysis, it's important not to miss the forest for the trees.

Technical Indicators Suppose a baseball player at bat happened to notice that almost every time the pitcher wiped his hand across his shirt the next pitch would be a fast ball. The batter might still strike out, but with this knowledge, he has a better chance for a hit. Analysts rely on technical indicators in much the same way. The use of these statistical tools as an aid in stock market timing is perhaps the most interesting and intellectually stimulating part of technical analysis.

There are literally hundreds of technical indicators. Most are derived from four primary sources:

(1) Business data
(2) Analysis of investor activity
(3) Market action
(4) Non-related coincidental factors

The indicators explained on the following pages have been fairly reliable in the past. Few, if any, work perfectly at every turn in the stock market. For this reason, an investor should maintain a portfolio of indicators or perhaps establish a composite index of several indicators.

Money Supply Indicators

Many Wall Street professionals believe there is a correlation between stock prices and the expansion or contraction of the nation's money supply. Indeed, a study of the four-decade period since the end of World War II suggests a definite correlation, especially if inflation is also taken into account. When money supply is increasing at a fairly steady rate and inflation is low and of little concern, stock prices tend to rise. On the other hand, either a contraction of money supply growth or an increase in the rate of inflation or both can be considered an unfavorable development.

The Money Supply Indicator is calculated monthly. It shows the year-to-year percent change in M2 (defined by the Federal Reserve as currency plus demand deposits plus deposits at commercial banks other than large CDs) adjusted for the year-to-year percent change in the Consumer Price Index (CPI).

To calculate the indicator, the percent change of M2 and the inflation impact (as measured by the percent change of the CPI) are added to or subtracted from 100. For example, if last month M2 increased 6.5% over the same month a year ago and the Consumer Price Index increased 4.0% in the same period, the Money Supply Indicator would read 102.5 for that month (100 + 6.5 - 4.0). On the other hand, if M2 advanced 3.0% while CPI increased 5.8%, the Money Supply Indicator would only be 97.2 for the month (100 + 3.0 - 5.8).

In the late 1940s, the Money Supply Indicator was frequently under 100 because the rate of inflation was greater than the growth of money supply. Corporate profits advanced but stocks remained dormant. Throughout most of the 1950s the indicator fluctuated in the 100 to 104 range. At that time, the money supply increased modestly while the inflation rate remained low. Stock prices rose.

In general, stocks can be vulnerable when the indicator declines, but seem to do well when it is steady or rising. An investor should be especially cautious when the indicator is declining while stock prices are advancing. This occurred in 1972, and again in mid-1987, prior to substantial market declines shortly thereafter. Conversely, if the indicator is rising sharply when stocks are declining, the market could be nearing a turn for the better.

The Money Supply Indicator can be a reliable tool during uncertain economic periods when money supply and inflation rate figures are in the limelight ... which seems to be most of the time.

There is another "Money Supply Indicator" that is easy to calculate and is also worth following. By subtracting and plotting the difference between M3 and M2, one can create another indicator that shows a fairly good correlation with stock prices. The Federal Reserve defines this difference between these two money stocks as "institutional money funds, and certain managed liabilities of depositories (that is to say, large time deposits, repurchase agreements and Eurodollars)."

The EPS/T-Bill Yield Ratio

One of the best methods of measuring the relative value of stock prices to other investment opportunities is the ratio of the S&P 500 earnings per share yield to the 3-month T-bill yield. This monthly ratio is easy to calculate and to maintain. It is constructed in the following manner:

(1) Divide the latest 12-month earnings per share of the S&P 500 Index by the monthly average price of the Index for the current month. The result is called the "earnings yield."

(2) Divide the "earnings yield" by the average yield of the 3-month T-bill for the same period.

If the ratio is .90 or lower, it is most likely a good time to sell stocks. When the ratio is 1.20 or greater, it is usually a good time to buy stocks.

Short Interest

At about mid-month, the New York Stock Exchange and other markets announce their short interest figures. These are shares that have been borrowed and sold by investors who believe the same shares will be available later for repurchase at lower prices. Although a large short interest indicates many investors anticipate lower prices, it also represents potential buying power. In years past, the NYSE short interest was a reliable market indicator – especially when short sale figures have been related to the number of shares traded.

The "Short Interest Ratio" is a measure of this relationship. It is calculated by dividing the NYSE short interest total by the average daily volume over the same period.

Historically, when the average daily volume exceeded the short interest figure (i.e., a ratio of less than 1.00), the indicator reading would be bearish. A short interest ratio of 1.00 to 1.60 was regarded as neutral and a ratio of more than 1.60 was bullish. For many decades, it was generally a good time to buy stocks when short interest was at least double the average daily volume (when the ratio was 2.00 or more).

Due to arbitrage and hedge fund activity, the short interest ratio has climbed to much higher levels than in years past. The ratio has been distorted by professional short selling funds that hedge their short positions with stock options.

Also, there are those who bloat the short sale figures with special dividend-capture or tax-avoidance strategies. In recent years the ratio has ranged between 3 and 5 and bears little resemblance to the original indicator. It can no longer be regarded as a reliable technical tool.

Odd Lot Investors

It is a widely accepted rule on Wall Street that the "odd lot" investor (defined as a buyer or seller of less than 100 shares), is almost always wrong. Yet, a close study of odd lot behavior does not bear this out entirely. The record clearly shows, for example, that odd lot investors were heavy net buyers at the market lows of 1966 and 1970, and were aggressive sellers at the highs in 1968 and 1972. Also, odd lot investors correctly used the 1987 stock crash as an opportunity to buy.

Nevertheless, small investors, like all participants who monitor the market's fluctuations and day-to-day activities, are motivated by greed and fear – and do tend to buy or sell incorrectly during times of extreme optimism or pessimism. One of the best barometers of this emotion is the Odd Lot Short Sale Ratio.

The ratio is calculated by dividing odd lot short sales by total odd lot sales. These New York Stock Exchange statistics appear in many newspapers daily. The weekly totals, two weeks old but more complete, are summarized each Monday in

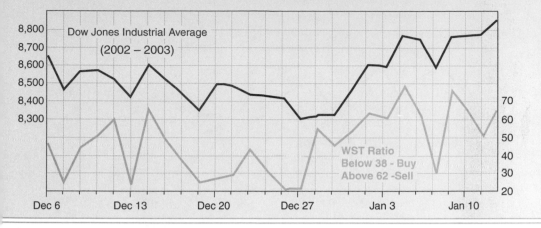

Dow Jones Industrial Average
(2002 – 2003)

WST Ratio
Below 38 - Buy
Above 62 -Sell

Dec 6   Dec 13   Dec 20   Dec 27   Jan 3   Jan 10

The Wall Street Journal or in *Barron's*, the popular weekly financial newspaper.

When the odd lot short sale ratio reaches or exceeds 3.0%, the indicator is regarded to be positive. When the ratio declines to 0.7% or less, the reading is negative.

It can be argued that stock options have diminished the reliability of this technical indicator and that the numbers are small, rendering the ratio irrelevant and not worthy of the time to compile it. Still, odd lot activity does seem to offer consistency.

Member Short Sales Ratio

Although two weeks old, the weekly NYSE round lot statistics that appear in *The Wall Street Journal* and *Barron's* on Mondays constitute a useful technical indicator. In addition to total shares purchased, sold, and sold short, this weekly report also shows the number of shares purchased, sold, and sold short for member accounts.

The specialists, floor traders, and "off-the-floor" traders involved in trading for member accounts are among the most astute people on Wall Street. When member firms' short selling is high relative to total short sales, the "Member Short Sales Ratio," as it is called, is bearish. Conversely, when member shorts are proportionately less, the indicator is bullish.

The Member Short Sales Ratio is calculated weekly by dividing all shares sold short for member accounts by total short sales for the same period. The indicator is negative when member short selling is 82% or more of the total and is positive when the ratio is 68% or less.

Technical analysts also use the Specialists' Short Sale Ratio, which is calculated in almost the same manner. However, this indicator may be less reliable than the overall member ratio because specialists are sometimes forced to go short. Traditionally, when specialists' short sales reach or exceed 60% of total short sales the ratio is bearish; when it drops to 40% or less it is bullish. Still, the principal argument against the use of this indicator is, like the Member Ratio, the lag time of the data reports.

The WST Ratio By far, the most reliable and effective technical indicators are found among stock options statistics. Options players are typically traders, they are highly receptive to short term stories, they are highly emotional, and, most importantly, they are wrong more often than they are right.

Put and call options, which are explained in detail in the next chapter, are contracts that allow investors an opportunity to buy or sell a stock, or an index, at a specific *price*, and

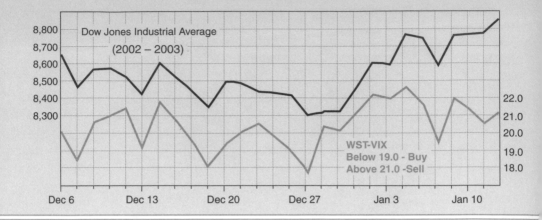

Dow Jones Industrial Average (2002 – 2003)

WST-VIX
Below 19.0 - Buy
Above 21.0 -Sell

at a specific *time* in the future. A *call* contract is purchased when the stock is expected to rise. A *put* is bought when the stock is expected to decline.

In 1996, the "Wall Street Trader," an inexpensive computer program, was first published by **BullsOrBears.com**. Thus, the "WST Ratio" was created.

The WST Ratio is a sophisticated measure of index option activity. The ratio is computed using Chicago Board Options Exchange (CBOE) intraday data, although the official daily WST Ratio is published at the end of each trading session. When the ratio is below 38.0, put buyers far outnumber call buyers and the reading is *bullish*. When the ratio is above 62.0, the call buyers dominate and the reading is considered *bearish*.

The WST Ratio is a short term indicator for predicting market swings of typically not more than one to three days. However, the WST Ratio 10-day moving average has some predictive value for the intermediate term (several weeks or more). A moving average reading above 60 (sell) or below 40 (buy) often coincide with important market reversals.

Spreadsheet data showing daily figures (either Lotus 1-2-3 or Microsoft Excel) can be downloaded from the BullsOrBears.com website at no cost.

The CBOE Volatility Index (VIX)

One of the most widely watched numbers today is the CBOE "VIX" (the Volatility Index) which is computed throughout the session and published by the CBOE at the close. The VIX Index measures the level of implied volatility of the U.S. equity market using real-time S&P 100 (OEX) index option bid and ask quotes.

By itself, the VIX has limited value as a technical indicator but it does show in broad terms the state of the market's emotion. The VIX will rise sharply to a peak when the market is in greatest despair and normally displays a low volatility when prices are near their highs.

There is another similar volatility index for the NASDAQ (called VIXN – pronounced "vixen") and moves in a manner identical to the more widely-followed VIX.

When the VIX is modified using the WST Ratio, a very useful short term indicator emerges. The WST-VIX, as it is called, is simply the Volatility Index weighted by the WST Ratio. This technical indicator can be calculated any time during the session and is published at the end of each day. The WST-VIX is positive when the reading is at or below 19.0% and negative when it moves above 21.0%. At least five years of daily back data can be downloaded free from the BullsOrBears.com website.

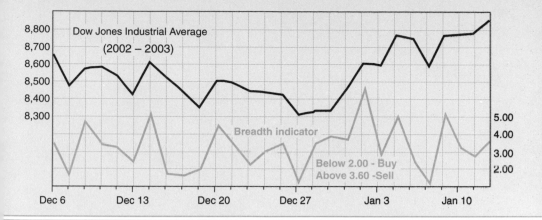

Dow Jones Industrial Average (2002 – 2003)

Breadth indicator

Below 2.00 - Buy
Above 3.60 -Sell

Dec 6   Dec 13   Dec 20   Dec 27   Jan 3   Jan 10

Market Breadth

Market Breadth One widely-followed technical indicator is called the ARMS Index. Named for its creator, technician Richard Arms, the ARMS Index measures the current condition of the market by relating the ratio of NYSE daily advancing and declining issues to the ratio of volume of shares rising and falling on the NYSE. As a general rule, an ARMS reading of less than 1.00 suggests buying demand; above 1.00 indicates selling pressure.

A variation of a moving average of the ARMS Index, called the "Market Breadth Indicator," produces buy and sell limits of 2.00 or less (buy) and 3.60 or more (sell).

Other Technical Observations

The use of indicators in technical analysis is limited only by one's imagination. These are several other ideas technicians use:

• Customers' margin debt on the New York Stock Exchange. A rising margin debt is considered positive; a declining margin debt is negative.

• Studies based on the inverse relationship between commercial paper rates and stock prices.

• The total market value of New York Stock Exchange stocks as a percent of the nation's Gross National Product. In the past, a ratio below 40% has been positive, above 70% has been negative.

• An analysis of personal buying and selling activity by company executives. These figures are reported to the SEC and are especially worth noting when three or more officers sell within a month of each other without any "insider" buying. The same rule applies to buying, but it is somewhat less reliable.

• The market value of $1 of dividends (the inverse to stock yields). Using the Dow Jones Industrial Average as a benchmark, the market has been fully valued at or above 30 times each dollar of dividends and at attractive levels at or below 15.

• The cash holdings of mutual funds as a percent of total fund assets. A 10% level or higher is thought to be positive while a level of under 6% is deemed unfavorable.

The statistical sources for these and most other technical indicators are plentiful. There are numerous online sources and most local libraries offer a variety of publications with business and economic data. Once all past figures have been collected, keeping the indicators current is an easy task.

Many market analysts are convinced there are other, unexplained forces that influence stock prices. For example, over the years there have been distinct seasonal trends. The best months for rising prices traditionally have been January, July,

November, and December. The worst months have been February, May, June, and October. This explains why buyers in May and June hope to see a "summer rally" and why October buyers look for the so-called "year end rally."

Short-term traders with years of experience are aware that, on balance, Mondays have been "down" days while Fridays have been "up" days. Also, when the market declines on Friday, there seems to be a strong tendency for prices to decline further on Monday.

Are there stock market cycles? Some analysts think so . . .

• Every "5-year" since 1905 has been a year of rising stock prices (1915, 1925, 1935, 1945, 1955, 1965, 1975, 1985 and 1995).

• Historically, the lowest price of every fourth year since 1930 has been followed by substantially higher prices (Note: 1934, 1938, 1942, 1946, 1950, 1954, 1958, 1962, 1966, 1970, 1974, 1978, 1982, 1986, 1990, 1994, 1998, and 2002).

• Finally, there is a very distinct 71-year pattern of highs and/or lows beginning with the 1903–1974 correlation. Other dates worth noting: 1911–1982; 1916–1987; 1919–1990; 1929–2000 highs with both cycles ending thirty-four months later. Market observers are forever arguing whether technical analysis is more of an "art" than it is a "science" (and some might insist it is no more than "voodoo"). The answer lies in the eye of the beholder.

The force of market psychology may never be understood, much less predicted, but the technical analyst is one step closer to harnessing it.

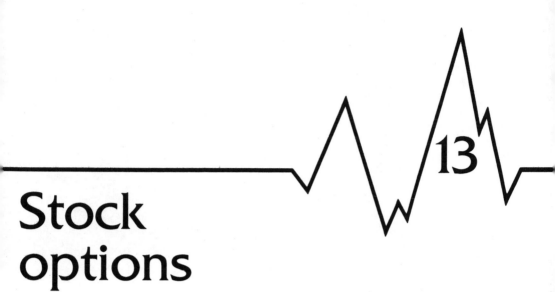

Stock options

Introduction Since April 26, 1973, when options, as we know them today, were first traded on the Chicago Board Options Exchange (CBOE), the growth of the options market has been significant.

The average daily contract volume on the CBOE was close to 10,000 contracts that year. Now, eighty times that activity is not unusual. Overall dollar volume, based on the prices paid for options, has increased from $448 million in 1973 to a multibillion dollar arena today.

Options had suddenly been discovered even though they had been trading quietly in the over-the-counter market for at least one hundred years. Some hailed them as the new way to quick profits in any type of market and many dismissed them abruptly as just another form of outright gambling. As they become more widely understood, however, options will undoubtedly be recognized for what they are: an additional investment tool and a means of managing risk for knowledgeable investors and seasoned speculators.

The mechanics of put and call options, suggestions for valuing them, and the methods for using them in a risk-manageable manner are among the highlights of this chapter.

Background A stock option is a contract that gives the owner the right to buy or sell a specific number of shares (usually 100) of a given stock at a fixed price within a definite time period. The stock involved is referred to as the "underlying security," the fixed price is called the "striking price" or "strike price," and the date the contract expires is called the "expiration date." For the privileges of the option, the buyer pays a "premium," another name for the option's "price." It is not a down payment. It must be paid in full in cash. The premium is the only variable in any option contract; all other items are fixed. And, like the price of a common stock, the premium is an equilibrium price reflecting the judgments of all buyers and sellers in the market at any given time.

An option conveying the right to buy stock from the option's seller (the "writer") is known as a "call" because it allows the buyer to call stock away from the writer. An option conveying the right to sell stock to the writer is termed a "put" because it allows the buyer to put stock to the writer. Either action by the buyer is known as "exercising" the option. Once an option has been written, the writer must abide by its stated terms. However, the writer can extinguish this responsibility, as explained later.

Stock options are currently traded on most of the national exchanges, including the Chicago Board Options Exchange and the American Stock Exchange (Amex). All are closely regulated by the SEC.

On the next two pages are examples of how options usually appear in a daily newspaper. These tables present price information from the previous trading session for each class of options as well as the closing prices of the underlying stocks. A "class" is comprised of all options, both puts and calls, covering the same underlying security. Thus, the options for Cisco, or for Citigroup, as they are illustrated on the next page, constitute a class. *The Wall Street Journal* publishes only the most active options in its tables. *Investor's Business Daily* and *Barron's* offer a much more complete listing. The formats are only slightly different as these examples for January 28 illustrate.

Several expiration dates can be given for each strike price. The tables here show the call and put options for the stock of Cisco Systems, trading on the NASDAQ, currently priced at $14.22. For most options, such as Cisco's, expiration dates are spaced over the next three consecutive months, as in this example: February, March, and April. In this case, the *Journal* also shows figures for July. Expiration dates are usually spaced in three-month intervals to as far out as nine months, the most distant expiration date now available.

LISTED OPTIONS QUOTATIONS

Tuesday, January 28

Composite volume and close for actively traded equity and LEAPS, or long-term options, with results for the corresponding put or call contract. Volume figures are unofficial. Open interest is total outstanding for all exchanges and reflects previous trading day. Close when possible is shown for the underlying stock or primary market. **XC**-Composite. **p**-Put. **o**-Strike price adjusted for split.

NOTICE TO READERS

The number of listed options quotations presented in the Journal has been pared to the top 100 most-active issues, from the top 350 issues. This recognizes the prevalence of online availability of these data. For full market coverage, go to the Online Journal at WSJ.com.

OPTION/STRIKE	EXP	-CALL- VOL	LAST	-PUT- VOL	LAST
AllgEngy 10	Jul	2501	1.30	2500	2.20
Altria 12.50	Feb	2074	0.20	40	4.40
38.38 40	Feb	1685	0.65	3142	2.20
Amazon 22.50	Feb	1868	0.80	2171	1.70
A E P 25	May	2024	1.85	10	3.10
Amgen 55	Feb	2690	0.60	110	3.90
51.59 55	Apr	1847	2	52	5.10
BP PLC 35	Jul	5	3.50	2000	3
36.49 40	Jul	2076	1.55	...	...
BankNY 25	Apr	1002	2.20	2206	1.90
BostSc 45	Feb	4511	0.35	6	4.20
Celgene 22.50	Mar	1735	1.10	460	2.10
CienaCp 7.50	Mar	2024	0.45	15	1.75
Cisco 12.50	Feb	401	2.05	2997	0.25
14.22 15	Feb	7535	0.50	490	1.25
14.22 15	Mar	5145	0.80	420	1.55
14.22 15	Apr	5376	1.05	28	1.80
14.22 15	Jul	1871	1.75	1050	2.50
Citigrp 35	Feb	2659	1.75	4745	1.40
CocaCola 40	May	91	3.50	7771	2.40

OPTION/STRIKE	EXP	-CALL- VOL	LAST	-PUT- VOL	LAST
32.66 35	Mar	8951	0.75	12	3.10
32.66 35	Jul	1709	1.70	...	...
Gen El 25	Feb	2209	0.35	273	2.10
23.15 25	Jun	2174	1.35	24	3.30
HomeDp 22.50	Feb	1846	0.25	243	2.20
IMS Hlth 25	Feb	12860	0.05	7278	9.10
Intel 17.50	Feb	12259	0.35	230	1.70
16.01 17.50	Apr	2329	0.95	287	2.35
16.01 20	Jul	1740	0.85	11	4.80
I B M 75	Feb	448	6.50	2026	1.50
80.11 80	Feb	3667	3.20	2930	3.20
80.11 85	Feb	2120	1.15	245	6
80.11 85	Mar	1782	2.40	42	7.20
80.11 85	Mar	1992	2.05	...	...
In Pap 35	Mar	...	...	1920	0.40
JPMorgCh 25	Feb	6731	0.55	387	2.10
23.51 25	Mar	4360	1.10	6315	2.50
23.51 30	Mar	3058	0.20	5	6.20
JackInBox 15	Mar				
JnprNtw 10	Feb	2136	0.30	305	1.05
KLA Tnc 35	Feb	684	2.05	2568	2.25
		983	2.40	2893	2.70
		3648	1.60	1926	2.85
		4067	3.50	355	4.60
		3113	0.70	34	11.60
		2221	0.30	301	16.20
		6	4.10	12319	0.35
		3337	2.20	19248	0.40
		7931	1.50	8982	0.70
		35762	0.95	7362	1.15
		8448	1.55	1859	1.60
		39864	0.55	6359	1.70
		26519	0.30	2749	2.45
		3036	0.65	250	2.70
		6636	0.30	7	4.60
		...	...	2520	0.90
		3	3.60	2650	4.80
		...	...	5305	0.50
		3574	2.05	2327	2.05
		1760	7.60	1760	3
		82	3	2183	1.05
		113	4.60	6394	2.55

OPTION/STRIKE	EXP	-CALL- VOL	LAST	-PUT- VOL	LAST
37.09 40	Mar	2116	1.35	43	4.40
Sanmina 5	Apr	5500	0.35	...	...
Sears 25	Feb	507	2	7513	1.35
SiebelSys 7.50	Feb	253	1.40	3759	0.20
Starbcks 25	Apr	4036	0.55	35	2.60
Texasinst 17.50	Feb	3982	0.30	263	1.60
16.00 17.50	Apr	3972	1.05	20	2.70
TycoIntl 17.50	Feb	1871	0.30	622	1.60
UPS B 60	Feb	1791	2	987	1
VeritasSf 15	Feb	10	3.70	2526	0.30
18.72 17.50	Feb	1021	2.10	2768	0.90
18.72 20	Feb	11964	0.85	4078	2.05
VerizonCm 35	Feb	239	2.30	2518	1.25
36.05 35	Jul	11	4	3815	3.50
ViacmB 35	Feb	5286	4.10	406	1.20
37.85 37.50	Feb	1940	2.40	1488	1.95
Yahoo 20	Feb	1962	0.50	157	1.90
18.63 20	Apr	3209	1.45	20	3

Volume & Open Interest Summaries

AMERICAN

	Vol		Open Int
Call Vol:	355,652	Open Int:	28,738,079
Put Vol:	181,456	Open Int:	21,476,934

CHICAGO BOARD

Call Vol:	531,599	Open Int:	41,862,861
Put Vol:	330,219	Open Int:	31,649,974

INTL SECURITIES

Call Vol:	373,393	Open Int:	35,543,282
Put Vol:	301,672	Open Int:	26,696,411

PHILADELPHIA

Call Vol:	161,115	Open Int:	42,765,925
Put Vol:	93,472	Open Int:	24,337,804

PACIFIC

Call Vol:	147,276	Open Int:	37,427,770
Put Vol:	119,947	Open Int:	27,728,623

TOTAL

Call Vol:	1,569,035
Put Vol:	1,026,766

OPTION/STRIKE	EXP	-CALL- VOL	LAST	-PUT- VOL	LAST
AllgEngy 10	Jul	2501	1.30	2500	2.20
Altria 12.50	Feb	2074	0.20	40	4.40
38.38 40	Feb	1685	0.65	3142	2.20
Amazon 22.50	Feb	1868	0.80	2171	1.70
A E P 25	May	2024	1.85	10	3.10
Amgen 55	Feb	2690	0.60	110	3.90
51.59 55	Apr	1847	2	52	5.10
BP PLC 35	Jul	5	3.50	2000	3
36.49 40	Jul	2076	1.55	...	...
BankNY 25	Apr	1002	2.20	2206	1.90
BostSc 45	Feb	4511	0.35	6	4.20
Celgene 22.50	Mar	1735	1.10	460	2.10
CienaCp 7.50	Mar	2024	0.45	15	1.75
Cisco 12.50	Feb	401	2.05	2997	0.25
14.22 15	Feb	7535	0.50	490	1.25
14.22 15	Mar	5145	0.80	420	1.55
14.22 15	Apr	5376	1.05	28	1.80
14.22 15	Jul	1871	1.75	1050	2.50
Citigrp 35	Feb	2659	1.75	4745	1.40
CocaCola 40	May	91	3.50	7771	2.40

STOCK OPTIONS

P/C Strike Price	Last Vol.	Price	Last Vol.	Price	Last Vol.	Price
	Feb		Mar			
Ciena			Close 6.31		**Apr**	
c7.50	407	0.20	2008	0.45	62	0.55
CirctCity			Close 6.30		**Apr**	
c7.50	104	0.10	no tr		16	0.30
p7.50	2	1.20	no tr		108	1.65
Cisco			Close 14.22		**Apr**	
c12.50	391	2	35	2.25	20	2.35
c15	7342	0.50	5128	0.80	5366	1.05
c17.50	44	0.05	582	0.20	342	0.35
c20	no tr		no tr		142	0.05
p12.50	2997	0.25	312	0.50	53	0.75
p15	380	1.25	420	1.55	28	1.80
p17.50	30	3.40	220	3.50	4	3.70
Citigroup			Close 35.46		**Jun**	
c30	102	5.80	40	6	no tr	
c35	2568	1.75	575	2.45	72	3.80
c37.50	869	0.65	324	1.75	1025	2.55
c40	382	0.20	275	0.60	1125	1.60
c42.50	no tr		126	0.55	212	0.90
p20	no tr		no tr		110	0.35
p27.50	no tr		1110	0.45	no tr	
p30	727	0.30	260	0.75	15	1.80
p32.50	1639	0.65	5	0.95	10	2.55
p35	4695	1.35	no tr		1345	3.50
p37.50	327	2.75	no tr		no tr	
CitrixSys			Close 13.45		**Jun**	
c10	75	3.50	no tr		118	4.20
p12.50	41	0.50	2	0.80	120	1.70

The February "series" will expire in the third week of February and the newspaper tables will be amended accordingly. Thus, when the Cisco February series ends, the tables will begin showing March, April, and May expiration dates. Depending upon the exchange and, of course, the time of the year, the option tables also show other consecutive series combinations. It is possible for options to be available and not be listed regularly in the newspaper. It depends on the level of activity and the degree of interest.

New options are introduced when the price of the underlying security advances or declines. This will usually occur at 2½-point intervals for stocks trading below $25 a share; 5-point intervals for stocks trading between $25 and $200 a share; and 10- or 20-point intervals for stocks trading above $200. For instance, if Cisco's common stock, last traded on the NYSE at $14.22 as indicated to the left, were suddenly to advance to about $19, new options would probably be offered with a strike price of $22.50 with the same expiration dates.

At times, no options are traded at an existing strike price under a given expiration date. This is noted in *IBD* by the words "no tr" in the tables. Thus, there were no trades in Cisco's February 20 and March 20 Calls. But some April 20 Calls did trade at $0.05. In general, new options are introduced as the expiration date changes or when the

stock price changes enough to warrant a new strike price.

Each newspaper, using its own method, summarizes the previous trading day's statistics for the options in each series. The interested options investor learns, for example, that the trades in the Citigroup February Call options with a 35 strike price took place at a premium of $1.75 per contract for the underlying stock. Since each option contract covers 100 shares of the underlying stock, the premium listed in the table must be multiplied by 100 to compute the actual dollar cost of a single option of any series. In this case, the premium would be $175.00 for one Citigroup February 35 Call. This cost does not include commissions and taxes.

To repeat, in every instance, these figures would have the same meaning if puts were being discussed rather than calls. Also, the published newspaper prices and volume might differ slightly due to the precise moment the data was collected at the close of the trading session.

Today's market contrasts sharply with the early days of options trading. In the 1920s, for example, most options activity took place in a small restaurant on New Street in New York's financial district. Each day a small cadre of options traders turned the restaurant into their own office, dining room, and after-hours club. They arrived early and

set up shop near the public telephone booths. Their pockets jingled with change for what was then a nickel telephone call. Some of the more prosperous brokers employed messengers who crisscrossed the Wall Street area trying to bring buyers and sellers together.

However, matching the buyer and writer was usually difficult and often impossible. It was a process that invariably required several telephone calls and exasperating negotiation to formulate terms agreeable to both the buyer and the writer. If an options investor decided the contract was no longer useful, it was even more difficult to sell it to someone else in a secondary market. The CBOE rejuvenated options trading when it standardized the terms of an option contract and when it created a central marketplace.

The trading floor of the CBOE was built in the airspace above the trading pits used by the commodities exchange. In this old section, a similar type of options trading has long been practiced in contracts for wheat, soybeans, potatoes, and other commodities.

There are currently eight oval trading counters on the floor of the CBOE. Options on several underlying stocks are traded at each counter. The traders group outside the counters watching each other for outcries of

interest as well as the television set display units above each counter. Up-to-the-minute pricing information on each option traded at the counter appears on the display units. The data includes the last premium trade, the current bid and asked quotation, and the underlying stock's trading information. When a trade is completed among the floor traders, the results are quickly passed to CBOE employees working inside the counter and the new trading information immediately appears on the screens above. Much of this data is also available on the electronic quotation machines used in brokerage firms throughout the country.

Representatives of the various member brokerage firms are stationed at communications booths that ring the trading floor. Messengers carry orders from the communication booths to the floor traders and soon return with the completed trade information. In this way, the firm's customers quickly learn the results of each transaction.

The Options Clearing Corporation, partially owned by the NYSE, serves as a giant bookkeeping operation recording the actions of all buyers and sellers. After the orders are matched on the trading floor the Clearing Corporation acts as the buyer to every seller and the seller to every buyer. It severs the relationship between the original writer and the original buyer. This combination of the

The Trading Floor at the Chicago Board Options Exchange

Clearing Corporation and the active secondary market makes it possible for an option owner to sell at any time and for an option writer to terminate the responsibility to deliver or accept stock at any time. The owner of an option instructs the broker to sell it in much the same manner as a common stock would be sold. This action is called a "closing sale transaction." The writer terminates the responsibility to deliver or accept stock through a "closing purchase transaction," also called "buying-in."

In this transaction, the writer buys an option identical in all respects to the option originally written except for the premium. The outstanding option is then offset at the Clearing Corporation with the option purchased in the closing purchase transaction. In each case, the profit or loss of either the writer or the buyer is determined by the difference between the original premium paid or received and the premium paid or received in the closing transaction. If only one investor liquidates a position as writer or buyer, it has no effect on the other investor. That is, if a call writer liquidates a position in a closing transaction, the owner of the call may still exercise it at any time.

Today option trading is linked between the five exchanges by an electronic network to further ensure the SEC's "best execution" rules.

Buying Options For buyers, options offer leverage with a predetermined risk. The option's cost is its premium and this premium is usually only a small fraction of the underlying stock's market price. Thus, the buyer participates in any price change in the stock without having to buy the stock itself, which would require a substantially greater investment. Further, the buyer knows that the maximum possible loss is the total amount of the premium.

In practice, most option buyers expect to profit from an increase in the premium. They are not interested in exercising the option to acquire the stock itself but are attracted by capital gains leverage and the limited capital exposure.

Here is a simplified explanation of how an option buyer can make or lose money on an option trade...

After studying the fundamental and technical characteristics of the ABC Company, a speculator concludes in late April that the company's common stock price will increase substantially in the next three months. The stock is selling for $40 a share.

The trader could either buy the stock outright or buy a call on the stock. Since the stock purchase would require an immediate outlay of $4,000 – excluding commissions – for 100 shares, the trader decides to take

	Stock		Call Option	
April	Bought 100 shares @ $40	$4,000	Bought 1 July 40 Call @ $4	$ 400
June	Sold 100 shares @ $46	4,600	Sold 1 July 40 Call @ $7	700
	Trading Profit	$ 600	Trading Profit	$ 300
	Less approximate commissions	135	Less approximate commissions	50
	PROFIT	$ 465	PROFIT	$ 250
	Net Return on Original Investment Before Taxes	11.6%	Net Return on Original Investment Before Taxes	62.5%

advantage of the inherent leverage of options. A July ABC 40 Call is purchased for a premium of 4.00 ($400 for 100 shares). The July expiration date was selected because, as the trader reasoned, the underlying stock would advance soon.

By late June, the stock price increased 15% to $46 while the option advanced to 7.00, a gain of 75%. At this point, the trader might want to sell the option in the secondary market to capture the 3-point increase in the premium. The comparison above shows how one can profit by either owning the stock directly or by buying a call. The degree of risk, however, is greatly different between the two.

The absolute dollar profit was less from the call option than from the stock; however, compared to the capital invested, the call option produced a greater profit at a much greater risk.

If the stock's potential had been misjudged and it declined rather than advanced, the maximum loss would be the entire initial premium of $400. Even though the stock could drop by more than the premium amount, the call buyer's loss is still limited to $400. Although the buyer might be able to reduce this loss by selling the call in the secondary market for whatever value remained, any loss to the call owner is an immediate out-of-pocket cash loss. On the other hand, the owner of stock only has a

"paper loss" and can hold the shares for future recovery.

Assuming in this example the trader expected the stock's price to drop sharply in the same short time period, the premium of a July ABC 40 Put would have increased in value as the underlying stock declined. Puts are calls turned upside down. And, like calls, puts offer leverage and limited loss of capital, but in reverse. Puts are appropriate in a declining market as opposed to the traditional method of profiting from falling stock prices by selling stock short. Stated differently, a put option is to a short sale as a call option is to buying the stock "long."

Under current margin requirements of 50%, selling short 100 shares of ABC at $40 in late April would have required a margin deposit of at least $2,000. If, two months later, the stock dropped 15% to $34 as expected, the trader would have had a profit of $600 or 30%.

The purchase of an ABC July 40 Put in late April at 4 would have produced a 75% profit in the same period if the premium had advanced to 7 as the stock declined – excluding commissions and taxes.

The put limited the buyer's potential loss to the amount of the premium while the short seller's risk was theoretically unlimited. Moreover, puts give the option trader greater psychological staying power. For example, if the stock had advanced before it began the anticipated decline, the short seller might have been tempted to cover prematurely. On the other hand, the put buyer, realizing that the total possible loss was limited to $400, could have endured the advance more easily.

It should be noted, however, that if the stock remained steady and did not decline to $34 until August, the short seller would still have made a 30% profit while the put would have expired worthless.

Speculators beware! When you buy a call or put option, THREE things can happen during the life of the option – and TWO of them are BAD!

Writing Options

Option sellers are called "writers" in a carryover from the early days of over-the-counter trading when the details of each contract had to be carefully written out by hand. Today, option writing is standardized but the term remains.

An option writer's primary purpose is to earn additional income through the premiums received from option buyers. This income can be a plus to the overall return on a portfolio. Premium income can also provide a "cushion" against an adverse move in the underlying stock – but only to the extent of the premium.

Assume an investor who owns CDE Company stock at a cost of $50 writes a CDE 50 Call and receives a premium of $5.00. If the stock does not move and the option expires worthless, the entire 5 point premium can be considered additional income. If the stock advances, it can be called away, which means the investor is, in effect, selling the stock for $55. The writer's maximum profit is, therefore, limited to the premium amount.

The premium also hedges the stock against a decline to $45. If the stock drops by more than the premium, the investor will suffer a loss, as before. Obviously, writing covered calls increases the total rate of return on a given portfolio only if the underlying stock neither increases nor decreases by more than the amount of the premium.

While all option purchases require a full cash payment, option writing involves more complex accounting. Most writing takes place in a margin account. The options written may be "covered" or "uncovered" (also called "naked"). A call is covered most simply if the writer deposits with the broker the exact number of shares of underlying stock to be sold if the option is exercised. A covered call writer can choose between delivering the stock on deposit or delivering stock bought in the open market when the option was exercised. Some writers who have a low cost on the stock already owned might select the latter method to avoid paying a large capital gains tax at that time.

A naked call (a call written against cash) can only be written in a margin account. A broker requires that adequate funds be on hand at all times to purchase stock in the open market if the option is exercised. A put is covered only when it is offset share for share by a long put having an equal or greater exercise price. The margin requirements for writing uncovered puts and calls are identical. Whenever a margin account is used, the investor should compute the transaction's ultimate rate of return based on the amount of capital deposited.

Naked call writing has much greater risk than covered call writing. If the stock either remains steady or declines, naked calls can produce large returns on the margin deposited. But if it advances, every point beyond the amount of premium initially received will be an out-of-pocket loss to the writer when the call is exercised. The naked call writer, like the investor who sells stock short, could have unlimited losses, but with greater leverage.

Some option investors, eager to increase their premium income, mix covered and naked calls in a strategy known as "variable hedging." The variable hedger writes more than one option for each 100 shares owned.

For example, an investor who owns 100 shares of EFG Company at $40 writes three EFG 40 Calls for a premium of $4 each or a total premium income of $12. By definition, one call is covered and two are naked. The $12 premium could offset a substantial decline in the stock owned to $28. However, if the stock were to rise, each 1-point advance beyond $46 would increase the variable hedger's loss by $2 until the calls are finally exercised. At $46, the $12 premium offsets the $6 increased cost for each share of stock underlying each naked call.

The variable hedge, then, has two break-even points and at any price between them, the hedger will make a profit. In this example, the two points were $28 on the downside and $46 on the upside. Each additional option written extends the downside break-even point but lowers the upside break-even point. The investor receives greater premium income but is also exposed to the substantial risk inherent in writing naked calls. This risk combined with the difficulty of predicting short-term price changes makes writing naked calls hard to justify. Even if it appears certain that the stock will collapse, writing naked calls is not the best method of exploiting the anticipated decline. Either shorting the stock outright or buying a put will produce greater profits from a steep price drop because the writer's maximum profit is always limited to the premium.

All writers can buy-in the option at any time rather than wait for the expiration date. For example, a covered GHI Company $50 Call has been written for a $5 premium. The underlying stock, which the writer owns at $50 a share, advances to $55 and the premium advances to $7.00. If the stock appears to be headed higher, the writer could buy-in the option at $7.00. This closing purchase transaction would produce a $2 loss on the option trade, but would leave a $5 unrealized gain in the stock with the potential for greater profits if it continues to advance as expected.

Put writers, like call writers, hope the premiums they receive will mean additional income. Since put writers buy stock rather than sell stock, the contracts they write are not covered by stock as they are with call writers. Although it is possible to write covered puts as mentioned earlier, most puts are uncovered and are written against cash. Actually, if a put and a call have identical premiums, exercise prices, and expiration dates, the covered call writer and the uncovered put writer will have the same maximum dollar risk and reward after the options are written. *If the options are exercised, the premium a put writer receives reduces the purchase cost of the stock just as the premium from writing a covered call is part of the proceeds of the sale.*

Put writing, like call writing, also finds its greatest utility when the underlying stock neither increases nor decreases by more than the amount of the premium.

For most investors or traders who are considering options, WRITING them is preferable to BUYING them ... It puts the trader on the most profitable side of the transaction – the side on which *time* is an *ally*, not an *adversary*.

Thus, for this reason, writing covered calls and writing naked puts (but strictly against shares the investor intends to purchase anyway) represent the two best and most consistently-profitable applications of stock options. In both cases, they can add to the profitability (the return) on a portfolio.

	XYZ Calls at 40 Strike Price	XYZ Puts at 40 Strike Price
	Stock Price	*Stock Price*
In-the-money	Over 40	Under 40
At-the-money	40	40
Out-of-the-money	Under 40	Over 40

Premium Valuation At any given moment, the amount of an option's premium is a function of the following:

(1) The relationship or expected relationship between the current price of the underlying stock and the option's strike price.

(2) The amount of time remaining before the expiration date.

(3) The volatility of the underlying stock.

(4) The dividend of the underlying stock.

(5) The level and direction of short-term interest rates.

These factors are built into the premiums of all options and if they change, the level of the premiums will also change.

In practice, once the underlying stock and its probable direction have been identified, there is still the problem of selecting one option out of the many available to obtain the best combination of risk and reward. To do this, the option buyer must begin by answering two questions:

(1) What is the extent of the stock's expected move?

(2) In what time period will the stock make its expected move?

Stated simply, option premiums in the same class are two-dimensional. There is a vertical dimension involving the stock price/strike price relationship and a horizontal dimension involving time. By answering the two questions, the options investor will be better equipped to cope with these two dimensions.

The Vertical Dimension

The relationship of the stock price to the strike price determines whether an option is "in-the-money," "at-the-money," or "out-of-the-money," as the table above illustrates.

A call is in-the-money when the stock price is *above* the strike price, at-the-money when the stock price and the strike price are *identical*, and out-of-the-money when the stock price is *below* the strike price. Puts are described with the same terms but in reverse.

An in-the-money call option is said to have "intrinsic value" by the amount the underlying stock is above the strike price. Thus, in the example above, with the stock selling at $44, a call option's intrinsic value would be $4.00. The term "intrinsic value" is used to denote the value that can be captured immediately by exercising the option and selling the stock.

	Stock Price	Price Concession	Intrinsic Value	Premium	% of Stock Price	Time Cost	% of Stock Price
	52	—	12.00	13.375	25.7%	1.375	2.6%
	50	—	10.00	11.75	23.5	1.75	3.5
	48	—	8.00	10.00	20.8	2.00	4.2
	46	—	6.00	8.125	17.7	2.125	4.6
	44	—	4.00	6.375	14.5	2.375	5.4
	42	—	2.00	4.50	10.7	2.50	6.0
Strike Price	40	—	—	3.25	8.1	3.25*	8.1
	38	2.00	—	1.75	4.6	3.75	9.9
	36	4.00	—	1.125	3.1	5.125	14.2
	34	6.00	—	0.50	1.5	6.50	19.1
	32	8.00	—	0.25	0.8	8.25	25.8
	30	10.00	—	0.125	0.4	10.125	33.8
	28	12.00	—	0.06	0.2	12.06	43.1

* The greatest amount of "real" time cost.

Just as "intrinsic value" is used when evaluating premiums of in-the-money options, the term "price concession" is used for out-of-the-money options. Price concession, also called "extrinsic value," is the opposite of intrinsic value. It is the amount by which the stock is below the strike price. A call with a $40 strike price would have a price concession of $2 when the stock is $38. Neither intrinsic value nor price concession is fixed. Their amounts depend upon the current price of the underlying stock and, thus, will change as the stock's price changes. Both "intrinsic value" and "price concession" also apply to put options but, again, in reverse.

Unfortunately, intrinsic value and price concession do not entirely explain this vertical dimension. A trader who buys a call option for $5.00, when the stock is selling $3 above its strike, is paying $2 above the intrinsic value of the premium. *This $2 is the cost of the time remaining in the contract*. In other words, the difference between the premium and its intrinsic value is its "time cost." Time becomes less important as the stock price moves higher and as the intrinsic value increases.

Conversely, when the stock price declines below the strike price, the premium is purely time cost since the option has no intrinsic value. Although, on the surface, the premium appears low, there is a hidden time cost (the price concession).

Unlike intrinsic value when the option is in-the-money, price concession is not included in the premium. Even though price concession is only a theoretical time cost and not a "real" time cost, it should not be ignored.

The table at the top of this page shows there is less risk and less reward for the XYZ Call buyer the further the stock price is above the strike price. It also shows greater risk and greater reward the further the stock price is below the strike price. As the option acquires intrinsic value, it loses leverage. The relatively larger premium reduces the option's sensitivity to further increases in the price of the underlying stock (i.e., the option's reward). At the same time, the presence of intrinsic value also reduces risk.

Similarly, as price concession increases, risk also increases because the probability of the option ever attaining intrinsic value decreases. The reward potential is also increasing because a small premium investment could produce dramatic gains if the stock were to advance substantially.

The further the stock is from the strike price, either up or down, the more the stock must move to justify the option price. And the probability of a stock moving, say, 10% in the course of a few months is much greater than the probability of it moving 30% in the same time period.

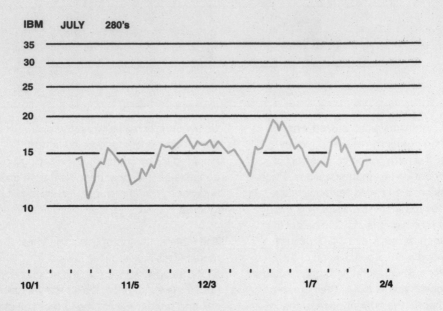

IBM   JULY   280's

35
30
25
20
15
10

10/1   11/5   12/3   1/7   2/4

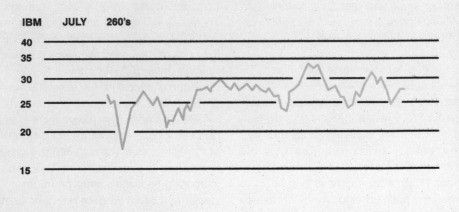

IBM   JULY   260's

40
35
30
25
20
15

10/1   11/5   12/3   1/7   2/4

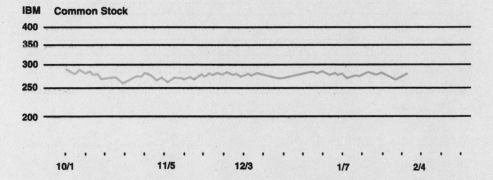

IBM Common Stock

400
350
300
250
200

10/1   11/5   12/3   1/7   2/4

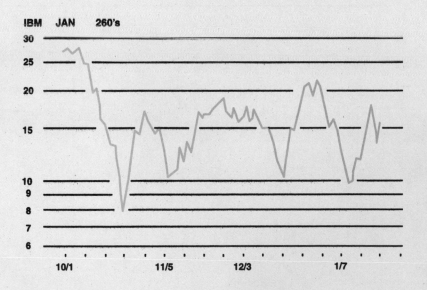

IBM   JAN   260's

30
25
20
15
10
9
8
7
6

10/1   11/5   12/3   1/7

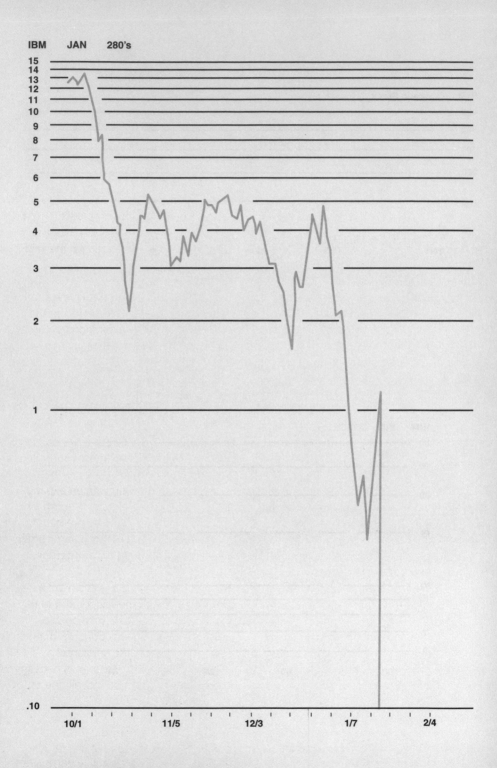

For these reasons, the buyer should choose an option that provides the best combination of a low premium and a low time cost as a percentage of the underlying stock's price. As the table suggests, the most favorable cost combination is generally found in a narrow band slightly above and slightly below the strike price.

The charts on the previous pages show the first three months of trading of the International Business Machines (IBM) July 260's and July 280's from October 1976 through January 1977 before the stock splits later in the 1990's. Throughout this period the July 260's were consistently in-the-money and the July 280's were consistently out-of-the-money. In these early months the percentage moves of the July 280's were greater than the July 260's. With both options having, or nearly having, intrinsic value, traders turned their interest to the option with the lower premium because they could participate in the stock's move for less money.

How far out-of-the-money should an option buyer go to obtain greater reward? The answer depends on the extent of the stock's expected move. Traders do not recognize an option's potential for attaining intrinsic value until the stock has moved closer to the strike price. In the meantime, other options in its class with strike prices closer to the stock price have outperformed it. This also explains why the volatility of a stock is a very important consideration in the valuation of option premiums.

The fate of an expiring out-of-the-money option can be seen by comparing the charts showing the expirations of the IBM January 280's and the IBM January 260's. The stock price was $275 when both expired in January.

The Horizontal Dimension

An option is a "wasting asset" because the time remaining up to the expiration date has a value that diminishes day-by-day. Clearly, an XYZ option with an expiration date only two weeks away is worth less (and should have a smaller premium) than another XYZ option with the same strike price but not expiring for six months.

It has been shown that a premium includes a time cost that varies according to the stock price/strike price relationship. This time cost also varies according to the time remaining. Hence, the horizontal dimension. For this reason, it is necessary to ask "In what time period will the stock make its expected move?"

The value of time can be seen by comparing the previous charts showing the early months of the IBM July 260's and the last few months of the January 260's. They traded side by side briefly at the same time. Each had the same strike price and the same intrinsic value or price concession at that given moment, but the premium of the July 260's was consistently $10 or more above the January 260's. Understandably, the January option was also much more sensitive to the stock's price swings.

Now, using the vertical and horizontal dimension concept, the investor can compare all options in the same class.

Consider the following real-life example, although the name has been changed...

On November 10, the common stock of XYZ Corporation closed at $47.75. An interested trader, believing the end of the stock's decline was near, glanced at the option tables in the newspaper. The following calls were available:

	January	April	July
XYZ 45	3.63	n/a	n/a
XYZ 50	1.13	2.13	2.63
XYZ 55	0.25	0.75	n/a
XYZ 60	no tr	0.25	0.75

The trader reasoned that the stock price would rebound 10% to 15% within the next two or three months. The analysis proved correct, but which option produced the maximum gain?

Two months later, on January 4, XYZ closed at $53.63, up 12%, and the XYZ call premiums closed as follows:

	January	April	July
XYZ 45	8.75	n/a	n/a
XYZ 50	3.88	4.88	5.50
XYZ 55	0.44	1.69	n/a
XYZ 60	no tr	0.31	0.88

From November to January, the XYZ calls increased by the percentages indicated below:

	January	April	July
XYZ 45	141%	—	—
XYZ 50	244%	129%	110%
XYZ 55	75%	125%	n/a
XYZ 60	—	25%	17%

The best results would have been obtained by purchasing the XYZ January 50's – the option with the strike price just above the stock price and with the shortest time period.

Many seasoned option buyers carry this idea a step further in a process called "walking up" an option. After the largest part of the premium's advance has been captured, the option is sold and the initial process is repeated over again. If the XYZ trader, for example, had expected the stock to continue its advance by another 10% to

15% in the January - April period, the January 50 Calls would be replaced by the April 55 Calls, available on January 4 for $1.69. The trader would hold the option until the stock was no longer expected to rise or until the stock crossed above the strike allowing the trader to walk up again.

This example enjoyed the benefit of 20-20 hindsight. In practice, correctly predicting a stock's short-term price change is considerably more difficult, often impossible. In fact, had the XYZ investor bought the April 55's, the outcome would have been disappointing.

Option buyers will find it easier to compare premiums than to value them on an absolute basis. While there are numerous sophisticated formulas and theories designed to compute theoretical premium values, even the professional floor traders and market makers of the leading options exchanges temper theoretical values with their trading senses. *Option buyers know how much can be lost but cannot say exactly how much might be made.*

Writers are in a somewhat better position to make value judgments because the premium received can be considered an investment return to be compared with other available short-term opportunities. *Option writers know how much can be made but cannot say exactly how much might be lost.*

The premium a writer receives is basically compensation for:

(1) Accepting the risk that the underlying stock could move adversely prior to the expiration date; and,

(2) Agreeing to support the option written with a reserve of either stock or cash during the option's life.

The premium compensation, expressed as an annual rate of return on the capital invested, will obviously be subject to change as the market environment changes. When interest rates rise and alternative investment opportunities become more attractive, a writer should either expect a greater return or consider placing the capital elsewhere. And the reverse is true when interest rates and other investment returns are declining.

There is significantly greater risk in writing an option than buying a Treasury bill, for example. Clearly, an option writer should demand much greater compensation. But whether the compensation must be double the Treasury bill rate, or triple the rate, before an investor is motivated to write options, will depend on that investor's perception of the risks and rewards involved. Some traders will simply accept a more modest return than will others.

Since option prices are equilibrium prices, a potential writer can quickly calculate what other option writers are demanding and buyers paying by reviewing the daily option quotations.

A writer, like a buyer, is usually faced with several strike prices and expiration dates. From these choices, the writer must select the option offering the best combination of risk and reward. For writers, as for buyers, this combination will most likely be found in the option that has a strike price slightly above or slightly below the current price of the underlying stock because, within this band, the writer will obtain the largest amount of "real" time cost.

The importance of real time cost is most evident when a covered call is written. In this instance, the writer's only possible net profit is, in fact, the amount of real time cost. For example, an investor buys IJK Company stock at $60 and, attracted by the large premium, writes an IJK 50 Call for $12. If the option is immediately exercised, the writer will deliver stock at $50. The $10 loss in the stock will be offset by the premium's $10 of intrinsic value. The writer's profit will be $2, or the premium's "real" time cost. If the stock had dropped to $50 and the option expired worthless, the net profit would also be $2. Of course, if the stock dropped by more than the total premium, the covered writer has a loss.

A writer's risk and reward combinations are the reverse of a buyer's ... the more in-the-money the option is when it is written, the greater the risk and reward; the more out-of-the-money, the less risk and reward.

The latest alterations in the tax laws changed the Internal Revenue Code which affects writers and other option investors. The combined impact of new and pre-existing tax laws on the economics of any options trade should be carefully reviewed by every options player with an accountant or tax advisor.

Reducing Risk One of the major attractions of options is their versatility. They can be used individually or combined in various ways to create strategies that modify an investor's risk/reward ratio. Many of these strategies are based directly on the relationships presented earlier. One very popular approach, called "spreading," involves the simultaneous purchase and sale of options on the same underlying stock. Of the numerous spreads available, two are frequently used in option investing: the vertical spread and the calendar spread.

The Vertical Spread

A vertical spread is formed by simultaneously buying (going long) and writing (going short) options on the same underlying stock with identical expiration dates but different strike prices. In a calendar spread, the options used have the same strike price but different expiration dates.

A premium is paid going long and a premium is received going short. Spreading takes its name from the "spread" or numerical difference between the two premiums. If the investor pays more than is received, the difference is called a "debit" and the investor is said to have "bought" the spread. A spread is "sold" with a "credit" if the premium received is greater than the premium paid. For example, a vertical spread created by going long IBM January 260's for 7.88 and shorting IBM January 280's for 2.13 would have been bought at a debit of 5.75. Reversing the transactions would yield a 5.75 credit. If a spread is bought, the difference between the two premiums must expand for the trader to profit. But if a spread is sold the difference must narrow. The increase or decline in the premium difference will depend on the movement of the underlying stock and the passage of time.

Vertical spread and calendar spreads can be designed to exploit either an increase in the price of the underlying stock or a decline. But "bullish" vertical or calendar spreads generally offer better risk/reward characteristics than "bearish" spreads.

The theory behind both types of spreads emphasizes the sensitivity of time cost to expiration date and to strike price, two familiar relationships explained earlier.

In a bullish vertical spread, the trader hopes to replace time cost with intrinsic value in the long option with the lower strike price. As the stock advances toward the higher strike price of the short option, and the expiration date draws near, the time cost of the long option will become an increasingly smaller percentage of the total premium. The short option, however, will only reflect time cost, since the stock has not crossed the higher strike price. As expiration approaches, the time value of the short option will decline rapidly and, unless the stock goes above the strike price, the option will ultimately expire worthless. In practice, however, the price change of the underlying stock might be the predominant influence rather than disappearing time cost. Secondly, spreads are frequently closed out before expiration.

In late October, when IBM was selling at $256.50, a bullish vertical spread could have been bought as follows:

Action	Option Series	Premium
Buy	January 260's	7.88
Sell	January 280's	2.13
		5.75 Debit

And, in late December, when the stock was 280, the spread could have been closed out at the following premiums:

Action	Option Series	Premium
Sell	January 260's	21.38
Buy	January 280's	4.88
		16.50 Credit

This spread, then, gave the investor a gross profit of 10.75 (the difference between the 16.50 ending credit and the 5.75 beginning debit) for a return of 87% on the 5.75 net investment before costs. Of course, in hindsight a trader can say it would have been more profitable to purchase the January 260 Call option alone. However, the point of spreading is to reduce the risk of a simple long or short position. By buying the spread for 5.75, the trader reduced the capital at risk by nearly 30% from the 7.88 premium of the single January 260 Call. And for this additional security, the trader accepted the certainty of a smaller reward.

With vertical spreads, both the maximum loss and the maximum theoretical profit at expiration can be determined from the outset. With bullish vertical spreads, the maximum profit is limited to the difference between the strike prices and the net premium paid. Should the underlying stock decline, the maximum loss would be the net premium paid. Thus, in the IBM spread the maximum gain could have been 14.25, the difference between 260 and 280, or 20, less the net premium paid of 5.75. Even if the underlying stock were to advance beyond the higher strike price, the gain could not be greater than 14.25 because the loss on the short option would offset the gain in the long option. And, if the stock dropped below the lower strike, the loss could be no greater than 5.75 since both options would expire worthless. These profit and loss boundaries are illustrated in the graphic. In addition, the chart shows that this spread would "break even" at 265.75, which means that the long option must acquire 5.75 of intrinsic value to offset the opening debit.

In a bearish vertical spread, the option with the lower exercise price is sold and the option with the higher exercise price is bought. As a result, the maximum theoretical profit at expiration will be the net premium received and the maximum potential loss will be the difference between the exercise prices minus the net premium received.

Maximum Theoretical Gain and Loss at Expiration Before Commissions and Taxes

Breakeven Point at 265¾

Maximum Gain 14¼

Stock Price

Maximum Loss 5¾

In selecting a vertical spread, the investor should follow these guidelines:

(1) The underlying stock should be able to reach or exceed the higher strike price in a bullish vertical spread, or a decline to or below the lower strike price in a bearish vertical spread.

(2) The debit, expressed as a percentage of the difference between the two strike prices, should be kept as small as possible in a bullish spread. The credit in a bearish spread should be as large as possible. Attractive percentages might be 30% or less for a bullish spread and 70% or higher for a bearish spread. In each spread a lower debit or a higher credit brings the break-even point that much closer.

(3) Perhaps stocks selling for $50 or more should be considered first, since the difference between the premiums will be $10 or $20 and commissions might be lower than for stocks selling below $50.

The Calendar Spread

While vertical spreading emphasizes the interrelationships of stock price and strike prices (i.e., the vertical dimension of options) the theory of calendar spreading stresses the importance of time (the horizontal dimension). In a calendar spread, the investor first selects the appropriate strike price and then builds the spread by using two of the three expiration dates in whatever combination that produces the greatest reward. In most calendar spreads, one option with a closer expiration date is sold short and the other option with a more distant expiration date is bought long. Almost all calendar spreads will begin with a debit since the longer term option will always have a larger premium than the nearer term option. As time passes, however, the spread between the two premiums should widen, allowing the investor to buy back the short option for significantly less while selling the long option for only slightly less than its purchase price.

The calendar spreader understands a simple fact of option valuation presented earlier, namely, that an option approaching expiration loses time cost far more rapidly than an option with several months of life remaining. This is particularly true for an expiring out of the money option, a condition dramatically illustrated on the chart of the expiring IBM January 280. The calendar spreader hopes the short option will share a similar fate.

A successful calendar spread might resemble the following example. In late June, these quotations appear in the financial section of a local newspaper:

Option	NYSE Close	Strike Price	Jul	Oct	Jan
KLM	$58.75	60	1.50	4.00	5.00

The trader, believing the underlying stock will remain relatively stable, buys a calendar spread for a debit of 1 by selling short an KLM Oct 60 at 4.00 and going long the KLM Jan 60 at 5.00. During the next several months, the stock has a series of small gains and losses but stays close to the strike price. Just before the October expiration, with the stock selling for $59, the October option is quoted at 0.50, while the January option is quoted at 3.50 since it still has three months of remaining life. At this point, the trader successfully closes out the spread with a credit of 3. The trader's initial $100 risk was able to produce a $200 gain (the difference between the closing credit and the beginning debit) even though the underlying stock remained steady. However, if the underlying stock had a large move, either up or down, most likely the spread would have ended in the loss of nearly the entire debit. The spread must widen in a calendar spread, but as the stock moves further away from the strike price, the spread will narrow.

Calendar spreads should be appraised with the following requirements in mind:

(1) The underlying stock should be expected to trade in a narrow band slightly below or slightly above the strike price. The effect of large unexpected moves in the underlying stock will always be greater than the effect of diminishing time cost. As noted, large moves either up or down may force the spread into a loss.

(2) The short option should have a large "real" time cost which, again, will be found in the option with a strike price close to the price of the underlying stock.

(3) The initial debit should be small relative to a realistic projection of the spread's potential gain. In other words, it is ill-advised to risk an opening debit of, say, 4 if the spread's ultimate gain will be a net credit of 1.

Although vertical and calendar spreads can produce nice gains, their effectiveness is hampered by three major drawbacks:

(1) **Commissions** A commission is paid every time an option is bought or sold. Opening and closing transactions on a typical vertical or calendar spread can, therefore, result in four commission charges. Even though commissions were excluded for simplicity in the examples of spreads just presented, the investor should always include this cost when computing any spread's potential gain or loss. In any spreading strategy, it is usually best to use

The Options Trading Room at the Philadelphia Stock Exchange

several options. For example, the commission expense for five short and five long options should be proportionately smaller than only one short and one long. Any spread that yields a profit only to have much of it consumed by commissions is appropriately known as an "alligator" spread.

(2) **Volatility** Judging the short-term price movement of the underlying stock is essential to the success of all option activity. Unfortunately, this is not as easy as it seems. Without knowing the volatility of the stock this task becomes even more difficult.

(3) **Exercise** The spreader may receive an exercise notice against the short option at any time. The probability of exercise increases as the underlying stock gains intrinsic value. Exercise radically alters the risk/reward ratio, which was the basis for the spread's creation. It leaves the investor with a simple long position. Depending on the circumstances, the spreader may respond to an exercise notice by:

- Exercising the long call and delivering the stock.

- Delivering stock already owned.

- Buying stock in the open market.

- Delivering stock borrowed from the broker by shorting the stock and maintaining the long call as a hedge.

Hedging

Options can be used as a hedge to reduce risk in much the same way an insurance policy can provide protection against a catastrophic loss. If an investor owns stock and does not want to sell it, even though it may decline in the near future, a put option could be bought as a temporary hedge.

Investors should carefully review the tax consequences of any hedge beforehand. In certain instances, the holding period of the stock owned could be altered. Nevertheless, hedging a long position is sometimes worth considering.

The benefits of a short sale hedge involving the purchase of a call against an ordinary short sale position might be more compelling. The short seller is mainly concerned with the potential "unlimited loss" that could result if the price of the short stock were to soar. A short "squeeze" is particularly unnerving because additional capital is required when the stock is covered at higher prices – as opposed to owning a declining stock outright. Short sale hedging can be especially effective during a bear market when call premiums are often depressed.

Puts and Calls Combined Often unpredictable corporate events place investors in a precarious position. They believe, or sense, that the price of a given

MNO Company
Straddle

Bought	Sold	Profit/Loss
April 50 Call @ $4.00 $6.50	April 50 Call @ $10.50	Profit +
April 50 Put @ $3.50 $3.00	April 50 Put @ $ 0.50	Loss −
Total Premium Paid $7.50	Total Premium Received $11.00	Total Gross Profit $3.50

stock is about to change substantially, but they do not know whether it will rise or fall. Such a situation might occur if a pending lawsuit is about to be resolved. If the company wins, its stock might rise sharply, but if it loses, it could drop precipitously. While many investors wait on the sidelines for the smoke to clear, a risk-conscious options investor might immediately use a strategy known as a "straddle."

A straddle consists of an equal number of puts and calls purchased or written simultaneously with identical strike prices and expiration dates. It enables the buyer to profit from a major price change in either direction while limiting the risk to the total combined premiums paid. Conversely, straddles produce substantial premium income for straddle writers who take the contrary view that the stock price will change little if at all.

Assume that the stock of the MNO Company has been trading steadily in early January at $50 a share awaiting certain corporate developments that could conceivably alter the price dramatically either up or down. An option buyer, convinced that a major price change will occur within the next three months, yet unsure of its direction, concludes that a straddle will be profitable. The MNO investor buys, simultaneously, an April 50 Call for 4 and an April 50 Put for 3.50. By early April, the stock has advanced 20% to $60 a share.

The call premium is now priced at 10.50, while the put premium has fallen to 0.50. If the straddle is now "unwound," that is, terminated, through closing sale transactions, the options investor would have a $3.50 ($350) gross profit on the initial $7.50 ($750) investment as shown in the illustration.

Depending on the amount of time remaining, it might be better to risk expiration rather than sell the put. It could regain some value if the stock were to drop suddenly.

Of course, the call could be exercised to acquire the stock which would then be sold to capture the profit. In practice, however, most straddles terminate in closing sale or purchase transactions.

If the stock had declined sharply instead of rising, the put would have been profitable, but not the call. A closing sale or exercise of the put would produce results virtually identical to those obtained from the profitable call.

This basic example provides the straddle buyer with several important guidelines:

(1) The total premium establishes the straddle's "break-even points." The underlying stock must rise or fall by an amount equal to the combined premium before any profits can be realized. In the

Here are simple graphics to demonstrate the profit and loss characteristics of each of these strategies:

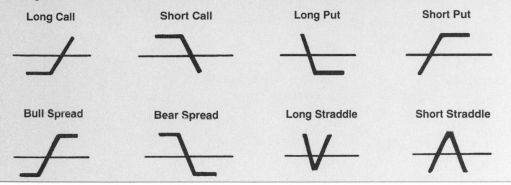

| Long Call | Short Call | Long Put | Short Put |
| Bull Spread | Bear Spread | Long Straddle | Short Straddle |

example above, the break-even points were 57.50 and 42.50 because the initial premium was 7.50 or 15% of the stock's price. The stock had to move at least 15% in either direction before the straddle was profitable. It is, therefore, important for the investor to keep the total premium as low as possible and the terms of the contracts realistic.

(2) A straddle involves "round trip" commissions on two options. As in other option strategies such as spreading and variable hedging, multiple commission charges must be computed accurately. Commission costs can easily turn a profitable trade into a loss. In addition, the trader should consult a tax advisor to anticipate the tax effects of any trade.

(3) While the prospect of a double premium is enticing, a potential straddle writer should remember that a sharp move can produce a substantial loss. If the stock is not owned and it rises sharply and the call is exercised, the writer would have to purchase the higher-priced shares in the open market. If the stock declines and the put is exercised, the investor might have to produce a large and immediate cash payment to pay for the put stock.

Above are simple graphics to demonstrate the profit and loss characteristics of several popular strategies.

Puts and calls can be combined in several other ways to create various risk and reward strategies as in the "strip" – two puts and one call; or the "strap" – two calls and one put. The possibilities are almost endless and their names are no less esoteric – long butterfly, short butterfly, long strangle, short strangle, ratio call spread, ratio put spread, call ratio back-spread, put ratio back-spread, and the box or conversion.

These and other exotic methods should be avoided until using individual puts and calls becomes second nature. And, even then, each new idea should be scrutinized carefully with special emphasis on tax consequences, margin requirements, and commissions. An investor might find in some instances that simply buying or selling an unadorned put or call is more effective than creating the complex web of a supposedly advanced strategy.

Index Options In recent years, the use of options has grown far beyond individual equity applications. Options are being offered on interest rates, currencies, and now, most importantly, stock indexes. With options on indexes, an investor can buy or sell calls or puts on groups of stocks or industries in the same way options are used for individual stocks.

These stock groups can be small and specialized, such as the index on the semiconductor stocks (the SOXX), or on large, highly-diversified market indexes such as the S&P 500 Index (the SPX), the S&P 100 Index (the OEX), or the Dow Industrial Average (the DJX).

Also, option contracts can be applied to ETFs. Among the most popular of these are the NASDAQ 100 Trust (QQQ), the S&P 500 Spider (SPY), and the DJIA Diamonds (DIA) offering leveraged ways to play market swings. In short, the investors and traders of today have a broad range of opportunities to buy or sell the "market," or segments of it, to hedge or to speculate, with varying degrees of risk.

The next page illustrates how the table for the OEX appears in a newspaper (in this case, the *Investor's Business Daily*). The table is similar to individual stock options. On this day, the OEX close was 426.68. The strike closest to it is called the "central strike" (the 425s) and any options above or below are either "in" or "out-of-the-money."

Program Trading This chapter would not be complete without including more on this increasingly-important market factor.

Program trading is defined as "strategies that involve the purchase or sale of 15 or more stocks with a market value of $1 million or more," program trading cannot be detected by simply reading the morning newspaper, although the statistics are published. However, the volatility and random swings that result can be seen by most investors every day.

One better-known example of program trading is "index arbitrage," which involves the purchase or sale of a basket of stocks in conjunction with the sale or purchase of a derivative product such as futures or options. The objective is to capture the difference between the two prices.

In 2000, about 25% of NYSE daily volume was due to program trading. Today, it is closer to 40%.

Index Options

P / C	Strike Price	Feb Vol.	Feb Price	Mar Vol.	Mar Price	Apr Vol.	Apr Price
SP100				Close 426.68 Apr			
c390		40	49	....	....	....	....
c400		....	....	2	43^{30}	....	....
c420		108	17^{50}	....	....	....	....
c425		154	14^{20}	....	....	....	....
c430		296	11^{60}	13	19^{20}	....	....
c435		464	9	2	19	....	....
c440		1174	7^{20}	7	17^{50}	....	....
c445		1129	5^{40}	....	....	....	....
c450		2285	4	47	10^{10}	....	....
c455		824	2^{80}	3	8	....	....
c460		1291	2^{10}	38	6^{80}	....	....
c465		399	1^{70}	6	6	....	....
c470		620	1^{10}	65	4^{90}	....	....
c475		1108	0^{75}	4	4^{30}	....	....
c480		615	0^{50}	52	3^{30}	10	6^{30}
c485		140	0^{40}	....	....	....	....
c490		1170	0^{25}	20	2^{05}	....	....
c495		15	0^{20}	....	....	....	....
c500		286	0^{16}	121	1^{20}	1	3
c505		35	0^{10}	....	....	....	....
c510		200	0^{15}	....	....	....	....
c515		63	0^{05}	....	....	....	....
c520		158	0^{05}	300	0^{45}	110	1^{35}

P / C	Strike Price	Feb Vol.	Feb Price	Mar Vol.	Mar Price	Apr Vol.	Apr Price
p300		210	0^{05}	208	0^{60}	201	1^{40}
p320		....	....	150	1^{15}	....	....
p340		100	0^{25}	103	1^{95}	10	3^{60}
p350		60	0^{50}	....	....	....	....
p360		22	0^{75}	2	4	....	....
p370		781	1^{30}	1	5	....	....
p380		359	1^{95}	202	6^{80}	....	....
p390		312	3^{20}	3	9	....	....
p395		261	3^{90}	....	....	....	....
p400		1509	4^{70}	1471	11^{50}	146	15
p405		147	6	....	....	....	....
p410		577	7	6	14	....	....
p415		108	8^{30}	....	....	....	....
p420		699	10^{30}	68	18	26	22^{90}
p425		340	12^{50}	10	20^{20}	....	....
p430		1124	14^{80}	22	22^{60}	9	26
p435		407	17	19	23^{30}	....	....
p440		198	20^{10}	24	27^{20}	6	29
p445		1	21^{20}	1	29^{50}	....	....
p450		54	28^{10}	109	33^{20}	....	....
p455		55	32	....	....	....	....
p460		152	36^{10}	55	40^{70}	4	39
p465		1	35^{60}	....	....	....	....
p470		86	40^{90}	....	....	....	....
p480		25	50^{70}	....	....	....	....

Conclusion Options present a special challenge. The investor must not only judge whether a stock is going up or down but when and roughly by how much.

It has been demonstrated that puts and calls can be used in any type of market. They can be used alone or in various combinations to create numerous risk and reward opportunities. But for the vast majority of investors reading this book, the two best and most consistently-profitable applications of options are:

- Writing covered calls; and

- Writing naked puts as a less expensive way to buy shares that would have been purchased otherwise.

Yet, in the final analysis, successful option investing ultimately rests on the accurate assessment of the underlying investment potential of the stock or index in question. And this is, after all, the entire reason for *Understanding Wall Street*.

Sources

14

annual meeting A stockholder meeting, normally held at the same time each year, to elect the company's board of directors and transact other corporate business.

arbitrage The practice of buying and selling two separate but related securities to profit from the difference in their values. An arbitrage opportunity often arises when two companies plan to merge or when one security is convertible into another.

asset Anything of value owned by a company. Assets can include cash, product inventory and other current assets, as well as land, buildings, equipment.

authorized See "shares authorized."

averaging down The purchase of additional shares of already-owned stock at lower prices to reduce the average cost per share of all shares held.

balance sheet A financial statement showing the company's assets (what the company owns), its liabilities (what it owes), and the difference, called "net worth" or "stockholders' equity."

bear market An extended declining trend in stock prices occurring usually in a time period of months or years.

beta (coefficient) The second letter of the Greek alphabet used by Wall Street to describe the volatility of a stock relative to a stock market index (market's beta = 1). The term is used to describe a stock's risk.

block A large amount of stock sold as a single unit. The term is most often used to describe a unit of 10,000 shares or more.

blue sky laws State laws designed to protect investors from "blue sky" (worthless) securities.

board of directors A group of people elected by the stockholders, usually annually, to exercise powers granted by the corporation's charter. These powers could include appointments of officers, issuance of shares, and declaration of dividends.

bond A certificate of indebtedness extending over a period of more than one year from the time it is issued. A debt of less than one year is usually called a "note." A bond is an obligation that must be repaid at a certain time. Meanwhile, the borrower pays interest to the bondholder for the use of the money.

book value The equity value of an outstanding share of stock. Book value is determined by dividing the amount of stockholders' equity to which each share is entitled by the average number of shares outstanding.

broad tape A news service used by brokerage firms and other business offices. The service provides a continuous printed stream of current business news items. The news is printed on a "broad tape" of paper.

bull market An extended rising trend in stock prices generally occurring within a time period of months or years.

buyout See "leveraged buyout."

calendar spread An investment strategy of buying and selling options on the same underlying security, with the options having identical strike prices but different expiration dates.

call option A contract giving the holder a right to buy 100 shares of a stock at a predetermined price (called the striking price) any time up to a predetermined expiration date. A call option is bought to profit by a rise in the stock's price.

capital gain A gain realized on the sale or exchange of securities, fixed property, or similar assets. Under current IRS rules, a capital gain is taxable.

capital loss A loss realized on the sale or exchange of securities, fixed property, or similar assets. The loss can sometimes be used to reduce taxes.

capitalism A profit-oriented economic system involving the private ownership of production and distribution in a competitive environment.

capitalization All money that has been invested in the business including equity capital (common stock and preferred stock), long-term debt (bonds), retained earnings, and other surplus funds.

cash flow Loosely defined as "net income plus depreciation." The term is frequently used to describe the amount of internally-generated cash available for dividends and/or for the purchase of additional assets.

class (of options) All options, both calls and puts, covering the same underlying security.

closed-end fund An investment company with a limited number of shares. To buy or sell, a shareholder must buy from or sell to another person, rather than deal directly with the investment company. Closed-end funds often sell at a market discount.

conglomerate A broadly diversified corporation that offers a large number of products and/or services in many unrelated industries. Rightly or wrongly, the term connotes a lack of corporate direction by management.

convertible debenture A debenture that is convertible into common shares at the option of the owner.

convertible preferred stock A preferred stock that is convertible into common shares at the option of the owner.

corner Such complete supply/demand control of a security that its price can be manipulated. The practice is illegal today and the term is primarily historic.

coupon A promise to pay interest when due, usually attached to a bond. When the due date arrives, the coupon is detached and submitted for payment. The term also refers to a bond's interest rate – and this is the more frequent use of the word.

current assets Assets that are expected to be converted to cash within 12 months.

current liabilities Obligations that will be paid within 12 months.

current ratio The ratio of current assets to current liabilities. The current ratio is calculated by dividing current assets by current liabilities. Current assets at least twice current liabilities is considered a healthy ratio for most businesses.

debenture An unsecured (without collateral) bond issued on the good word and general credit of the borrower.

deflation The economic condition of falling prices for goods and services. It is the inverse to inflation – an increasing buying power of cash and a substantially reduced amount of currency in circulation.

depreciation The estimated decrease in value of property due to use, deterioration, or obsolescence over a period of time. Although depreciation does not require a cash outlay, it is a cost of doing business.

derivatives A wide variety of financial instruments whose value is determined in part from the value and characteristics of another security (the "underlying security"). Options and futures are examples.

discount The amount below the list price or face value. A bond discount refers to the excess of the face value over its current market price. A bond that sells below 100 (below par) is said to be "selling at a discount."

disinflation A condition of inflation, but at a declining rate as witnessed in the 1981 to 1986 period.

dividend A payment to stockholders, usually in the form of a quarterly check. The dividend is declared by the board of directors and is normally determined by the level of the company's earnings.

dividend reinvestment plan or **"DRIP"** An investment plan involving the automatic reinvestment of stock dividends, usually sponsored by the company declaring and paying the dividend.

dollar-cost-averaging An investment approach that involves consistently buying uniform dollar amounts of a security regardless of the price. When prices are low, more shares are bought than when prices are high.

dual listing The same security listed on more than one exchange.

earned surplus Another term for "retained earnings."

earnings The amount of profit a company realizes after all costs, expenses, and taxes have been paid. See also "net earnings."

earnings per share The net earnings divided by the average shares outstanding.

EBITDA A term popular with analysts that refers to "earnings before interest, taxes, depreciation, and amortization."

equity See "stockholders' equity."

expiration date The date on which an option expires. In recent years, the expiration date has been designated as the Saturday immediately following the third Friday of the expiration month.

extrinsic value Another term for "price concession."

Fibonacci series A series of numbers, popular among technical analysts, that is defined by each new number being a sum of the prior two. For example: 1, 2, 3, 5, 8, 13, 21, 34, and so on.

financing The sale of new stock or bonds by a corporation in order to raise capital.

float The number of shares currently available for trading. The float is calculated by deducting, from the shares outstanding, the number of shares closely held by individuals or institutions not likely to sell immediately if the stock price rises.

free cash flow Defined as "net income plus depreciation, less the total of dividends, capital expenditures, required debt repayments, and any other scheduled cash outlays." Also loosely defined as "cash flow plus after-tax interest plus any non-cash decrease in net working capital."

front-running The illegal practice by a specialist to buy or sell for his personal account ahead of a customer.

fundamentalist One who believes that stock prices are determined by the future course of earnings and dividends. The fundamentalist studies, among other things, economics, industry conditions, and corporate financial statements.

futures A contract specifying a future date of delivery of a certain amount of tangible or intangible product. Such products might include commodities such as grains or metals; and financial instruments.

going public A term used to describe the initial sale of shares of a privately held company to the public for the first time. In more recent years, the term "Initial Public Offering" (IPO) has been used more often.

government-sponsored entities (GSE's) Government-sponsored mortgage resellers such as Fannie Mae and Freddie Mac. GSE paper is not government-guaranteed.

greenmail The unethical act of buying stock in a company, threatening to take control, then demanding that those shares be purchased by the company – usually at a price higher than other shareholders can obtain on the open market.

gross profits Profits earned from a basic manufacturing or service operation – before selling costs and other expenses are deducted and before taxes are paid.

hedge fund A managed portfolio created for 100 or fewer (usually-wealthy) clients to provide various methods of offsetting excessive market risk elsewhere. Hedge fund activities can involve short selling, program trading, swaps, and derivatives.

income statement A financial statement that presents a company's business results over a specific period of time, usually quarterly or annually. It shows, in dollar terms, all revenues, costs and expenses, taxes, and earnings.

index The measure of a combined, representative value of a group of stocks, bonds, currencies, commodities, or other interests. An index is ordinarily expressed in relation to its original "base" value.

index option A call or put option having an index (rather than an individual stock) as the underlying security. Index options are similar in many ways to listed stock options except that exercising is settled with a cash payment rather than receiving or delivering stock.

inflation The economic condition of rising prices for goods and services. Inflation refers to a declining buying power of cash and a substantially greater amount of currency in circulation. It is generally the result of excessive government spending.

initial public offering (IPO) See "going public."

insider An officer or director of a company – or another person having access to corporate information not available to the public.

Instinet A subscriber service for displaying tentative bid and ask quotations.

institutional investor A bank, mutual fund, pension fund, insurance company, university, or other institution that invests in the securities markets.

interest The compensation a borrower pays a lender for the use of money borrowed.

interim report A company report, usually quarterly, that presents a company's business results (income statement) for the period and usually the current financial condition (balance sheet). During the year a company will normally issue three interim reports and one annual report.

intrinsic value The amount by which the current price of the underlying security is above the call option's strike price (or below the put option's strike price). An option that has intrinsic value is said to be "in-the-money."

"irrational exuberance" A term made famous by then Federal Reserve Board Chairman Alan Greenspan in the early days of the dot-com bubble in late 1996.

junk bonds Bonds that are issued having little or no collateral or liquidation value. Junk bonds typically offer high interest income and very high risk. Bonds of this type have been popular instruments in buyouts, corporate mergers, and acquisitions.

leveraged buyout Acquiring control of a company, usually using debt. Typically, the stock is purchased by employees or a group of investors with the help of an investment banker.

liability Anything a company owes. Liabilities can include current liabilities as well as debt to be repaid in later years (e.g., bonds).

liquidate The action of selling assets or securities to obtain cash.

liquidity The ability of a stock to absorb a large amount of buying or selling without disturbing the price substantially.

load mutual fund An open-end investment company that charges the investor a fee when the investor buys the fund shares. This fee (or "load," as it is called) is used primarily to compensate salespeople selling the fund.

long term debt Liabilities that are expected to be repaid after twelve months.

margin account An account, typically with a brokerage firm, that allows an investor to buy or sell securities on credit. An investor can, depending on the rules, borrow up to 50% or more of the investment value.

market breadth The extent or scope of change in stock prices. Market breadth is most often measured by the number of stocks that advanced or declined during the period and their volume, or by counting the number of stocks hitting new highs or new lows over the past 52 weeks.

market order An order to buy or sell at the best possible price as soon as it can be accomplished.

municipal bond A bond issued by a state, territory, or possession of the United States or by any municipality, political subdivision, or agency. Included are bonds issued by cities, counties, school districts, and authorities.

mutual fund An open-end investment company. A mutual fund offers the investor the benefits of portfolio diversification (i.e., owning more shares to provide greater safety and reduce volatility).

NASDAQ (pronounced "nazdak") The computerized National Association of Securities Dealers Automatic Quotation system that provides brokers and dealers with price quotations of securities traded over-the-counter.

net earnings or **net income** or **net profit** The profit a company realizes after all costs, expenses, and taxes have been deducted from revenues. See also "earnings."

net profit margin The profitability of a company after taxes are paid. The net profit margin is calculated by dividing net earnings by total revenues (sales and other income).

net worth See "stockholders' equity."

no-load mutual fund An open-end investment company that allows investors to buy and sell fund shares without paying a fee (called the "load"). A no-load fund is sold by word-of-mouth and advertising since it typically has no salespeople.

odd lot Any number of shares less than a round lot. Normally, an odd lot is 1 to 99 shares with a round lot being 100 shares or a multiple of 100 shares.

odd lot differential A small extra charge an investor pays if an odd lot is purchased. The amount is ordinarily $0.125 per share.

open-end investment company An investment company that uses its capital to invest in other companies. Its shareholders can participate directly because the open-end investment company will sell or buy its own shares at book value. See also "mutual fund."

open order An order still pending or on the books to buy or sell a security, but not yet executed. An open order will remain in effect until it is either executed or cancelled.

operating profit The profit a company earns from operations before taxes are paid. It is the remainder after deducting all operating costs from sales.

operating profit margin The profitability of a company's operations before taxes are paid. The operating profit margin is calculated by dividing operating profits by sales.

option A contract allowing an investor to purchase or sell 100 shares of stock at a predetermined price any time up to a predetermined expiration date.

Option Clearing Corporation (OCC) The central bookkeeping operation that issues standardized options and matches the buyers and sellers of options. The OCC is a clearing agency, regulated by the Securities and Exchange Commission.

outstanding See "shares outstanding."

paper profit A profit that has not been realized. In most cases, the term "paper profit" refers to the profit an investor has on a security that was purchased earlier but has not yet been sold.

par value In bonds, par value refers to the stated value of a bond (usually $1,000 or 100). In stocks, par value is an arbitrary value primarily used for bookkeeping purposes.

pattern day trader A trader who buys and sells the same stock on the same day at least three times in a five day period. An equity balance of no less than $25,000 must be maintained in the margin account.

payout ratio The proportionate amount of earnings paid out to stockholders as a dividend. For example, a company that pays a $0.25 dividend out of every $1.00 of earnings has a payout ratio of 25%.

pink sheets A daily list of over-the-counter stocks not traded on NASDAQ and the broker/dealers making markets in them. The pink sheets normally show the bid and asked prices of the prior day.

preferred stock A stock that has prior claim on dividends (and/or assets in the case of corporate dissolution) up to a certain amount before the common stockholders are entitled to anything.

premium The amount above the list price or face value. A bond premium refers to the excess of the market price over its face value. A bond that sells above 100 (above par) is said to be "selling at a premium."

premium (of an option) The market price of an option. This is the price that the buyer of an option pays and the writer of an option receives. The premium is determined by the supply and demand of the option's buyers and sellers as they assess the future market value of the underlying security.

pretax margin The profitability a company before taxes are paid. The pretax margin is calculated by dividing pretax profits by total revenues (sales and other income).

pretax profits The profit a company earns before paying taxes. It is the amount remaining after deducting all costs and expenses, other than taxes, from total revenues.

price concession The opposite of intrinsic value. It is the amount by which the current price of the underlying security is below a call option's strike price (or above a put option's strike price). An option having a price concession is said to be "out-of-the-money."

price/earning ratio or **P/E ratio** The relationship between the price of a stock and its earnings per share. The P/E ratio is calculated by dividing the stock price by the earnings per share figure. A stock selling at $45 with earnings of $3.00 per share has a price/earnings ratio of 15.

private placement A stock or bond issue that is sold by a company directly to an investor or a group of investors without involving an underwriter or registration with the SEC.

profit margin The profitability of a firm measured by relating profits to revenues. The three most common profit margin calculations are: operating profit margin, pretax profit margin, and net profit margin.

program trading Computer-driven, automatically-executed securities trades (usually in large volume) of a basket of 15 or more stocks. Also, with index arbitrage, the objective is to capture the arbitrage profits available when, for example, stock indexes and their futures are being traded.

prospectus A document issued by a corporation at the time securities are offered providing buyers or potential buyers with pertinent details and data on the corporation and the security being issued. Also see "red herring."

proxy A written authorization by a stockholder allowing a representative or someone else to vote for or against directors and business proposals at the annual meeting. The results of these votes are usually announced at the meeting.

proxy fight Two or more groups soliciting signed proxies from stockholders to gain a voting majority. Usually it is to win control and oust the incumbent management.

put option A contract giving the holder the right to sell 100 shares of a stock at a predetermined price (called the striking price) any time up to a predetermined expiration date. A put option is bought to profit by a decline in the stock's price.

quick-asset ratio or acid-test ratio Current assets less inventories as a percent of current liabilities (i.e., current assets minus inventories divided by current liabilities). Some accounting experts prefer dividing the sum of cash and marketable securities by current liabilities. A company's position is considered healthy when quick assets exceed current liabilities.

random walk A stock market theory based on the belief that stock price movements are completely random and unpredictable.

red herring A preliminary prospectus easily identified because much of the cover is printed in red as a warning to investors that the document is not complete or final.

Regulation T The FRB regulation that sets the minimum margin requirement.

reinvestment rate The internal growth potential of a company. The reinvestment rate is calculated by multiplying the firm's return on equity by the retention rate.

retained earnings Earnings that have been reinvested back into the business after dividends are paid to stockholders. Retained earnings is often an important component of a company's stockholders' equity figure. Another name for retained earnings is "earned surplus."

retention rate The percent of net earnings available for reinvestment into the company after dividends are paid to stockholders. The retention rate is also the inverse of the payout ratio. If the payout ratio is 25%, the retention rate is 75%.

return on equity The rate of investment return a company earns on stockholders' equity. Return on equity is calculated by dividing net earnings by the average stockholders' equity figure.

revenues or **total revenues** A term used loosely to describe the income sources of a corporation (i.e., sales and other income) before any costs or expenses are deducted.

reverse stock split The opposite of a stock split. A 1-for-10 reverse split, for example, is analogous to receiving a dime for ten pennies. A reverse split is usually done to raise the stock's market price.

round lot A standard unit of trading or a multiple thereof. Generally speaking, the unit of trading is 100 shares in the case of stocks and $1,000 par value for bonds.

Rule 13-d An SEC rule requiring the disclosure of beneficial ownership of 5% or more of any security registered with the Securities and Exchange Commission.

sales The total dollar value of products sold. It is the number of units sold multiplied by the sales price per unit.

Sarbanes-Oxley Act of 2002 A new law that addresses a wide range of corporate-accountability issues. Among them, CEOs and CFOs must certify their companies' annual and quarterly financial reports subject to civil and criminal penalties.

secondary A large block of stock purchased by a securities firm or a group of firms for resale, usually in smaller lots at a fixed price. The stock is purchased from existing stockholders, not the company.

Securities and Exchange Commission The SEC was established by Congress to administer the Securities Act of 1933 and several other investment related acts.

senior securities Bonds and/or preferred stocks within the capitalization of a corporation. These securities are considered "senior" to the common stock.

series (of an option) Options that cover an underlying security and that expire on a specific month (e.g., the "July" series).

settlement date The date on which money or securities are due once securities have been purchased or sold (three business days after the trade date).

shares authorized The maximum number of shares allowed to be issued under a corporation's charter. Additional shares require a charter amendment.

shares outstanding The number of authorized shares that have been issued and are now in the hands of owners.

shelf registration A registration of a new issue that can be prepared up to two years in advance to make funds available when the market conditions are right.

short "against the box" A short sale involving stock that is already owned (rather than borrowing it). This trading technique, no longer allowed, was once used primarily for tax reasons.

short interest Shares that have been sold short but not yet repurchased.

short sale A trading technique typically used when a stock is expected to decline in price. A short sale involves selling borrowed stock anticipating that the same number of shares will be repurchased later at a lower price. The repurchased shares are then returned to the owner from whom they were borrowed.

sinking fund An arrangement whereby a portion of a bond or preferred stock issue is retired periodically prior to its fixed maturity date.

soft dollars A payment, typically for research services, by using commissions or underwriting fees in lieu of cash.

spread The difference between two values; most often used to describe the difference between the "bid" and the "asked" prices.

statement of income See "income statement."

stock dividend A dividend paid in securities rather than cash.

stock split A division of a company's shares into a greater or lesser number. A 2-for-1 stock split, for example, is analogous to the division of a dime into two nickels.

stockholders' equity The difference between a company's total assets and total liabilities. Stockholders' equity, sometimes called "net worth," is the stockholders' ownership in the company.

stop order or **stop-loss order** An order to buy or sell that becomes a "market order" when the stock sells at or through a specific price (called the "stop price"). A stop order is typically used to protect paper profits or limit the extent of possible loss.

straddle An investment strategy of simultaneously buying or writing both a call and put on the same underlying security, with the options having identical exercise prices and expiration dates.

"street" name A term that applies to securities held in the broker's name rather than in the customer's name. Securities purchased on margin are held in street name. The customer can request street name for convenience or other reasons.

striking price The predetermined exercise price of a stock option. It is also frequently called the "strike price."

swap(s) An exchange of stream of payments over time according to specific terms. For example, an interest rate swap is one in which one party agrees to pay a fixed interest rate in return for receiving an adjustable rate from another party.

technical analyst or **technician** One who studies all factors related to the actual supply and demand of stocks, bonds, or commodities. The primary tools of a technician are stock charts and various technical indicators.

tender offer An offer by a company or a special group to purchase stock of another company. Usually the tender is made at a price above the prevailing market price.

third market The buying and selling of exchange-listed stocks in the over-the-counter market.

tout A slang term referring to a highly biased recommendation to buy a stock.

trade date The date on which a transaction takes place. Three business days later is the settlement date. The trade date (no longer the settlement date) is now the cutoff point for tax purposes.

----

treasury bill An obligation of the U.S. Government with a maturity date less than one year from date of issue. A treasury bill bears no interest but is sold to the investor at a discount prior to maturity.

----

treasury stock Issued stock that has been reacquired by the company from the stockholders. These shares may be held by the company indefinitely, reissued to the public, or retired. Treasury stock is not eligible to vote and receives no dividends.

----

triple witch The day on which stock options, stock index options, and stock index futures all expire simultaneously.

----

unit investment trust A registered load investment company that buys and holds a generally fixed portfolio of either stocks or bonds with a stated date of termination. "Units" in the trust are sold to investors.

----

up-tick or **plus-tick** A term used to describe a transaction made at a price higher than the preceding transaction price

----

vertical spread An investment strategy of simultaneously buying and selling options on the same underlying security, with the options having identical expiration dates but different strike prices.

VIX or **Volatility Index** A figure introduced by the CBOE in 1993 that measures the level of implied volatility of the U.S. equity market using real-time S&P 100 (OEX) index option bid/ask quotes. VXN is an identical formula for the Nasdaq-100 Index. They are calculated continuously.

----

volume The total number of shares traded, of an individual security or in the entire market, in a given period of time.

----

warrant A certificate giving the holder the right to buy securities at a predetermined price within a predetermined time limit or perpetually. Warrants are issued directly by the company. In contrast, call options are written on stock already outstanding.

----

wash sale A fictitious and illegal purchase and sale of stock to create market activity, prohibited by the NYSE in 1817. The term also applies to the repurchase of shares within 30 days, which automatically disallows a loss for tax purposes.

----

when-issued The abbreviated form of "when, as, and if issued," which refers to a security authorized but not yet issued.

----

wire house A stock brokerage firm having many branch offices linked by a communications network. The term is now primarily of historic significance.

----

working capital or **net working capital** The excess of current assets over current liabilities.

----

writer (of options) The seller of an option is called the "writer." The writer receives the premium from the option buyer.

WST Ratio A sophisticated ratio of puts and calls that measures the emotions of index option traders. The WST Ratio has a positive reading at or below 38.0 and a negative reading at or above 62.0.

----

yield The annual return on an investment (from dividends or interest) expressed as a percentage of either cost or current price.

----

yield curve The yield difference between short term Treasury notes and long term Treasury bonds. This indicator is watched closely by economists and analysts.

----

yield to maturity The yield of a bond also taking into account the premium or discount of the bond and the amount of time to its maturity.

Sources

Between corporate websites on the internet, local public and college libraries, as well as brokerage firms, investors can obtain all the necessary information on companies, industries, and the economy that will ever be needed.

Once an investor learns how to use these sources on a regular basis, valuable information and data can be found quickly and easily. Better libraries subscribe to numerous resources and investment services and some are quite expensive. Most individual investors can neither afford them all, nor absorb them all, on a regular basis. The internet is the place to start, but a visit your local library is almost always time well spent!

Here are just a few of the many valuable publications and services available to independent investors:

Publications and Subscriptions

Barron's
200 Burnett Road
Chicopee, MA 01020

www.barrons.com

Business Week
1221 Ave. of the Americas
New York, NY 10020

www.businessweek.com

Economic Indicators
Superintendent of Documents
U.S. Government Printing Office
Washington, D.C. 20402

http://bookstore.gpo.gov

The Economist
North American Office
P.O. Box 58524
Boulder, CO 80322

www.economist.com

Forbes
60 Fifth Avenue
New York, NY 10011

www.forbes.com

Investor's Business Daily
12655 Beatrice Street
Los Angeles, CA 90066

www.investors.com

Kiplinger Newsletter
1729 H Street
Washington, DC 20006

ww.kiplinger.com

Statistical Abstract of the United States
Superintendent of Documents
U.S. Government Printing Office
Washington, D.C. 20402

http://bookstore.gpo.gov

The Wall Street Journal
200 Burnett Road
Chicopee, MA 01021

www.wsj.com

Investment Services

Moody's Investors Service
99 Church Street
New York, NY 10007

www.moodys.com

Standard & Poor's
55 Water Street
New York, NY 10041

www.standardandpoors.com

Value Line
711 Third Avenue
New York, NY 10017

www.valueline.com

Business Organizations

American Stock Exchange
86 Trinity Place
New York, NY 10006

www.amex.com

Chicago Board Options Exchange
LaSalle at Van Buren
Chicago, IL 60605

www.cboe.com

Federal Reserve Bank of New York
Public Information Department
33 Liberty Street
New York, NY 10045

Investment Company Institute
1401 H Street, N.W. Suite 1200
Washington, D.C. 20005

www.ici.org

Nat'l. Assoc. of Investors Corporation
P.O. Box 220
Royal Oak, Michigan 48068

www.better-investing.org

Nat'l. Assoc. of Securities Dealers (NASD)
P.O. Box 9492
Gaithersburg, MD 20898

www.nasd.com

New York Society of Security Analysts
1601 Broadway, 11th Floor
New York, NY 10019

www.nyssa.org

New York Stock Exchange
Eleven Wall Street
New York, NY 10005

www.nyse.com

Leading Brokerage Firms

Charles Schwab
120 Kearney Street
San Francisco, CA 94108

www.schwab.com

Goldman Sachs Group
85 Broad Street
New York, NY 10004

www.gs.com

Lehman Brothers Holdings
3 World Financial Center
New York, NY 10285

www.lehman.com

Merrill Lynch
4 World Financial Center
New York, NY 10080

www.ml.com

Morgan Stanley
1585 Broadway
New York, NY 10036

www.morganstanley.com

Salomon Smith Barney
388 Greenwich Street
New York, NY 10013

www.citigroup.com

T.D. Waterhouse
100 Wall Street
New York, NY 10005

www.tdwaterhouse.com

UBS PaineWebber
1285 Avenue of the Americas
New York, NY 10019

www.ubspainewebber.com

Wachovia Corp.
One First Union Center
Charlotte, NC 28288

www.wachovia.com

Other Useful Online Addresses

EDGAR (SEC's searchable database)
www.edgar-online.com

Chicago Mercantile Exchange
www.cme.com

New York Mercantile Exchange
www.nymex.com

Securities Industry Association
www.sia.com

Other Online Brokerage Firms

Accutrade
www.accutrade.com

Ameritrade
www.ameritrade.com

Brown & Company
www.brownco.com

DLJ Direct
www.dljdirect.com

Dreyfus
www.edreyfus.com

E*Trade Securities
www.etrade.com

Fidelity
http://personal.fidelity.com

Muriel Siebert & Co.
www.msiebert.com

Quick & Reilly
www.quick-reilly.com

ScoTTrade
www.scottrade.com

T. Rowe Price
www.troweprice.com

Other Online Addresses

Fortune Magazine
www.fortune.com

Money Magazine
www.money.cnn.com

Appendix

Year	DJIA Close	DJIA Earnings	DJIA Div.	Payout Ratio	Avg. P/E	Div. Yield	% Chg. CPI
1945	193	10.56	6.69	63%	16.4	3.9%	2.3%
1946	177	13.63	7.50	55%	13.8	4.0%	8.3%
1947	181	18.80	9.21	49%	9.3	5.3%	14.4%
1948	177	23.07	11.50	50%	7.8	6.4%	8.1%
1949	200	23.54	12.79	54%	7.7	7.0%	-1.2%
1950	235	30.70	16.13	53%	7.0	7.5%	1.3%
1951	269	26.59	16.34	61%	9.7	6.3%	7.9%
1952	292	24.78	15.43	62%	11.1	5.6%	1.9%
1953	281	27.23	16.11	59%	10.1	5.9%	0.8%
1954	404	28.18	17.47	62%	12.1	5.1%	0.7%
1955	488	35.78	21.58	60%	12.2	4.9%	-0.4%
1956	499	33.34	22.99	69%	14.7	4.7%	1.5%
1957	436	36.08	21.61	60%	13.0	4.6%	3.3%
1958	584	27.95	20.00	72%	18.3	3.9%	2.8%
1959	679	34.31	20.74	60%	18.3	3.3%	0.7%
1960	616	32.21	21.36	66%	19.4	3.4%	1.7%
1961	731	31.91	22.71	71%	21.1	3.4%	1.0%
1962	652	36.43	23.30	64%	17.3	3.7%	1.0%
1963	763	41.21	23.41	57%	17.2	3.3%	1.3%
1964	874	46.43	31.24	67%	17.9	3.8%	1.3%
1965	969	53.67	28.61	53%	16.9	3.2%	1.6%
1966	786	57.68	31.89	55%	15.1	3.7%	2.9%
1967	905	53.87	30.19	56%	16.0	3.5%	3.1%
1968	944	57.89	31.34	54%	15.6	3.5%	4.2%
1969	800	57.02	33.90	59%	15.2	3.9%	5.5%
1970	839	51.02	31.53	62%	14.4	4.3%	5.7%
1971	890	55.09	30.86	56%	15.9	3.5%	4.4%
1972	1,020	67.11	32.27	48%	14.3	3.4%	3.2%
1973	851	86.17	35.33	41%	10.7	3.8%	6.2%
1974	616	99.04	37.72	38%	7.4	5.1%	11.0%
1975	852	75.66	37.46	50%	10.0	4.9%	9.1%
1976	1,005	96.72	41.40	43%	9.7	4.4%	5.8%
1977	831	89.10	45.84	51%	10.1	5.1%	6.5%
1978	805	112.79	48.52	43%	7.3	5.9%	7.6%
1979	839	124.46	50.98	41%	6.8	6.0%	11.3%
1980	964	121.86	54.36	45%	7.2	6.2%	13.5%
1981	875	113.71	56.22	49%	8.1	6.1%	10.3%
1982	1,047	9.15	54.14	50%	100.9	5.9%	6.2%
1983	1,259	72.45	56.33	78%	16.0	4.9%	3.2%
1984	1,212	113.58	60.63	53%	10.4	5.1%	4.3%
1985	1,547	96.11	62.03	65%	14.2	4.5%	3.6%
1986	1,896	115.59	67.04	58%	15.0	3.9%	1.9%
1987	1,939	133.05	71.20	54%	16.4	3.3%	3.6%
1988	2,169	215.46	79.53	37%	9.4	3.9%	4.1%
1989	2,753	221.48	103.70	47%	11.1	4.2%	4.8%
1990	2,634	172.05	102.00	59%	15.6	3.8%	5.4%
1991	3,169	49.27	95.18	50%	57.3	3.4%	4.2%
1992	3,301	108.25	100.72	50%	30.1	3.1%	3.0%
1993	3,754	146.84	99.66	68%	24.0	2.8%	3.0%
1994	3,834	256.13	105.66	41%	14.7	2.8%	2.6%
1995	5,117	311.02	116.56	37%	14.6	2.6%	2.8%
1996	6,448	353.88	131.00	37%	16.4	2.2%	3.0%
1997	7,908	391.29	136.10	35%	18.7	1.9%	2.3%
1998	9,181	383.35	151.13	39%	21.4	1.8%	1.6%
1999	11,497	477.22	168.52	35%	21.6	1.6%	2.2%
2000	10,787	485.14	172.08	35%	22.1	1.6%	3.4%
2001	10,022	369.51	181.07	49%	26.2	1.9%	2.8%
2002e	8,342	393.00	189.68	48%	22.8	2.1%	1.6%

| 58-year Average | 7.2% (annual growth) | | | 52% | 14.4 | 4.1% | |

Illustration Credits

Index

About the Authors

Jeffrey B. Little began his Wall Street career in the early 1960s. He has worked as an accountant in the margin department of a retail brokerage firm, as an instructor of technical analysis in a brokerage training center, as a highly respected securities analyst of technology stocks, and as a portfolio manager and advisory committee member of one of largest no-load mutual funds in the country. Mr. Little is a finance graduate of New York University and has been a Fellow of the Financial Analysts Federation, a member of the New York Society of Security Analysts, and a vice president of T. Rowe Price Associates, a prominent investment counsel firm in Baltimore. Mr. Little is currently a writer and a publisher of non-fiction books and computer software in Boca Raton, Florida where he and his wife, Judy, now reside.

Lucien Rhodes, an economics graduate of Dartmouth College, has several years experience as a securities analyst and portfolio manager in both commercial and investment banking. He has been registered on both the New York and American Stock Exchanges and is a past member of the Baltimore Society of Security Analysts. Mr. Rhodes is also a respected financial journalist. His articles have appeared in various well-known publications including *The Baltimore Sun, Fortune, Wired,* and especially *INC.* magazine where he received a national journalism award for his work. In addition to his background in finance, he is also expert in various computer technologies. In recent years, he has combined these interests to serve as an Internet consultant to financial service companies and venture capital start-ups based in California's Silicon Valley. Lucien Rhodes lives near San Francisco with his wife, Nancy.

Understanding Wall Street
4th Edition Video

The highlights of this classic book are now available in a VHS, DVD, or CD-ROM format for your viewing pleasure. This two-hour video begins with the startup of a new business and the colorful history of Wall Street, tracing its origin as a dirt path, along with an explanation of the exchanges and over-the-counter market. You will also learn how to read the financial pages and what to look for when evaluating a company for potential investment. This up-to-date video explains Wall Street in its contemporary investment arena, as it is today with the internet and computerized trading.

The *Understanding Wall Street* video is perfect as a home reference or as an educational medium. It can be ordered quickly and easily with an 800 number and any one of the three major credit cards.

Thank you, but I would prefer to order by mail.

_____ copies of the new Understanding Wall Street video

( ) VHS   ( ) DVD   ( ) CD-ROM

Enclosed is $39.95 plus $5 shipping and handling for each video ordered.

_____ Visa   _____ Master Card   _____ Amex   _____ Check or Money Order

Credit Card Number _____   Expires _____

Name _____

Address_____

City _____   State _____   Zip _____

Signature _____

Mail To:

LIBERTY PUBLISHING COMPANY, INC.
P.O. Box 4248
Deerfield Beach, FL 33442

Toll-free call for immediate service: **(800) 251-3345**
Company Offices: (561) 395-3750

Liberty Publishing Company can also be reached at **BullsOrBears.com**.

(Florida residents please add applicable 6% sales tax. Prices are subject to change. Orders outside the U.S. must be prepaid with int'l. money orders, payable in U.S. $.)